Confessions of a Lighthouse Keeper

GREG APPEL

Guthugga Pipeline Press

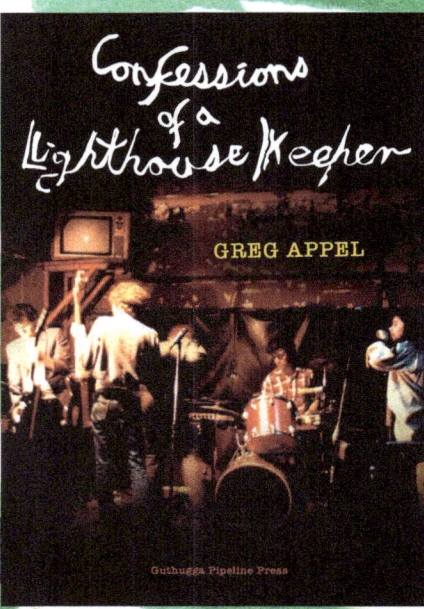

Confessions of a Lighthouse Keeper
ISBN: 978-0-9587956-9-2
©2020 Greg Appel
Published by Guthugga Pipeline Press
Book design and production: Eddy Jokovich/ARMEDIA
Greg Appel: www.spontaneousfilms.com.au

Thanks to Sarah Macdonald for her evocative writing. Thanks to Frances Green and graphic artist 'George Lazarides' for the TTNP image. Thanks to all the photographers that have contributed: Darian Turner, Robert Fretwell, `pling, Bleddyn Butcher, Paul Clarke, Jake Lloyd Jones, Steve Appel and quite a few we couldn't work out. The band took quite a few themselves. Also Fran, Claudia and John Paul Young. On yas!

 A catalogue record for this work is available from the National Library of Australia

Dear reader,

I'll try and keep this short. You can jump ahead if you don't like things in italics.

This is a very personal book and I'd like to thank everyone who's helped me out. This would start with my mother and father for conceiving me and giving me the best possible start in life. There may or may not be entities to thank before this? Grandparents, cave people, dividing cells, and before that?...

But back to the point.

There are people who may wonder where the hell they are in this story. And possibly, people who wish they weren't in it. You are all part of my life, and I can always put you in the sequel. What I've tried to do is write a personal tale, of interest to a wider group of people than my conceiving parents.

I'm quite a private person and many in this book are like me. That's probably why we cluster together.

We live in an age of self-promotion and I can't pretend I'm not part of this. However, I feel this book is about you as well. You people—that have made my life what it is. Some of you have even written large sections. Some of you are barely mentioned. And some of you are in here just the right amount.

I'd particularly like to mention my immediate family. Amanda and I have been together since these musical days, but she is only a fleeting character. Our son Anders is barely in this book, but large in my life. Our daughter Zelie—she's in it plenty. Juliet, another private person, has helped make my life very good. I sincerely hope she's one of the ones who's in here just the right amount.

My friends are many, but often distant—which is mainly my fault. And I believe my enemies are few.

The people that helped edit this book include Bob, Deirdre, Zelie, Amanda, David, James, Liane, Clinton, Hairy, Roger, Blue, Juliet, Eddy, and my sister Margie (who will be surprised by the abbreviation of her name).

There's just so many people who I could thank.

And you, dear reader, are one of them...

Precis

This memoir is more than an insider's account of a mid-eighties Australian independent band. *Confessions of a Lighthouse Keeper* provides multiple insights into the broader music and entertainment world—in a country that has mixed feelings about the arts. It's atmospheric, light, self-deprecating and full of musings from others who have travelled this road—over the last fifty years. The Lighthouse Keepers are sentimental favourites amongst the generation who came of age in the inner cities of Sydney, Melbourne and even Canberra—during the 1980s.

The book is written in an engaging style and features personal interviews, diary entries, and writing contributions from other witnesses, all linked by Greg Appel's very personal text. After all—he has spent a fair part of his career linking the rantings and musings of Australia's entertainers in TV and radio programs.

Interviews include:

LINDY MORRISON, the Go-Betweens
JAMES CRUICKSHANK, Widdershins, the Cruel Sea
ROB McCOMB, the Triffids
MURRAY COOK, the Wiggles
JOHN PAUL YOUNG, legendary Australian popstar
STEVE KILBEY, the Church
KEN GORMLY, the Cruel Sea
CLINTON WALKER, writer
DAVID NICHOLS, writer/academic
JULIET WARD, the Lighthouse Keepers
SARAH MACDONALD, journalist/broadcaster

…with a foreword by

TANYA PLIBERSEK, Australian Labor Party, Member of Parliament

Poster: Chloe Brookes-Kenworthy

LIGHTHOUSE KEEPERS

GREG APPEL

The Lighthouse Keepers were an Australian country and indie pop band formed in 1981 in Sydney. The Lighthouse Keepers combined a 'loosely rehearsed, casual ethos' with humour, punk attitudes and pure pop song craft. While sounding unlike anything else at the time, they were very successful on a cult level. In November 1984, the group issued their debut studio album, *Tales of the Unexpected*, and a single, 'Ocean Liner'. In 1985, the band toured the United Kingdom and Europe, at times supporting their fellow label mates, the Triffids. 'They are the perfect group with the perfect pop songs, songs about heartfelt passions with simple intelligible lyrics...These people know what they are about, they know how to touch us lesser mortals right at the heart. Pure genius,' raved Jane Wilkes in the UK's *New Musical Express*. But after this one European sojourn, the ensemble disbanded in 1986, releasing a compilation album, *The Imploding Lighthouse Keepers*, in November that year.

(from Wikipedia)

The author

Perhaps as a punishment for his sins in this indie world, Greg Appel ended up as the producer of the ABC TV rock history *Long Way to the Top* and has created numerous other music programs and events. As a guitarist/songwriter for the Lighthouse Keepers in the mid-eighties, his interest in music has often influenced his work. His diverse documentary work has included awards in Australia and directing *The Team That Never Played*, an international documentary about apartheid-era football in 2010. His documentary on bossa nova music in 2008, *Bossa Nova: the sound that seduced the world* premiered at the Sydney Film Festival and was broadcast on ABC1 and ABC2. He has also produced many feature documentaries for ABC Radio National. Greg brings to this tale a unique perspective on the music business, public broadcasting and program-making. From putting on family shows at caravan parks in his youth, he has come full circle to putting on shows about caravan parks in the fraught world of live theatre.

CHAPTER BREAKDOWN

All chapters are named after Lighthouse Keeper's songs, with a fairly linear narrative from the sixties, all the way to nowadays.

INTRODUCTION

1. ODE TO NOTHING — the Lighthouse Keepers break up after an onstage brawl in Hamburg.

2. DISHWASHING LIQUID — a dreamy Canberra childhood, followed by a not-very-good punk band.

3. LIGHTHOUSE KEEPERS — early history in Sydney independent scene interviews, diaries.

4. WE'VE GOT A GIG — the Lighthouse Keepers play a lot, the inner-city scene explodes (sort of), interviews, diaries, records of live shows.

5. SPRINGTIME — the Lighthouse Keepers play even more, interviews, diaries, records of live shows.

6. WHEELS OVER THE DESERT — the Lighthouse Keepers go overseas and try their luck with mixed results: interviews, diaries, records of live shows.

7. TORTURE ROAD — one big tour to Europe: interviews, diaries, records of live shows.

8. BAD MOOD — the end of the road for the band: interviews, diaries, records of live shows.

9. A TIME OF EVIL — another band: the Widdershins is formed, some darker times including witchcraft, drugs and even sex.

10. MARCH OF THE GREEN MEN — Greg Appel starts to work at the ABC and begins to make documentaries.

11. CRUISING — Greg works on various ABC TV shows including *King Street, Newtown* and *A Long Way to the Top*.

12. SHADOWLANDS — the story of *Van Park* — a musical comedy about some old musos stuck in a caravan park starring John Paul Young and Steve Kilbey.

13. RETURN OF THE KING — putting on live shows and making docos is occasionally rewarding.

14. LOVE BEACON — flashes and reflections.

15. HOOGLE WALTZ — what goes around comes around, a life in the arts in perspective.

FOREWORD

"Most days resemble other days. They fall in rows, mowed down by time. One does not regret the loss. But a few glorious days stand out in the memory, days where each moment shines separately, like cobbles on a strand."

Jay Parini

The inner city of Sydney in the 1980s was like that for me. And the music of that time transports me back in a heartbeat. Hearing the first few bars of 'Ocean Liner' takes me right back to the share houses on Watkin Street; Crown and Cleveland Streets. The terraces filled with flat-mates' parents' hand-me-down furniture, scuffed lino and parties with flagon wine (and the rest).

I was in high school, but my beautiful big brother, ten years older than me, used to sneak me in to the Hopetoun, the Graphic Arts Club, the Trade Union Club, the Sandringham, the Strawberry Hills Hotel, and parties. He used to take me on Saturday mornings to Redeye Records, where we would stand side by side for hours, listening to songs from the new records on headphones. Two or three hours to buy a record seemed like a great investment of time.

His favourites and mine were Australian bands: the Triffids, Laughing Clowns, Go-Betweens, Ed Kuepper, Paul Kelly and the overseas acts like the Violent Femmes who played with them.

And of course, the wonderful, the magnificent Lighthouse Keepers.

Juliet Ward's voice and Greg Appel's lyrics still go straight to my heart. So much longing. So wistful. So bittersweet.

Always, always unrequited love.

As Juliet says in this book, 'always looking for that great party and never quite finding it'.

They say of travel that half the pleasure is anticipation and the other half recollection.

That's true of teenage love too—and that's what these songs have for me, still today.

No matter how broken-hearted we were, there was the anticipation of the great passion just around the corner. And now the memories of the friendship, love and partying. The days weren't all great but the anticipation then and the recollection now each have their own sustaining pleasure.

It's such a pleasure to read the inside story of a band that has always been one of my favourites. Let's hope future generations of young Australians will get the chance to enjoy Australian music in local venues.

Thank you Lighthouse Keepers for being part of the soundtrack of my youth.

Tanya Plibersek

INTRODUCTION
Confessions of a Lighthouse Keeper

Dear reader, I wish I had something more substantial to confess to you, like that saucy British 'Confessions Of' series from the 1970s. But there's not quite enough there. Sadly, the best I can do is group sex. It's a long time ago. The four of us drunkenly look around at our naked selves, someone says, 'this is the sort of thing that we're going to talk about when we get old.' We all agree!

But like much in life, the reality doesn't always compare with fantasy. I recall that incident had some ramifications that weren't so saucy. They wouldn't make for a very thrilling read either. I might have also realised in that moment that I just wasn't cut out for the swinger's life after all—damn that brain wiring! The other participants all would have much better confessions too. But I'll do what I can for you with the material available. This is more about what my beady eye observed in the little grotto of the Australian entertainment scene that I have inhabited for most of my life. It can be an ugly place—but sometimes a beautiful creature emerges. They may even be naked.

Indeed, the Lighthouse Keepers song 'Gargoyle' came to me as a teenager one summer's night in 1981, in a brightly lit, hot bedroom in middle-class Canberra. At the time I thought the spooky lyrics came from some other astral plane but I now realise the song was all about having sex with a real live na-

ked girl. After my 'beady eyes' watched her, I obviously decided to take up her offer and descend the stairs down to the backroom... So perhaps this memoir might have a few confessions, in the 1970s sense. Back we go to a time and space re-enacted many times now on various screens. Back then, I recall watching *Happy Days*, that nostalgic television fantasy of middle America in the 1950s, and promising myself that I wouldn't forget the actual seventies. They weren't that happy, although I, perhaps, was almost happy when I wrote 'Gargoyle'. It was one of my first songs, and I had a good feeling about it as I sat in my hot bedroom. It felt new.

But read on. We're going on a journey, a

literal one. We will travel across Australia and beyond, and traipse through my memories of distant times. To do this, I have had help from others I've met along the way. Just like in my real life, people will appear at odd times, then disappear. And as I search for my earlier self, they will provide different insights into a world that gets harder to remember all the time. I've always obsessively kept a collection of writings and archival bits and pieces. I've added to these with text, diaries and interviews from people I've met, many I'd call friends. It's come together to make something larger than my own life. I'm just the spider in the middle of the web. So what are we waiting for? Let's get entangled!

CHAPTER 1
Ode to Nothing

Amanda, Hamburg, 2014.

18.12.14

As I write, I'm on a train going through Hamburg's bleak and wintery suburbs with my partner Amanda and daughter Zelie. We have grown a little weary and I reflect back to that possibly drizzly *nacht*—when it all fell apart…

The beginning of the end

It's always the beginning of the end, isn't it? But let me open with the end of the Lighthouse Keepers. It was the thirteenth of November 1985, at a venue in Hamburg, Germany.

There were about twenty people in the room, waiting to be entertained. There were a few Australians in the audience. Somehow

Lighthouse Keepers on tour in Europe.

they'd found out the Lighthouse Keepers were playing a few sets in a narrow bar, somewhere in deepest Hamburg. We'd been in Europe and the UK for about a month and away from home a lot longer. We'd left from Sydney via Perth, playing a few shows in outback towns along the way. That was how you got to Europe, right?

The Lighthouse Keepers were a rather pathetic bunch. Always very nervous on stage, we'd look down a lot. We'd change instruments or tune unnecessarily, anything but look at the audience. Juliet was our singer and, perhaps, as part of her stage persona, she might make eye contact with a few members of the audience. I think this was her ritual for overcoming fear. 'Dangerous,' I thought as I focused my eyes on some not-very-difficult chords. This was particularly dangerous on a night like this. Was it raining outside? I think it must have been.

In retrospect, we hadn't been away from home long. We weren't like those hardier Australian bands, the Triffids or the Go-Betweens who lived for years in cold squalor in London, and toured for as long as it took. After six months, we were tired and the close contact with each other was already wearing thin.

Backstage, one of us was especially drunk. S. O'Neil, better known as 'Hairy', sometimes drank himself into an altered state. When intoxicated, he was usually a fairly harmless being: gentle, touchy feely, and inclined to nod off easily. But on this night, walking was a challenge—so was any sort of movement. He stumbled like a zombie from a bad film. I knew then there was no chance he could play the bass, the guitar or any other sort of instrument. And since he was our best musician, I knew we had a problem.

It is not unusual in a touring band for tensions to build up on the road. Some characters just rub each other up the wrong way. Hairy and Steven Williams, the drummer, were polar opposites in character. As well as the drummer, Steven Williams was pretty much the manager—although why anyone would want to manage a rock band is a mystery. But we didn't stop him. We just whinged like brats: 'Where's my money? Where's my dinner? Where's the rider?' And so on. If Steven was the capitalist, Hairy was the left-wing radical, or perhaps the maverick independent. He was uncompromisingly Stalinist about musical correctness. He hated cover songs, loved obscure punk and new wave music and was generally against 'the man'. Sometimes, he saw 'the man' in our drummer. As the tour wore on, they gravitated to the opposite ends of the grubby Kombi

Chapter 1 : Ode to Nothing

van. By the time we got to Hamburg, Hairy and Steven Williams were barely speaking. Now at the show, I glimpsed a scary monster deep inside the drunken Hairy. It wanted to do bad things.

So we started off with some 'acoustic' songs, leaving Hairy to sober up back stage. We often did acoustic songs, so it was nothing unusual. Steven Williams joined us on brushes. But the tension rose as the monster began to stir. Hairy picked up his bass and walked on stage. He flapped the strings and a horrible noise came out. It bore no relation to the song we were playing. He staggered around the stage, continuing an improvised slap solo, with a malevolent look on his face. Drums and bass are the engine of a band, but our managerial drummer was not feeling the groove. He was thinking how hard it was going to be to get money out of the club, with such a small audience too.

Halfway through the song, he jumped from behind his drums and attacked Hairy, punching and pushing. But the monster fought back. This wasn't in the set list. Perhaps the show had not been advertised as well as it could have been: a couple of Australians belting the hell out of each other on stage.

It was a strange sight, and I'm sure the few people in the room thought so too. The Lighthouse Keepers could be called 'Emo', if such a classification had existed at the time. Now we were fighting onstage like heavy metal musos. But it was never going to be a fair fight, as our drummer was built like a boxer and much less drunk. The intoxicated Hairy could only lurch and throw his limbs about, like he was trapped in a net. The band retreated backstage and the two fighters fell around a bit more, before the drummer left the stage with a look of contempt. The sound of feedback and freeform slap bass concluded the show.

Lighthouse Keepers European tour van.

Many years later, I asked Hairy what was going on that night. He said he didn't remember a thing. Was this one of those rare psychological cases where people enter a dissociated state and forget who they are? Perhaps the creature that lurked within Hairy is worth investigating. An unpredictable, sometimes lascivious animal, that would appear as if from nowhere. Even at a badly attended show by an Australian indie band.

But what are we doing when we go out to see a band? We want something special to happen. Musicians and audiences are forever poking at the beast that possessed Hairy. Intrigued, yet horrified when it suddenly appears on stage. Many years later, my cousin married a girl whose relative had been in that room, and the story was related back to me via this intermediary. A sad tale about that night in Hamburg, when pressures of the road became too much for the Lighthouse Keepers...

While my own band decided it was all too difficult after one stormy European night, there were other Australian acts from the time with more of a work ethic. They might have fought amongst themselves, but they kept on touring.

In the three decades since my years as a Lighthouse Keeper, I've had a whole other life. Some days, I'm called a documentary maker. On others, just a videographer—a new category that means general dogsbody with a camera and microphone. Haggard celebrities, whacky entertainers, construction workers, psychics, I've videographed them all.

So I've taken this approach to put together this book. With a camera, a recorder and a phone, I've interviewed people from my past. Sometimes, I took my daughter, Zelie, along with me. She was now a young woman with an offhand interest in the scene I'm writing about. I had previously met Lindy Morrison briefly on a few occasions. The band she drummed for, the Go-Betweens, were a band that inspired the Lighthouse Keepers. We were both too alternative for the mainstream, but didn't neatly fit into any Australian underground scene either.

I'd also met Lindy, during the making of ABC Australian rock series *A Long Way to the Top*. So I thought I'd bring everyone together. We all enjoyed a glass of wine as Lindy took us back to the days that the Go-Betweens toured Europe themselves.

You're talking about ten years of my life: it was good, it was bad, but mostly it was living the dream.

Lindy was happy to hand out advice to Zelie. Most of it, about not throwing your life away in the music biz, but then there were good times.

It's all about the gang, and I miss that gang. But the gang is like a family. A family becomes dysfunctional when certain people outgrow their roles. And that's what happened in the band, ten years with the same people, in the van, backstage, onstage, in the hotel lobby, in the studio, it kills you, girl... haha

Lindy's transcribed laughter brings us to the musician's lifestyle, a choice that can end in tears. It is the well-known, almost boring truth, that musicians are generally alcoholics, often with multiple other drug habits. Some cope by renouncing alcohol and/or drugs altogether; they are a common sight at AA and NA meetings. But not every muso embraces destruction and redemption with such gusto. Quite a few regulate their pleasure in a controlled manner, and have done so for many years. After all, drugs do have medicinal benefits. They can cure, as long as you don't have too much medicine...

'Evil' Graham Lee is a distinctly un-evil looking character. Graham chose the perfect instrument for a keen drinker. Sitting on a chair behind a lap pedal steel guitar.

Lindy Morrison with Zelie Appel.

Chapter 1 : Ode to Nothing

Graham Lee and Rob McComb.

I've crossed his path on the road to nowhere a number of times, but mainly with the Triffids, often with his partner in crime, bass player Martyn Casey. Graham was feeling nostalgic when I caught up with him recently in Melbourne.

> I remember one particular day. It began on a bar in a Scandinavian ferry, Marty and I, we were with some truck drivers and some women who looked like gypsies. None of them could speak English and we're there having a riotous time. Marty got refused service. The next day we had to play in Finland at a festival and, of course, we started drinking again. It was outdoors—beautiful with streams and things, then there were all these people even drunker than us, throwing up in the streams. But I listened to a recording of it not long ago—it actually sounds good. After the show, Marty got assaulted by a guy with a knife. Wild times... But I don't look back at it as a really bad day... it was one of the best days of my life. Those days... you don't get in any other profession.
>
> 'Evil' Graham Lee, the Triffids

On the other side of the stage, often enveloped in a cloud of aromatic smoke, was the Triffids' violinist and guitarist, Rob McComb.

> **It was like a wandering minstrel lifestyle, it was really just looking at a map and the day was only as good as how the publican treated you.**
>
> Rob McComb, the Triffids

Communications in the eighties were non-existent by today's standards. Someone back home who knew your itinerary might send a letter to the main post office of a city ahead of time. Overseas phone calls were totally out of reach for musicians. You were out there together—alone.

> Everyone had some kind of poison. I don't know how you could have done it otherwise. The music scene was being out on the tiles four to five nights of the week. I don't think I could have done it without some help. You never read that in the job description of a touring band. Long stretches of boring nothing being away from home. Is it any wonder that people fell prey to drugs?
>
> Clinton Walker, 2016

Many rock critics have a band in their past. In the eighties, Clinton Walker played with the Killer Sheep, before turning his attentions to writing about other bands. He is proud of his time in this druggy wilderness. His choice of drug was heroin.

> [Heroin] users may have looked like zombies to you but they were actually functioning...I was always personally amazed about people like you that I heard many years later were getting up in the morning and going to university! But there was no less discipline for me. I would get up in the morning, at a decent hour...you can't turn out the millions of words I did without it... you just chugged through whatever you did, whether you were in a band, a journalist, or a would-be filmmaker.
>
> Clinton Walker, 2016

Some people look back on their drug-taking past as the best days of their lives. Personally, I was very wary of heroin, but I have had some great moments helped along by various other medicines. Unfortunately or not, my personality meant that I did all this in moderation and was always in control. But this nostalgia is not shared by all of the survivors from this era.

> **Drugs—it's been done to death. Everybody knows that everyone was doing a lot of smack and they were sharing needles. I'm a social worker with Support Act, the industry charity. No one thought that sharing needles would spread a blood disease. We were just so cavalier in those days, a lot of people have health problems right now, a lot of musicians that I hung out with are affected.**
>
> Lindy Morrison, the Go-Betweens

But the universal drug of choice for musicians was alcohol—as much as you could possibly drink. After the Lighthouse Keepers' drunken Hamburg brawl, I did my best to patch things up between Hairy and Stephen Williams in the Kombi van the next day. Collectively, we decided complete silence might be the best option. So I did the only thing I could: I stuck my head down and scribbled in the tour diary I had started back in Australia. The 'Eating Guide to Roadhouses of the World' was my humble attempt to turn the tedium of the road into something more interesting. A lazy sort of creative writing.

Tuesday the 19th of November 1985

It's a fair amount of kilometres and Europe that have passed under the pages of this novelette since me last entry. And here we are in Bergmen (approximate spelling) (I just ate a meal, not a bad one either cooked by old Blue) hating each other quietly as the end is in sight. In fact, soon we will be driven over the Alps to Zurich with our trusty driver Claus at the wheel. Then we'll fly back to Perth and hence begin the pleasure of returning home

Chapter 1 : Ode to Nothing

via a few choice venues. Physical violence has broken out only once in Hamburg. But hatred fosters also, in the intimate atmosphere created in the Kombi van.

Since last entry, we have played at Passau at the festival of a small Anarchist pub. It's a good place where the drinking never stops. Hamburg, Carpi and Milano. There's a fair distance in between and a lot of coldness to be endured as the weather has turned snowy, to say the least. A million floors have been slept on, and a thousand buns with cheese and stuff in them consumed, plus a hundred 'how do you say this in German? Italian?' have been asked.

The audiences have been generally good and we've played quite well through stone age equipment (barring one minor incident with a little excess alcoholic fluids) but the reason for our mission has possibly been forgotten somewhere with the personal space. Not to say misery has finally struck, far from it. I've learnt even more about people getting on together, probably more than I wanted, and everyone looks forward to getting home. It just happens at the moment of writing I'm bored of humans and what they do to each other. This has probably been brought on by excess herbal remedy which me and trusty Claus had last night.

This was the second-last entry in my roadhouse guide…

We all decided to wind things back once we got home. Pathetic, maybe. Australian life was just too easy, and hanging around with a bunch of grizzling weirdoes wasn't fun anymore. It was the end for me and Juliet as a couple too. But still, it was a great way to see Europe. Way better than backpacking alone, which I'd done at eighteen.

I never married the Lighthouse Keeper that I lived with back then, but have remained in touch with Juliet Ward over the years.

Juliet and Wolfgang, Blue Mountains.

Interview, Bermagui 2015

> Me: People often asked me after the band split up, 'What happened to Juliet?'
>
> Juliet: I got sick of people being horrible to each other.
>
> Me: But you've got quite a story there. Witchcraft, drugs, lesbianism...

At a certain point in our mutual history, she would have rolled her eyes and lapsed into a stony silence. But no. One of the joys of putting this together is that people, even Juliet, answered me. Especially when I had a camera pointed at them. This is one of the good things about making documentaries—something unexpected may occur.

> Juliet: I remember walking everywhere,[1] a litre of Coca-Cola for breakfast every morning, 'roll your own', lots of beer, always wanting to go to that party that was really good but never quite finding it, but for all that bullshit that went on... so much fun.

[1] barefoot.

A lot of artists are fascinated by their own story. I know, because I've interviewed so many. Sometimes, I only need to ask, 'Tell me about yourself?' and follow it up with a, 'Can you expand on that?', if there are any gaps. But with many artists, there are no gaps. They are their own muses.

I've had mixed feelings about writing this memoir. Is there enough in my life to be of interest? Beyond of course, my own self-fascination. Am I even an artist? Obviously, since you're reading this, I forged ahead with the project. The internet suggests that there is a potential audience of perhaps 500. That's good enough for me. And perhaps a few more—you never know.

There were some little signifiers and daggers thrown at me that made me start to write. I was half-way through a book by one of the Scared Weird Little Guys, an Australian musical comedian who had run a marathon in Antarctica, when I realised that I could do this too. I'm not really sure what drew me to this book in the first place. The middle-aged male confessional isn't really my genre, but I was aware of books like *Fat, Forty and Fired*... this sort of title. I had reached a 'certain age' (sadly, way past forty). I'd done interesting things, met interesting people...sort of. And a small circle of people are still interested in our old band, the Lighthouse Keepers. In fact, it's amazing how often my muso background comes up in unexpected and positive ways. Like during scary meetings with important people. But what was my insurmountable obstacle that I could conquer and emerge out the other end, a finer human being? And what humbling lessons had I learned?

Then it came to me. After the Lighthouse Keepers, I had plugged away at a musical comedy called *Van Park*, for nearly twenty years. Why? I don't really know anymore. Perhaps it was because no one had told me to stop. Getting it produced was my seemingly

Chapter 1 : Ode to Nothing

insurmountable middle-age obstacle.

I took the fully developed vehicle to Melbourne and unleashed it on the Comedy Festival. Already a 'hit' at the Sydney Fringe Festival in 2010 (pretty much true), it couldn't fail in Melbourne. They cared about music there. They still had a music scene, and a story about old washed-up musicians in a caravan park would resonate with those well-dressed entertainment connoisseurs. Wouldn't it?

I was a week into a two-week run and getting nervous. The box office receipts looked scary. Modern technology enabled me to see every ticket purchased—virtually live. It was enough to drive anyone insane. The venue manager assured me two weeks was the right length for a run. Everyone did it that way. You had to build an audience, get reviews, and get them talking. That's how theatre worked.

The Melbourne *Age* published the first review: two-and-a-half stars. A momentum killer. The insurmountable obstacle was... insurmountable. Fuck theatre, I thought.

This story has no happy ending. As you will see, it is a metaphor for life. When I think about it, my life in the arts had been a bit of a two-and-a-half star run. I enjoyed some success, but was I talented enough? As a musician, I'd gone about two-and-a-half stars of the way. Come to think of it, the average review of my bands weighed in at three stars—reserved praise kind of thing. I'd somehow ended up in the television documentary world, and eked out a living. Again the reviews were generally positive, but never over the top—never unmitigated praise.

The Lighthouse Keepers were rarely a critic's favourite. We were a little on the wet side, with no literary pretensions. Of course, it's possible the critics didn't actually like us that much. But over time, it has become apparent that we do have some fans in high places. The current Australian Labor Party MP, Tanya Plibersek, named us her second-favourite

Hairy on the Canberra train.

band on Triple J not that long ago. We never topped this list or that. But Tanya put us in the same hallowed box as our old mates the Triffids—a current mainstay of any critic's Top Australian All-Time Geniuses list, along with the Go-Betweens. Neither of those bands were hugely popular when they actually plied their trade in the eighties. Indeed, I had played my own little part in both these bands' historical rebirth when I produced the Australian rock series *Long Way to the Top* for ABC TV in 2001. It wasn't like they were ever as popular as Cold Chisel or even Icehouse.

> **When we got inducted into the Aria Hall of Fame in 2008, I remember looking at Richard Wilkins in the audience and thinking, 'you don't even know who we are'.**
>
> 'Evil' Graham Lee, the Triffids

Perhaps I'm the Salieri in the Mozart story. I'm referring here to the eighties film

Amadeus, where Mozart's annoying genius is tracked by a sullen Salieri, who is now a virtually unknown composer (except for his part in this film) but, at the time, was his rival. Did my band, the Lighthouse Keepers, play Salieri to the Triffids and the Go-Betweens?

But did the Triffids, in turn, play Salieri to Nick Cave? And the Go-Betweens to REM or whoever? But then again, REM were the Salieri to U2, and on it goes—U2 now find themselves the Salieri's of Alt-J or Coldplay or whoever holds the international sensitive-but-rocking baton of the period.

Is this not the artist's lot? As you will learn, most musicians don't really like other musicians, at least not their music. You have to believe that your own stuff is better, otherwise why get out there, against insurmountable odds, and play those mournful songs? Most of us dwell in Salieri's creative twilight zone.

I always say the Go-Betweens were a B-grade cult band. If I had any fame, it was in a really minor way. But I think I earned the right to be recognised. I think that the work the Go-Betweens did was so authentic and so original that I'm not surprised that people want to chat to me about that time.

Lindy Morrison, the Go-Betweens

I'll do the complicated maths for you. If the Go-Betweens were a B-grade band, then the Lighthouse Keepers were a C, which is a three-star rating. But wherever we fall in the critical universe, I still feel good when I hear one of our old songs. They sound rough but beautifully formed. The music stills mean a lot to me, as I'm sure it does to all those who saw the light back then. And, as I try to illuminate those long ago days, I promise I'll avoid any more lighthouse metaphors.

CHAPTER 2

Dishwashing Liquid

Enough speculating. Let's get into some fine detail. Hang in there, dear reader. I grew up in Canberra, Australia's most recently built capital. A slightly spooky place that gets very hot and cold. A city filled with people with great work conditions but tedious jobs. But back then, it seemed like a paradise to a small child.

While they were still toddlers, I liked to ask my own children where they were before their conception. Unfortunately, they never had an answer. It was the kind of question that made them glaze over and look bored.

When you're just coming into your consciousness, you have no control over your entrance point. If you have shelter, food and parents that treat you well, you're generally happy. My parents just happened to be Caucasian doctors that had settled in the barren but prosperous new suburbs of Australia's capital. The local public school was filled with kids just like me: white, Anglo–Saxon, and often Protestant. Perhaps we were different in our own ways. So a strange but not-too-weird outlook in a child was tolerated, even celebrated.

Me with the love heart, Gavin Butler up the back with the blond hair.

I was a popular story writer at school. In my Year 6 Composition book, I wrote a piece that went down an absolute treat. The secret lay in writing key members of the class into the stories, then taking the plot over the top. I still preach this style to anyone who will listen and perhaps it is the key to any creative endeavour. That is: to win over an audience, put as many of your audience in the story as you can.

Gavin Butler, Aurora Hatzel and the rest of 6 Blue may be interested in reading on…

Easter by Greg Appel 6 Blue

It was Easter at Goulburn Prison. Gavin had been put in jail for murder of his wife. In jail, Gavin was fed one of the baddest eggs from the farm nearby and one millimetre of water from the Parramatta River. He was whipped two hundred times a day. Easter was a bad day for Gavin, as the guy whipping was in a bad mood and he was whipped a thousand times. Gavin was only given a crust of bread that day.

That night, a bony figure crept up behind one of the guards. It was Gavin and he drove his knife into the guard's back and pushed it through his heart and out the other side. There was a deep thud as the dead guard hit the ground. A siren screamed through the air but it was too late and Gavin escaped into the dark of the night.

Next morning, Gavin was deep in the Australian bush and about a mile from the sea. In an hour he had reached the sea. Joyously, he rushed down the beach and swam into the ocean. Down below he could see many brilliant coloured fish. When he clambered out of the sea he saw that he had nearly been eaten, by a shark. Far down below, a grey figure was circling around him. He made a bed out of sand and just before he was asleep, he saw a figure which looked like his wife. He drew his knife but a voice spoke at him.

'It is your wife, Aurora. Do not try to kill me again.'

After a while his wife sat down with him and they talked for a long time about what they had been doing all the years.

That night Gavin Butler was stabbed in the heart by his wife. No trace of either of them was found, except Gavin's Diary.

I don't know if my writing got any better than this. I still remember Aurora Hatzel's glorious hair and beautiful form. I was probably trying to destroy the blossoming romance between her and my friend Gavin, but I'm sure it had the opposite effect. He was a popular kid with his long straight blond hair. His mum let him grow it long, and my mother tried to keep me away from him. He was from a 'broken home' and his cats had ringworm! His separated parents also had something to do with the Labor Party.

The most alien people I ever saw were the Catholics who wore purple uniforms, and were a race unencountered generally. I didn't actually know what they were, but somehow my parents inveigled in me a suspicion of their ways. I guess it was an old sectarian suspicion that dated back to the Reformation. But in Canberra, we dealt with it in a much more civilised way than Henry the VIII and all. No massacring, we just kept our distance.

Over at the Catholic kids' school, they probably had their own heaven on earth. Canberra was a pre-planned suburbia, full of clean wide streets, big backyards, and only nesting magpies to trouble us. Does a child care about design or urban ambience? Not much. Did I know or care about white middle-class privilege? But with my four siblings, dogs, cats and all, a happy world was created, that Henry the

Chapter 2 : Dishwashing Liquid

The Canberra Times was Canberra's *Sydney Morning Herald*.

VIII and his seven wives could only dream of. Sometimes I would wake up and think: Have I been born in the best place ever?

Our house was like something from *The Brady Bunch*, except my parents were still married. It was architect-designed and everything, and stood out from the many government houses in the area. It really looked like the seventies with orange and brown all over the place. *The Canberra Times* spread the word:

> 'Some people live in houses and some people have homes. Doctor and Mrs. Denis Appel[1] of Garran definitely fall into this second category. You know that theirs is a happy home the minute you walk through the wooden gate and into the courtyard entrance…'

1 This should actually be Dr and Dr Appel, although Mum was taking a bit of time off to raise five children.

If all this happiness leaves you feeling nauseous, rest assured, there are darker days ahead. although, by international standards, perhaps the skies become just a little overcast. Indeed, my mother dates Christmas 1975 as the beginning of the end when my father re-gifted me his barely strummed acoustic guitar, although she played a part, organising guitar lessons at home every Wednesday afternoon with a vaguely sinister-looking man who got around in long socks and shorts. In our middle-class world, all good parents gave their children tennis and music lessons. And so teaching these things became a great job for anyone who was 'interested' in the young.

My sister doesn't agree with me about the scale of damage our music teacher, Mr.

A classic Appel action shot; performance art combined with photography.

Cranfield, did to our young psyches. He didn't discriminate between the sexes either. I just knew when he sat next to me, and the creeping hand came out, I felt uncomfortable and moved a bit further down the couch. It was only years later when we talked about it that I realised what was going on. And justice was eventually dealt out to Mr. Cranfield. He apparently ended up in prison, where he died. But that was the start of my relationship with the guitar. I didn't really enjoy the lessons that much, and Mr. Cranfield didn't seem that interested in music, but I had a guitar—which I've still got.

I began to realise that you could play other sorts of music on the guitar than the pieces in the lesson book. You could make random things up that sounded quite nice. It wasn't long before I asked my mother to stop music lessons. I could do it myself, thanks very much. Perhaps I should have said this to Mr. Cranfield.

But back to our happy family. Being the oldest of five children was both a responsibility and an opportunity. Once I was rid of the annoying guitar lessons, I was free to use the instrument as a tool for more important activities, such as putting on shows. I liked nothing better than organising a small cast, then aiming for the sky. Our theatre was the backyard and our lighting was the harsh Australian sun. My sister was the next down from me in age, my constant aid in getting the younger boys in order. She was a solid producer, perhaps the best I've ever had, with absolute faith in the material.

In the photo sequence on the opposite page, we're dabbling in a bit of performance art. A difficult medium, nevertheless, fully mastered here. Note, the ensemble cast are in full Sunday School outfits. I don't think Mum was able to keep this going much longer.

We staged some amazing shows, and produced some incredible cassettes. Especially once I began recording with two cassette machines—one to play the sound effects, the other to record. I'd repeat the process and build a wall of sound that would make Phil Spector proud: vast soundscapes of screaming crowds, only spoiled by the cursed hiss of cassette tape. Dolby noise reduction made no difference.

The sixties mostly bypassed my parents, except for a few signs in their music collection. Dad had an eight-track cartridge machine installed in this Land Rover (he was ahead of the SUV pack by decades). And, like many gentlemen his age, he was hip to Neil Diamond's *Hot August Night*, and everything by Cat Stevens and, of course, the Beatles *Abbey Road*. I must say, these works still sound pretty solid, although *Abbey Road* might not be peak Beatles. I managed to ferret out some odd entities at the back of his record collection in the living room cabinet that went even further back in time. There were a few hits from the fifties: like Bill Haley and the Comets, or Frank Sinatra. But one that stood out for me was Elvis Presley's 'Baby Let's Play House'. Dad had somehow obtained a single of this early Sun recording. I would play it over and over, and really get down, on our deep white shaggy carpet: much like Tom Cruise in *Risky Business*, although I'd be in my Adidas tracksuit, not underpants. I wasn't hooked on rock and roll, but I did like it. Dad said the Elvis record was popular at resident parties when trainee doctors would get together. I feel we're getting deep into video montage territory here.

In fact, my family always had good cameras and we have 16mm footage going back to the forties. I'd also developed an interest in amateur photography. Perhaps it never really left me. It's just that everyone else is doing it now.

I was fond of my guitar. It even came on holiday trips, along with Dad's piano accordion. I still remember sitting on a pile of suitcases on the concrete driveway, waiting to leave but filled with joy at what lay ahead. Two weeks could feel like two years in today's world! I can even remember the smell sometimes. Roses, mixed with kangaroo grass and just a hint of dog faeces. Weird what stays with you.

We would go on holidays with other doctors' families. You might call us upper-middle class, if you wanted to be divisive. Our only cousins

My first electric guitar.

were also doctors' children and lived nearby. Canberra's scorched inland location meant that the ocean took on a mystical significance. Apparently, Australia's 'founding fathers' considered putting the national capital somewhere near Eden, on the NSW South Coast, but decided to build it in a random group of hills, well away from the surf. The Federation people sure got the location wrong. How different our Parliament and politicians might have been. Back then, the beach was the only prerequisite for a holiday. It had to be coastline. Snow, perhaps, could be included—after all it was made of water.

Mum's Church of England values also brought us together with the odd family in dire need of a holiday. Canberra was the sort of place where you might encounter the architect of Medicare (highly unpopular with most doctors) and find him in a broken marriage. My mother decided we should bring him and his kids along for camping therapy. My parents also made friends with another family, the Leans, during a light plane trip *en route* to an island holiday and, by the end, we were friends for life. They were there for all future camping trips. I can't imagine that happening anymore. One of the traveling hordes of kids, Sarah Macdonald, another doctor's child, wrote an article about one of our trips. By the time she wrote this, she had become a media personality. I later ran into her in the fractious world of ABC youth TV. I didn't know she could write this well. It brings it all back with beautiful clarity.

An ancient selfie.

Greg, Steve, Margie and Rob Appel (Dave must have been in his crib at that stage).

Those lazy, hazy, crazy days…

By Sarah Macdonald

Sandbar was a camping ground north of Myall Lakes on the mid-north coast of NSW. It was down a dirt track that branched off a scenic route of the Pacific Highway.

The camp site was a flat grassy area between the warm waters of Smiths Lake and the surf of Sandbar Beach. Melaleuca, twisted angophoras and gums shaded the tents. Stained white sand ringed the lake. Nearby was a pocket of temperate rainforest and a swamp full of frogs.

Our holiday was a group affair. Six adults and 18 kids pitched tents in a big circle around a 'No Camping' sign and a fire that smoked all day long. We created a world bordered by a kitchen tent, a wall of eskies, a grove of paperbarks and the brackish lake.

In this planet of childhood perfection there were two tribes: 'Kids' and 'The Olds'. We met up at mealtimes, when we children would swarm upon our parents to gobble and hop. Our backs were smothered with sunscreen, while our bites were disinfected and our cuts were covered. We ran wild the rest of the day: paddling or sailing, swinging from trees, wading through the swamp, catching waves, and fishing from sharp rocks. We'd gossip in age-based factions, our words swept up with the shrieks of cicadas, bower birds and kookaburras.

As the bush turned black and the sky pink, we'd unload firewood, consume cinder chops splattered with tomato sauce, and share the breathless thrill of ghost stories. We'd struggle to bed bone sore, our skin brown and scratched, our hair sticky with salt. We'd surrender to sleep while serenaded by the parents' camp-fire singing. The lilo would be deflating, and the sleeping bag would be itchy. My brother was always snoring, yet in the place that straddles dreams and consciousness, I would float high on happiness, nurtured by a deep love for a place and time.

Here I first felt the flush of romantic love (or at least hormones). He (I still dare not use his name) was the perfect object of affection

Chapter 2 : Dishwashing Liquid

Camping at Sandbar; Simon Pickworth on left, Steve Appel in middle with assorted Macdonalds, Deebles, Pickworths and Leans – me on right (or stage left?).

for a prepubescent. Part *Skippy*'s Sonny Hammond, part his older brother, Matt, he was a little bit Shaun Cassidy and a lot Leif Garrett. His oval face was tanned and smattered with freckles. Stringy blond hair fell into eyes of soft green. From his skinny chest hung a Bonds T-shirt of the same colour. Faded and floppy with wear, it emitted a smell I found intoxicating: a combination of burnt skin, Aeroguard, musty boy breath, salt spray and camp-fire cooking. He retained a detached indifference to life that I found dead sexy.

I fell in love with him on our last holiday at Sandbar. The giddiness I felt has ensured I remember it as my favourite trip, but there were other events that marked it as special. The level of the lake was so high the sandbar to the sea had to be opened. As soon as the bulldozers finished the dredge, the ocean began to suck the lake low, forming rushing rapids. The tribe of children built a flotilla that took us to the action. We were led by a motorboat containing a couple of The Olds.

Next came two 16-year old boys in a sailing boat, pulling two sets of 15-year-old girls in smaller boats. My friend Beth and I came next in a dinghy. The spunky boy and his younger brother shared a lime canoe tied to our stern. Behind them was a small tinnie full of little kids. My younger brother, Angus, came last, gripping his bucking lilo as he rode our wash, his laughing mouth filling with water, his limbs akimbo and his tiny brown body shining with wet.

The toddlers waved sadly from the sand, their hands held by mothers whose smiles were stretched tight with concern. I don't remember riding the rapids but my sister insists there were sharks waiting at the end of them.

That night our bodies were so swollen with swallowed sea water that the full moon seemed to turn a tide in our brains. After all the other campers had gone to bed, our tribe crept up to the toilet block, divided into gender-based gangs, and snuck inside. We each went into a loo or shower cubicle, locked the door and crawled out underneath so the 'occupied' sign remained showing. We galloped home whooping into the sky and sharing manic grins of thrill. In the morning we returned to watch those lesser beings (the children of the campervan families) stand with legs twisted and faces pinched while waiting for a toilet that would never be free.

The owner of the camping ground didn't take long to realise it was us. He berated our parents while we hid in the trees, trying desperately to not laugh. As I stuffed my fist in my mouth and wrapped a leg around a branch. I saw an expression on the parents' faces as they earnestly assured him we would be punished. They were trying not to giggle; one father seemed puffed with pride.

The camping ground owner may have hated us kids, but he didn't like the Olds much either. Every night they'd pull out an accordion, a guitar and a gallon of port and sing Bob Dylan's 'Blowin' in the Wind' and 'Hey, Mr Tambourine man', as well as 'Morning Has Broken' and 'Moonshadow' by Cat Stevens. Their musical taste and ability may have irritated the Sandbar owner, but it humiliated the teenage boys. Greg and Simon would stand behind the Oldies' sing-alongs rolling their eyes and muttering, 'Old hippies.' One night my mother decided that she had had enough of their teenage scorn. 'For God's sake, guys, if you're so cool, then show us! We'll do a concert on Friday night, and you kids do one on Saturday night,' she declared. 'The team with the best concert wins the right to bag the other.'

Simon and Greg took up the challenge and wrote an entire rock opera in two days. We all rehearsed madly. My elder sister, Sue, and Simon's sister Lucy stage-managed, choreographed and directed the production – and they promised to make my friend Beth and me stars.

On the second-to-last night, the parents sang

Foster/Tuncurry/Sandbar tourism brochure.

Chapter 2 : Dishwashing Liquid

their usual hippie songs, as well as some Aussie ballads, such as 'Inglewood Cocky'. They then performed a shadow in a tent, which involved miming a surgical operation that they thought was hugely hilarious. The Olds' last act involved my mother, Beth's mother and the boys' mother all standing with their hands like the children in *The Sound of Music*. They sang to the tune of 'Oh Dear, What Can the Matter Be':

> 'Oh dear, what can the matter be,
> Sandbar ladies locked in the lavatory.
> They were there from Friday to Saturday.
> And nobody knew they were there.'

We kids squirmed like snakes.

The next night was our show. The toddlers formed a rock group, whilst the adolescent boys performed a gymnastics display. The tweenies mimed ABBA's 'Rock Me' whilst Beth and I were the last act. The tape began and we emerged in our string crochet bikinis, which were covered in silver foil. We were gymnasts, yet our prepubescent, skinny, angular bodies had yet to be touched by any sense of rhythm. We were unaware of just how much we resembled praying mantises. We were also clueless about anything sexual and therefore willing to perform a song from the *Rocky Horror Picture Show*. We twisted our stick like limbs, thrust out our bony pelvises and gestured suggestively as we mouthed the words, 'I'm just a sweet transvestite. From transsssexual Transylvaniiiiaaaa...'

Our act ended with a cartwheel that landed in the splits. I looked up to see the Olds rapturous in their applause. I realise now they must have been killing themselves laughing on the inside. For a finale we all joined together for one song about our toilet raid: 'Midnight stampede, we're to going to get you and you and you and you and you'.

As the chorus reached its crescendo I looked at the dark shadows of the bush and the camp-fire-lit faces around me. I smelled the smoke and the gum trees. I tasted the salt on my lips. And I realised then that I would never forget this time and this place.

Sarah's article brings back those memories vividly. I can still hear the tune to 'Midnight Stampede'—heavily inspired by the Status Quo signature guitar riff. Every schoolboy guitarist could do that, along with 'Sunshine of Your Love' by Cream. The slightly pungent young boy was obviously Steve, my brother, who would go on to play in King Curly, as well as with me in the pretty much unknown One Head Jet. A bad name for quite a good band.

I digress. We return to sun-blasted Canberra, where I'm still growing up—enjoying life in this concrete and eucalypt paradise until...

Lizard sitting on a rock
Pulling away at his big cock

I think I quote correctly from Gavin Butler's poem. My primary school friend and I were in the final years of high school—or college as it was called in the ACT, which has stand-alone Years 11 and 12. Since Year 6, we had grown meaner—especially Gavin, although now I called him 'Gus'. My career as a name-maker-up had just begun.

Together, Gus and I would write and record rock operas—that's what we called them anyway. Monty Python's innocent English humour inspired our works. We'd leave school during our seemingly endless free periods, go to someone's house, eat hot chips—the one dish we had perfected—and listen to Monty Python records, which reliably reduced us to guffawing tears. Only another burning hot chip stuffed into our adolescent mouths could halt the mirth. They inspired our rock operas and got us writing. Gus's lizard lines, many years on, still work for me. It's got everything: Australian wildlife, landscape and a heavy sexuality that would soon overcome us.

To say that the dawning of this sexuality brings some negatives is putting it mildly. The devil must have brewed up testosterone one particularly inspired night, dousing all innocence in its intoxicating fluids. My memories of Canberra from the period just prior to the Lighthouse Keepers now go gloomy. I guess that goes with the music I started hearing at the time. But after an idyllic childhood, the nation's capital turned into a strange place to be at sixteen. Gus was a punk now. Somehow, the English working-class phenomenon resounded in

Guthugga Pipeline review, *The Canberra Times*, 1980.

Canberra's suburban wastelands—at least for a few.

It may have just been the bit about boredom that we focused on. *New Musical Express*[2] magazines were piled high in Gus's exposed besser brick bedroom. He even had badges. I couldn't quite go that far, but I did still sneak a look at his *NME*s. Full of important information about bands like X-Ray Spex, Sham 69 and The Undertones. Gus led the way into the dark world of punk rock, but I still enjoyed a little Elton John on the side. I was perhaps more interested in the post-punk scene, as there was such a diversity of music. We all went along to the Canberra Theatre to see the Stranglers and Graham Parker. Then there was the Australian National University Bar. Here you would find mainly Australian bands, anything from the Dynamic Hepnotics to Jimmy and the Boys. Ignatius Jones fronted this brave

---

2 In 2017 the *New Musical Express* finally closed shop. An era over. I guess the market for bitchy English reviews was swamped by internet ranters.

with the wine stains, there was always a bit of blood on the carpet. Somehow, I was always the one putting ABBA on at the end of the night. It went down well too. It seemed these punks wanted a Swedish high just the same as everyone else.

Like a lot of my friends, I still lived at home, where the middle-class life went on, despite punk. My mother did have a word to me about getting a job one day when I was lolling about in a hammock on our large backyard deck. It was kind of annoying, but times were different for school leavers in those days. I'd forgotten! I'd done a federal public service test. Someone sent me a letter and I was suddenly a well-paid Grade 4 Clerk, where I quickly learned from my superiors how to look busy while doing very little. It was amazing money, and I was quickly promoted to Grade 3 from some other exam I'd forgotten I'd done. Even less work, and more sitting down in that one. We spent most of the time watching a thermometer on the wall, because at a certain temperature you could go home. Sometimes, they just let you go anyway. Ah, flexi time—if only I'd stayed on—I'd be in an un-nameably high grade with enough super to cruise out the rest of my life. But I didn't. Can I blame punk rock? I don't think so. Possibly the broader concept of music, combined with meeting a girl called Juliet Ward. If so, thanks to both of you.[3]

band, doing the whole camp rock thing to pre-diversity pub rock audiences around the country. There was plenty of yelling about 'poofters' from the audience.

I had spent some time at an all-boys private school, which was a sudden descent into an old-world masculine environment that really stung. Aurora Hatzel and Jackie O'Callagan seemed a long way away during that period. And it all happened as the hormones hit. High schools back then had an atmosphere of brooding violence, both public and private. I later fled to the ACT public school 'college' system for the last two years. But I couldn't say it was that much more fun. The damage was done. We were all adolescents—doomed to wander the earth in a state of confused despair.

Once we left school, I remember visiting various rented government houses on barren lawns, where ten or so of us would gather to drink goons (flagons of cheap wine). Along

This was the end of the seventies and I played with Gus, in Guthugga Pipeline along with our new mate 'Hairy', an artsy type who had appeared in the last years of school. It was punk-inspired Anglo-boy stuff. Guthugga Pipeline was our first attempt at a band and it sounded like that.

We probably devoted more time to the name than the music. This was a period when I briefly did wear a badge. This was because we'd come up with a name for our

---

3 Cue ABBA: 'Thank You for the Music'?

Confessions of a Lighthouse Keeper: Greg Appel

Guthugga Pipeline, watched by their usual large crowd, at Garema Place in Canberra, with Bill the Busman on bench, facing band.

band that was represented by a blue square. The name could not be spoken, let alone written, just seen. We were far ahead of Prince and his symbol period with that one. But we soon got sick of explaining it to people and reverted to Guthugga Pipeline, a misspelling of the Snowy Mountains hydroelectric tunnel thing not far from Canberra. I'm pretty sure I came up with that inspired name.

I cast my mind to other punk-inspired bands in Canberra at that period. The Young Doctors, who changed their name to the Young Docteurs for a reason that still escapes me. The Vacant Lot, Myxo, and Tactics, who I recall reprimanding us for playing 'Road Runner' by the Modern Lovers when we supported them. It was their cover! The singer, David Studdert, used a high-pitched yelp to deliver what seemed to be an angry political discourse. He's still going for it on Facebook. I found this on the Lighthouse Keepers page.

I was there from the beginning I am so fucking bored with middle class wanna be's trying to re-invent themselves as past life exciting people in compensation for their shitty current lives. What a pillock.

David Studdert, Tactics, via Facebook[4]

Probably a good example of the camaraderie amongst Canberra punks. It was a small, divided scene. The photo says it all—playing to two people in an otherwise empty Garema Place in bright sunlight. You can see our number one fan—the one actually facing the band. Bill the Busman[5] was a little like Rainman, as played by Dustin Hoffman. He was known around town as an odd guy who was always on the local 'Action' buses, and could also tell you any time and bus route detail you might care to know.

---

4 Facebook, you know, that thing people stare at on their phones. I think he was actually getting stuck into another Canberra band, but on the Lighthouse Keepers page, so seems at least semi directed that way.

5 Bill has been sited fairly recently, reportedly identifying as a female.

Chapter 2 : Dishwashing Liquid

He also attended every local punk-related gig and had an encyclopedic knowledge of these acts. He had an interesting little dance. Punk events were really the only place where his straitjacket jerk might go unnoticed.

Often, he was the only one moving to the angsty beats. Bill was an under-appreciated figure. You need these people when you start a band. They're called fans.

No doubt that night a cover band would be playing in the same spot, pulling hundreds of happy yobbos (or booners, as we called them). We did play cover songs too— it's just no one outside a very small circle of like-minded people had heard them. Twenty years later, punk somehow became the number one music of choice for yobbos. At least we gave it a go. And Bill the Busman was streets ahead of his time.

I had started to write songs for Guthugga Pipeline which would fit in with the punky stuff. One day, I wrote something different inspired by a girl I had just met. She looked raggedly radiant on the couch in some blood-splattered living room. Long jet black hair (dyed of course), pale skin, a cigarette in one hand and a coffee cup of wine in the other.

Little beady eyes are watching her for sometime

They come in close but she says she doesn't really mind

The secret plan is underhand he takes his aim

He takes her hand and says to her 'what can I say?'

When I read these lyrics now, I realise it was obviously me who was the Gargoyle that watched Juliet through beady eyes (I think some kid on the bus to school had said I had

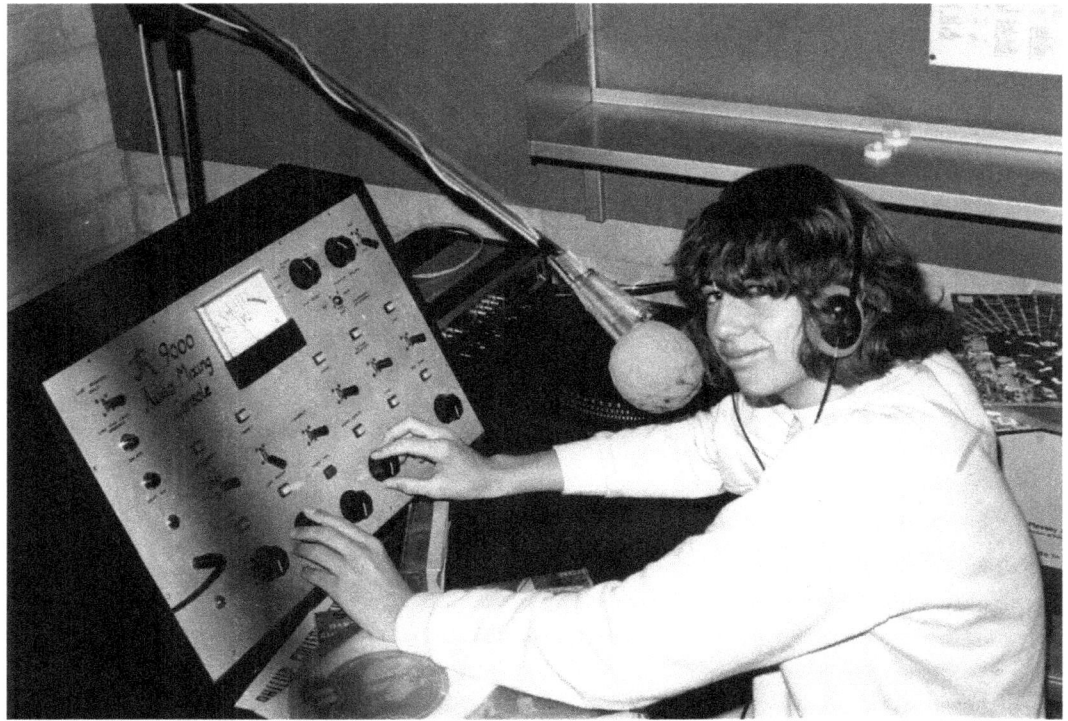
Me pretending I know what I'm doing with these dials.

goggly eyes—I didn't have a comeback despite the fact that he was a not-great-looking redhead). Eventually, we recorded the song in Sydney and put the record out as The Lighthouse Keepers—and 'Gargoyle' it was indeed named—on our very own Guthugga Pipeline records.

And step by step he takes her down and down the stairs

Is this heaven or hell?

Because I can't tell

But I don't seem to care[6]

I remember vividly, if a bit foggily,[7] the night I went down those stairs referred to in the song lyric. Because when I first met Juliet, she lived under a house. Literally. If the roles had been reversed and it had been a man leading a woman into this dark space, I don't think the outcome would have been so positive. I don't know if she paid rent, but she'd set up a bed on the dirt amongst the brick columns that formed the foundations of this group house. There were a few scary objects scattered about in the gloom—lit by a few candles in bottles, possibly some bones, perhaps a Patti Smith poster glaring at me from the dark. In fact, it looked a little like a serial murderer's lair (as depicted in movies anyway). But luckily Juliet was a female and to me it was a wonderful place—I loved the decorations and the whole spooky vibe.

This was a period before the phrase 'self harm' came into being. I also understood that Juliet didn't want to talk about it, not that I really wanted to. With all the punk aesthetic around us and the general undercurrent of suburban gloom, it just seemed to fit in. Some people would do this sort of thing for fun of an evening.

While I didn't feel like slashing myself,

6   Teenage lyrics can be a little cringeworthy!
7   There may have been real fog around—being Canberra.

Juliet playing Pacman.

I had a few suspenseful nights back at my parents' house, where I still resided. I waited to see if Juliet was interested in continuing what I thought was a very promising relationship. And a few days later, she turned up. Amongst the bushy Australian native garden at the front of our house, I watched the twin silhouettes of Juliet and her dog Chaos—a good looking golden retriever—coming down the drive! Our dog at the time was a vicious but faithful black Labrador cross called Pluto. Creatively named by a previous owner who'd obviously done a few bad things to him. As the two dogs tore each other apart downstairs, I realised Juliet's visit meant she was interested in me as an object.

Perhaps the Lighthouse Keepers really started near Bermagui. It's a wild, sparsely-populated area on the NSW South Coast, made slightly famous by Salman Rushdie,

Chapter 2 : Dishwashing Liquid

Me, Juliet and Chaos; Bermagui, 1983.

because it's such a good place to hide. Juliet's parents had a shack there, just a few hours' drive from Canberra. Once there, we would play all sorts of songs on our acoustic guitars—weird and wonderful things learnt from Juliet's father's eclectic reel-to-reel tape collection. These were cover songs again, but way back—before punk, even before the sixties, where I thought musical time had begun. 'St James Infirmary Blues', 'Blood on the Saddle', 'King of the Road'. The songs still come back loud and clear. By the warmth of an open fire, I discovered Juliet had a hauntingly beautiful voice with an edge. Happy times for me again. That burden of sexuality suddenly all made sense.

If the beginnings of the band were in the wilds of the NSW South Coast, the group as an entity came together in Sydney. By the end of the seventies, the six-hour drive from Canberra had been cut down, courtesy of some new bits of freeway. But taking the trip there in my old VW Beetle from my middle-class world could be quite confronting.

Sydney was hot and smoggy, and strangely alluring. Its streets were full of thick smells, people and all sorts of stuff. After years of mixing in a fairly homogenous world, my eyes were suddenly opened. I started to go there as much as I could, strongly motivated by primitive instincts—i.e. Juliet was ensconced there. Tagging along with her softened the blows a lot.

If Canberra had a wilder side, she was already walking on it. She had gathered a group of friends from her days at an even more alt-Canberra school than me. AME[8] was a radical place built on the sixties dreaming of some longer-haired public servants. I don't think the kids had to go to class much at all. There seemed to be a lot of expressing of oneself involved in the curriculum, if Juliet's stories were true, plus a lot of bitching. She was heavily into animals and rode horses. Perhaps it was her way of escaping the heavy school vibes.

A few of her old classmates were involved in our punky world. Some of them were very advanced in their drug use, and their parents were also pretty good about them having sex in the house. Hairy even got a girlfriend from this group that performed this very act with him—for at least a few weekends. Pink had gone seamlessly from hippie to punk (just like Johnny Rotten, I believe). She had the fashion spot on, with carefully positioned safety pins, and looked very 'Anarchy in the UK'. I'm sure Hairy appreciated her open attitudes to sexuality like every young man would, though I never asked him. We just looked on with slight awe at our friend's unexpected success in the pine-bunked bedroom.

I certainly felt this aspect of sixties counter-culture was generally positive! Our group of friends were almost nerds, but not quite that focused or intelligent. But then again

8 The Association of Modern Education School.

it was my mate Gus, the composer of the Lizard poem, and now Guthugga Pipeline's singer,[9] who was the dux of Garran Primary. Nevertheless, girls were pretty hard to come by. Alternative types were our only hope.

This was all happening at the tail end of the 1970s and, as we move into the eighties, it might be useful to set the scene of the times with the Top 40 of the first year. These are the songs that were actually popular with the masses, and not the sort of things me and my associates were listening to. Or were we?

Is the Top 20, or whatever they call it now, still this good? There's not really all that much that's really awful amongst this. I don't much care for 'Another Brick in the Wall' by Pink Floyd, but it's kind of catchy in a supermarket setting. There's a few overly soppy ballads. But… there was a lot going on.

So not only was there action in the popular music sphere that we pretended to ignore, the world was changing. In Australia, we had the Lindy Chamberlain dingo baby thing—an episode that seems more meaningful in retrospect. John Lennon was shot in New York at the end of that year. I remember I was playing with Hairy in the Grant Brothers, (a short-lived band named after two brothers who never actually joined) at the Griffin Centre. This was a venue that looked like a Soviet-era block of flats in the empty heart of Canberra's CBD. The news came through to us at some point during the proceedings. There was one Grant sister called Jane, who despite her brothers' non-appearance, had turned up at the show. I clearly remember her saying loudly, 'Oh, well, he was getting ugly', in reference to the deceased. I realised that she was doing this for dramatic effect, but thought perhaps she

---

AUSTRALIAN TOP 20 CHART 1980

1. I GOT YOU .... Split Enz
2. TURNING JAPANESE .... The Vapours
3. CRAZY LITTLE THING CALLED LOVE .... Queen
4. ANOTHER BRICK IN THE WALL, PART 2 Pink Floyd
5. BRASS IN POCKET .... The Pretenders
6. CAN'T STOP THE MUSIC .... Village People
7. SPACE INVADERS .... Player
8. MORE THAN I CAN SAY .... Leo Sayer
9. FUNKYTOWN .... Lipps Inc.
10. PLEASE DON'T GO ...... KC and the Sunshine Band
11. TIRED OF TOEIN' THE LINE .... Rocky Burnette
12. DON'T STOP TIL YOU GET ENOUGH ....
.... Michael Jackson
13. WHAT I LIKE ABOUT YOU .... The Romantics
15. UPSIDE DOWN .... Diana Ross
16. MOSCOW .... Genghis Khan
17. YOU'VE LOST THAT LOVIN' FEELIN' ...... Long John Baldry & Kathi McDonald
18. HE'S MY NUMBER ONE .... Christie Allen
19. CALL ME .... Blondie
20. BABOOSHKA .... Kate Bush

---

was going too far, and she better stop yelling about it. Maybe she was channelling punk.

I think in a time not too far from now, the Beatles will become an actual religion. There's everything there, the hymns, the creed, the crucifixion—and what's more, it's all properly recorded on tape and film. This was not possible in real biblical times, where things were only written down hundreds of years after, then transcribed into Greek, Latin and the rest.

I think this was the same night when another violent incident shook our little world. It was definitely at the Griffin Centre with the Grant Brothers anyway. There were a few other bands on the bill making up most of the small uninterested crowd. The central location of this venue meant that local yobbos (we used to call them 'booners' in the ACT) could get to it easily. For instance, there

---

[9] Perhaps vocalist is a better word—a character vocalist—as per the spirit of punk.

Chapter 2 : Dishwashing Liquid

The Grant Brothers; Hairy, Tony and me.

was a gang led by 'Red Fox' who got around in a yellow panel van that often pulled up around the front of the building. These kind of thoroughbred thugs loved to terrorise the new wave and punk followers. They knew that beneath the badges and safety pins, a weedy wimp could always be found. With a few exceptions...

There was a guy from that period called Trogg, who I think was into punk. Anyway, he seemed to decide my old mate Gus/Gavin was a good drink and drug buddy, and therefore hung around with us. He had an extremely wild look in his bloodshot eyes. Images of sitting in his share house flood back to me. He was 'married' to a tiny girl called Kim, who sat silently on the couch with him. Blood from weeks ago was caked on the cork-tiled floor. No one was ever going to clean it up. A stained Radio Birdman record cover was on the floor. (Strangely, Rob Younger from this band was to become a good family friend later in life.)

Since Trogg was part of our world at the time, he'd often come to shows like the Griffin Centre events. With people like Red Fox circling the building, there was always the potential for trouble. Sometimes, drunken punks decided they were feeling a bit tough too, and used their puny fists to do battle amongst each other. Trogg was a reasonable size, however, and his studded leather jacket with matching wrist-bands gave him a formidable air. But trouble was about to come from further afield.

I've referred to my cousins earlier. We'd all grown up together and got on well. They were a family of four boys and, perhaps because of this, they seem to have an extra air of masculinity. They were even good at sport. Their dad had been an athlete and they all had big chests and hints of what would be called a sixpack now. My cousin Peter had been a good companion as we grew up, and could be described as a sort of enlightened yobbo at the point he enters the story. He even considered himself *au fait* with new wave and punk. I remember he had a bit of a confused cassette collection of 'G' tapes that included some authentic punk works, but then might throw to a dodgy seventies artist that was not credible on any level, such as Warren Zevon. Anyway, as a musical connoisseur, what better night to see what his cousin was up to at the Griffin Centre? (his mate Tony was also the Grant Brothers drummer).

Peter had a bit of an attitude and his own entourage. People knew it when they entered a room. During one of the other acts, there was an attempt at pogoing, probably pretty pathetically. But the bouncing led to bumping and somehow a scuffle broke out. I hadn't formerly introduced Trogg and my cousin Peter, but now they seemed to be getting to know each other—in an intensely physical way. The fight got pretty wild and the dance floor was cleared as these two tribal leaders battled it out.

I couldn't help but be a little proud of my cousin as Trogg was reduced to a quivering wreck. But I didn't think it wise to let Trogg know I was related to his new arch foe. And the legend of 'Pete the Basher' grew amongst my friends. And people say, Canberra's a boring place! We had to make our own fun. I'm sure this sort of fun went on with young people all over the country. This all-pervading atmosphere of youthful violence has diminished considerably over the years, though the media like to pretend otherwise. However, I don't feel nostalgic for it, like I do about smoking. Such was Trogg's legend that rumours abound. Someone said he was all better now after a time in Goulburn Jail. Another said he was a Christian. Good old Jesus.

At the time, I didn't really question all this juvenile delinquency that was happening around me. It just seemed to be what you did. It didn't seem out of place when one of our mates got into smack, turned yellow with hepatitis and got a prostitute for a girlfriend. Well, apparently he did—I don't think I ever saw her—I just heard all of the difficulties he was having with the relationship (as you can imagine).

It wasn't only Sydney that I was coming to terms with. I'd already decided that I wanted to travel to the old country, the UK. I'm not quite sure why. It seemed you just did it if you were a young Australian, a colonial pilgrimage. I could see some of my punk mates rotting on couches in both Sydney and Canberra and I didn't want to do that. I'd already booked the tickets and planned it all out when I got together with Juliet. So it was extremely bad timing. Would she be there when I returned from abroad?

Cat with whisky.

Hairy.

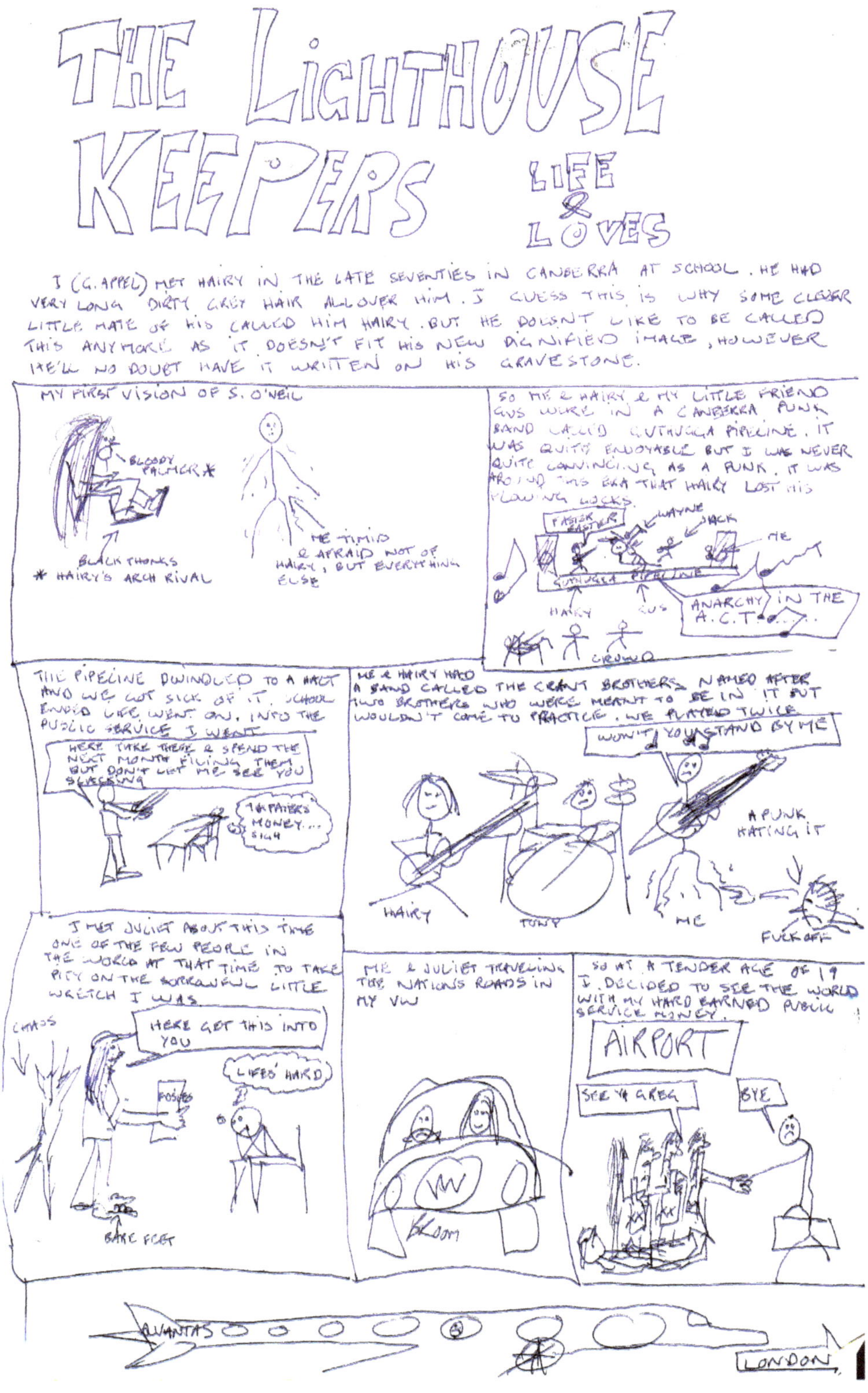

Chapter 2 : Dishwashing Liquid

THE LIGHTHOUSE KEEPERS LIFE & LOVES

I (G. APPEL) MET HAIRY IN THE LATE SEVENTIES IN CANBERRA AT SCHOOL. HE HAD VERY LONG DIRTY GREY HAIR ALL OVER HIM. I GUESS THIS IS WHY SOME CLEVER LITTLE MATE OF HIS CALLED HIM HAIRY. BUT HE DOESN'T LIKE TO BE CALLED THIS ANYMORE AS IT DOESN'T FIT HIS NEW DIGNIFIED IMAGE, HOWEVER HE'LL NO DOUBT HAVE IT WRITTEN ON HIS GRAVESTONE.

CHAPTER 3

Lighthouse Keepers

Photo: Bleddyn Butcher.

I returned from my grand tour of Western Culture—the UK, Europe and back through America. It was somehow good for me to deal with travel, unpleasant English types, and know I could survive. The real English punks on the Tube were truly terrifying and I found most of the music scene there pretty ugly. Europe was a bit more fun. By the time I got to America, I was just plain homesick. Enough was enough and I returned to sunny Australia. I was happy to get back.

We didn't have the internet in those days, and my contact with Juliet had been limited to very expensive phone calls and actual handwritten letters. Really, I had no idea what to expect when I returned. Indeed, Juliet was making some strange connections back in Australia.

In our country, there is a rather tedious tradition of calling redheads 'Blue'. And Juliet had become acquainted with one of these characters in the Sydney suburb of Ultimo, where she was living at the time. He got about in an Afro, like punk had never happened.

> The first time I met Juliet Ward was 1980 or '81. I was sitting in the Glasgow Arms Hotel (later dubbed 'the legs' by Juliet) with some of the people I lived with. She looked a bit different from the usual crew in the back room near the jukebox and video

games. I remember her wearing black jeans, a light blue Mobil oil work shirt and having bare feet. Chaos, Juliet's golden retriever, followed her past me towards the bar and ignored me when I tried to pat him. Juliet also ignored me, but I was pretty shy, so I can't say that I would have tried to talk to her.

Blue, Lighthouse Keepers

Blue was just one of, what seemed to me, a slavering pack of men who were hanging around Juliet in my absence. Indeed, it was dogs that would break the silence between them. Blue had a small black dog called Bubbalouie that would yap at Juliet's dog, Chaos, safely behind a corrugated iron fence at the back of Blue's group house. Unluckily for Bubbalouie, the incline of the yard and a hole in the fence meant that Chaos could piss on the irritating animal. And so Juliet and Blue got talking at the local pub. But Blue had a few more conversation starters as back-up. A steady supply of cheap wine and a harmonica.

> Juliet would often tell me about a mythical Canberra band called Guthugga Pipeline [sic] and of its nucleus, Hairy, Gus and Greg. These superheroes seemed to be giants or gods and often, I would listen to their live performances on Juliet's tapes in between her Stiff Little Fingers albums. Eventually, Greg returned from his solo world tour. He didn't look ten-foot tall and five-foot wide at the shoulders.

Blue, Lighthouse Keepers

To quickly remove any suspense from this saga—once I returned to Australia, me and Juliet took up where we left off. I shook Blue by the hand in a manly way, and we partook of alcohol together. By that stage, Juliet was living in a group house that included Jack from Guthugga Pipeline's sister, Megan. She came with a leather-trousered guy—one of

Andy Hall, my colonial friend beginning his stockbroking career in London. His goal was to make enough money to retire at 40. Pretty much achieved!

her many boyfriends. Australia's colourful characters seemed almost tame compared to the evil English fellows that I'd dealt with—such as the flatmates of my expatriate friend, Andy Hall, in London. These nasty fellows were far enough up the extremely complex British class ladder to look down on colonials like me.

Now back in good old Sydney, everyone was much friendlier. Megan's boyfriend suggested having sex with me one evening, when no one else was sitting on the grubby couch with us. I politely declined but, after he stole the giant 'Silver' brand cassette player I had lugged back from Asia, I took steps to minimise the numbers in the household. Juliet was in agreement and gleefully got a few more cats so we didn't feel lonely. But Juliet's new friend Blue liked to drop in unannounced and make himself at home—as was the fashion in those times.

Chaos.

> I remember being at Juliet and Greg's house, blind drunk and playing my harmonica, when they returned home. Greg then complimented me on my playing. He later invited me to play at a talent contest and I was in the band!
>
> Blue, Lighthouse Keepers

Now to the Lighthouse Keepers' opening show. Yes, it was a talent contest! I had begun studying at what is now called UTS, but was then the NSW Institute of Technology. It was an insubstantial but very enjoyable course that would eventually give me a Bachelor of Arts in Communications. The talent contest was put on by the Student Union in a carpeted concrete bunker of a bar, usually full of drunken engineering students. I don't know what possessed me to enter us in the contest.

Me and Juliet both loved novelty songs—good ones anyway—though this was an unspoken love, a bit like our own emotional relationship. Novelty songs are now a dying art form—poor old serious world. But these songs formed the core of our repertoire for the talent quest. We had Blue on the harmonica, and Juliet's dog Chaos barking along as a bonus. I had purchased a cheap twelve-string guitar, which would serve me well for many years. At that time, we also had Tim Palmer on bass. Now he's a Walkley award-winning ABC journalist—more on that species later.

Tim was also 'studying' communications and we were drawn together by a passing obsession with trucking music. Drunken nights listening to songs like 'Give Me 40 Acres and I'll Turn This Rig Around' and 'The Woman Behind the Man Behind the Wheel'—classics that I still remember note for note. For the talent quest, we chose the name Tex Truck and the Semis. I think Tim was 'Tex'. Our finale was 'Cigarettes and Whiskey and Wild Wild Women', an atmospheric American novelty song. Tim sang 'cigarettes!' with the best hillbilly twang he could muster. It be-

Chapter 3 : Lighthouse Keepers

came 'Higarites' yelled in a loud raspy voice. Adding a certain strangeness to an already strange show, Tim played the bass exactly like his hero, Steve Kilbey from the Church. Exactly like how he imagined Steve Kilbey played it anyway, with an ethereal pout and bass hanging low. Occasionally, to keep up appearances, he'd make contact with the strings. It was better this way, I think. But he yelled 'Higarites!', to perfection. At the time, the real Steve Kilbey was a serious and remote Bohemian creature in a paisley shirt. I've got to know him a little since then. He has a more nuanced off-stage alter ego and doesn't mind a bit of slapstick humour. Australia is a small place and its music people bump into each other like asteroids from the eighties video game.

Tim didn't last long on the bass but, like me—against all odds—he ended up with a career in the industry that our Bachelor of Arts degree was supposedly preparing us for. I sometimes bump into him in the ABC Ultimo lifts, just across the road from where the UTS talent quest was held in 1982. My mind almost never goes back to the time when Tim was Tex, rasping away at full volume, the dog barking and the engineers in hysterics, as we romped home with first prize. From these dizzying heights, the Lighthouse Keepers came into being.

Once Tex was gone, we all agreed that we needed a better name. And luckily, my early instincts to archive my life have left me with hard empirical evidence, like name lists. At the top of the next column is the original list of names, with votes.

How nice to have enough free time to take a band name list seriously. These days, tax returns, washing dishes and general mind-numbing tasks take over the mind along with a little terror! Back then, the washing-up could wait another day at least. From all this list-making, we actually came up with a good name.

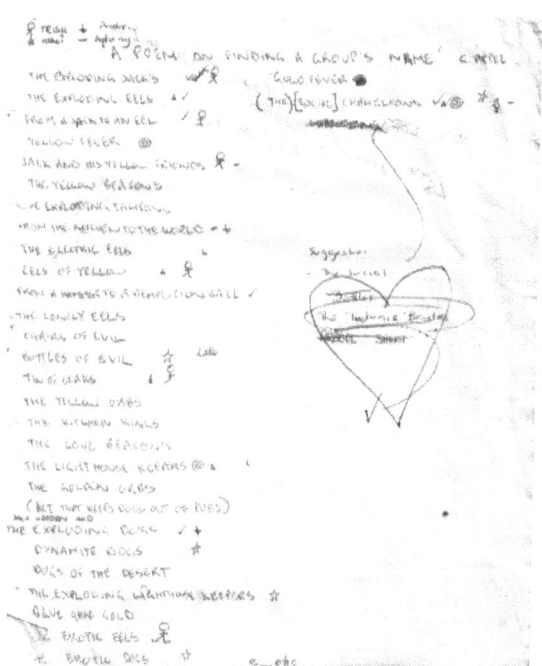

Original list of names, with votes.

I think the names of my bands slowly degenerated after this. Our next band, the Rainlovers, turned into the Widdershins, then after Hammerhead there was One Head Jet. You might be unfamiliar with these excellent bands—all world-class acts. But the one most people remember (though not that many) is the Lighthouse Keepers.

The Lighthouse Keepers were a pretty apolitical band but we did have amongst us a real old-fashioned communist. It turned out Blue had a red side. He was a lapsed communist by then but, as we got to know him, he regaled us with tales of Australia's left-wing past. He was a little older than us, so was easily placed in the ranting old man category and, sadly his stories of revolution largely fell on drowsy middle-class ears. To give you a sense of his conversational technique, let's wind forward to 2008, when none of us had heard from Blue for about fifteen years. The rumours he was in Italy proved to be true. On his return, I made contact.

Blue, Britannia Hotel.

By this stage, I'd had children, made a few documentaries, and done all sorts of things, but I knew I had the old Blue on the phone when he ignored all formalities and launched into an obscure anecdote about his Italian acquaintances, often breaking into actual Italian. But I'll let Blue speak for himself. He has written his own version of some of the events about to unfold. His style can be rambling and he is still 'enamoured with Marxist approaches to studying the past'. But read on—this is one of the gifts that the completely free university education of this period has made to the future.

> And so, I now know a bit about history, the construction of identity and personal beliefs. Not that it has done me much good: my identity and personal beliefs came into contact with a market-driven, profit-maximising, top-down managed private training company so much so that I now find myself unemployed and at the tender age of sixty, facing a very uncertain future. So don't be surprised if I occasionally

Hackett Street, Ultimo.

digress to lay the metaphorical boot into the couple of bullies I encountered in my recent work.

I had drifted into university in the mid to late seventies. Like most Western world youth at the time, I was interested in music, and due to the influence of Chris Winter in his pre-Double J days and Bob Hudson on early JJ, as well as shows like *GTK* on ABC TV, I was enamoured of the blues or what is now sometimes called 'roots' music. So much so that I could annoy people on both harmonica and badly tuned acoustic slide, or bottleneck guitar.

By this time, I had become resigned to living on the 'dole' in cheap share houses in inner-city Sydney. At this time of high unemployment, the late 1970s and early 1980s, there was a lot of free music in the pubs, wine bars and cafes ('hippy' cafes) of inner-city Sydney. In the inner city, the cost of living was relatively low and, probably most importantly, grog was cheap. There was also a lot of live music in the suburbs. Another big influence was the media: from articles and gig guides in the newspapers to community radio, 2SER and, most importantly, JJ, was just up the road in Forbes Street, Darlinghurst.

It was also possible to live on the 'dole' and the student study allowance which in a sense subsidised a lot of this 'lifestyle': lifestyle in inverted commas because the word probably wasn't used much at the time. What was happening was not really considered a permanent choice for most people. People drifted into music because it was possible, and into the inner city attracted by cheap rents and cost of living, a sort of communal life and a relative freedom to indulge in sex, drugs and rock'n'roll.

Blue, Lighthouse Keepers

Dear reader. Are you with us still? Blue writes much like he talks. I have foggy memories of his endless yarns during long trips with the band or during those frequent moments in the music world where you're just waiting somewhere… But I always found there was something enlightening in his wide-ranging ruminations. Almost by accident, he'd stumble across something interesting.

This was a period where Juliet and I would get out of the house a bit and socialise with other people, some who didn't even come from Canberra. There were people from all over Australia, and even Sydney itself. Blue, for instance, came from the city's southern suburb of Bexley, as he repeatedly told us in many anecdotes. Sydney at the time seemed a vastly different city to the cranky real-estate-obsessed place it has become. This was perhaps because we were all young and never had a thought about investing in property or flashing our car lights at strangers—besides, we were very pleasant natured.

Our inner-city scene was a scene within a scene. It was a small world but bigger

The Britannia Hotel, Cleveland Street.

than punk in Canberra. It was also quite diverse and punks were a minor part of a kaleidoscope of creatures. Some in paisley shirts, some in cheesecloth, some in leather. Traditional garb like flannelette was popular too. Sydney smelt different. Leaded petrol fumes, wisteria, cigarettes, beer. There seemed to be other young people everywhere and not a lot of effort was required to engage with them. Everyone was your friend. Everyone also seemed to be in a band. You didn't have to like their band—you probably didn't—but you'd go and see them anyway. We were also united by an antipathy to whatever what was perceived as mainstream.

> I think there was a certain hatred of music as well as the love for it. They have *Countdown*[1] reunions now, but all we did every Sunday night was sit around and say how fucked everyone was. The whole nation did it.
>
> Juliet, Lighthouse Keepers, 2015

[1] The ABC TV show, of course.

While I still kept a few ABBA records in my record collection, Elton John's were quietly left back in Canberra. Whether we loved it or not, there was a lot of music going on. Some bands such as Hunters and Collectors or Do-Ré-Mi might present an anti-commercial attitude, but this could get confusing if they became popular. Legend would have it that this thriving scene was supported by the Federal Government, with their handy universal arts grant, 'the dole', as Blue has just told us. It is kind of true. We all complained this amount was not enough, but in retrospect it was pretty adequate. If you had a reasonable rent situation, you could somehow go out and get quite drunk most nights of the week. A small side job could make for a decent financial situation. Even better was playing in a band, where your entertainment for that night was already sorted, with unlimited free beer if you got a crowd. Consequently, many musicians have bad alcohol problems for life. My own could be called mid-level by Australian

Chapter 3 : Lighthouse Keepers

standards and serious by American. I sometimes wonder if there is a class action that musicians could bring against the breweries and/or venues. Strangely, the Lighthouse Keepers had a lot of lawyer fans (well, a few anyway) but class action has never transpired. I wouldn't do it to you anyway, Carlton United Breweries. You've been a good friend…

The post-punk mood in inner Sydney also meant a wide variety of bands recorded their work and put out records themselves. These were now called 'independent' records on 'independent' labels. When I come across some of the music from this scene now, it sounds enthusiastic, but thin. Tim Pittman was a music fan from back then, who turned into a promoter. He refers to himself as a professional gambler.

> For independent acts in the eighties, it was a real struggle to get a decent sound. A lot of those early records don't sound that great. Everyone was trying to stamp their authority on sound but no one really knew how to do it. I like lo-fi. With real garagey punk—it works. But trying to do it with something a little more sophisticated like dance music or something with a few different melodies going on—that doesn't really work.
>
> Tim Pittman, promoter (still)

Hairy.

The Australian music scene at this time was large and diverse, with a healthy mainstream that was just getting into those snare drum sounds that reverberated out of FM radio, laden with expensive effects. It was the signature sound of the times. David Nichols was another music fan who was around in those days. I met him when he was writing a fanzine called *Distant Violins* that featured a lot of the lo-fi music in this book. He remembers the time when Australian recording studios finally got the international stamp of approval.

> Duran Duran came to Sydney to record at EMI in 1983. That was a big moment—when Australia was deemed to have the required facilities to do those kind of world-class albums.
>
> David Nichols, some sort of academic

But the Lighthouse Keepers themselves sound like they were recorded in the sixties, or perhaps before then. In fact we recorded our music in the same 'new romantic' period as Duran Duran. Big studio drum sounds might have been all the rage—but they were out of our price range. And it was for a budget-priced recording session that the Lighthouse Keepers truly came together as an original band.

Recording Gargoyle

Well Greg and Juliet had a friend named Keith, who recorded the two of them doing a version of "I fall to pieces" on a four track tape recorder. I think Juliet met him first as he looked after her when she used to get drunk at Laughing Clowns concerts, when Kei was mixing for them, and Greg was away touring the world solo.

Keith at the mixing desk: Dream Studios.

The key to this was my band mate from the punk days in Canberra, Hairy. Luckily, Stephen O'Neil still has a lot of hair, and therefore can still carry off the nickname which has remained with him, just like the hair. He was—and still is—an excellent instinctive musician. He seemed to be able to play everything. Despite his long mane, Hairy had always been more of a punk than I was when we were both in Guthugga Pipeline back in Canberra. At school, he'd been the keeper of authentic rock knowledge. He had a good collection of records that went deeper than the Sex Pistols and the Clash. We learned about the Stooges, the Modern Lovers and all sorts of stuff from him. Me and Hairy had a few side projects like the Grant Brothers too and now, both in Sydney, we decided to record some of the songs from this short-lived band. In addition, I wanted to record something with Juliet. So it all kind of merged together.

Another of Juliet's new friends who appeared during my overseas sojourn was a guy called Keith Hale. He'd been round the traps a bit in the sixties, and lived in a Chinatown warehouse with some counter-cultural types. It was here that they'd set up Dream Studios. Keith was quite idealistic about recording and must have seen something in us. He certainly stayed up very late into the night, recording our not-very-tight band and keeping us motivated. There were no lines of coke in sight, just cans of it. Around this time, I remember Keith slipping me a Gram Parsons record. I didn't realise what he'd given me 'til much later. But Keith knew we loved country music, as the first thing we recorded with him was a version of Patsy Cline's 'I Fall to Pieces'.

> Dream Studios was in an old Haymarket warehouse. It consisted of a small room downstairs with a hole in the ceiling where the microphone leads ran through to the mixing desk and tape machines that were upstairs. I remember a lot of running up and down the (rather steep and long) staircase between each take to have a listen and decide if we were happy with the results.
>
> Hairy, Lighthouse Keepers

I'm using some of Hairy's extensive archives from this period to go into fine detail about our first recording. They reveal that we began on the tenth of January 1983, and paid Keith $100, to record four songs for us. The cover of 'I Fall To Pieces' and three of my songs, including 'Gargoyle'. We then borrowed $500 from Hairy's parents to press the records. To save money, we bought some plastic sleeves and some wholesale paper to make covers by decorating them individually by hand.

Today, there is a generation of 'retro' enthusiasts who lust for analog recordings and vinyl. They would be wide eyed at what was going on when we mastered *Gargoyle* with Don Bartley at EMI's Studio 301. It was all about lathes and tracking the groove, while

The Lighthouse Keepers inspect *Gargoyle*, Australian National University.

VU meters jerked about. But this warm and fuzzy technology was not always trouble-free, as Hairy records:

> The Big Day, Monday 7 March 1983—went to get the records, brought them home and found 300 were warped, and 200 had dreadful surface noise. We sent them back!
>
> We eventually got our 500 unwarped records and began the laborious task of making the individual covers.
>
> By the time we had put all our drawings and marks on the covers, we were reluctant to part with them. Ap[2] generally did stick figures, sometimes in perverse situations, whilst Blue provided dreams of the Apocalypse and witty social comment. In fact, Blue was having a lot of nightmares at the time. Juliet did heavily detailed and very stylised drawings, while mine were generally abstract. We also roped in various other helpers, with Greg's brothers springing to mind.
>
> Hairy, Lighthouse Keepers

2 This was my nickname.

Our commercial activities were all very eco-friendly. We physically took our records to shops like Phantom, Redeye, and Scratches in Sydney. We also posted them to Greville in Melbourne and Impact in Canberra. In addition, we'd sell records at shows. Months of toiling over the covers and heartbreaking separations from the artworks followed, until all were sold. Later in the year, we pressed a further 500, all of which had sold by early 1984. Later in May 1984, Hot Records re-released it. Our ecological footprint would never be the same. But Blue, our harmonica and slide player, cannot help looking back at these times from a Marxist perspective.

> So, there were these ideas, very self-contradictory ideas, of small enterprises battling the majors, professionalism versus do-it-yourself and self-expression, commercialism versus authenticity, and mainstream suburban versus 'street cred'. I listened to people extol the virtues of small-scale produce and craft markets, and the sense of ownership and control over your own creativity and life that this

gave. Having studied economic history, I was wary of this: markets, being what they are, would tend to lead to concentration of ownership, money and control. Without a more democratic exercise of decision-making and power, markets would eventually replicate the rise of new privileged monopolising elite who would most likely be co-opted by the major companies.

Blue, Lighthouse Keepers

But, happily, we made enough money from this inner-city micro economy to pay back the $500 borrowed from Hairy's parents. Hairy's father had actually been an active communist—perhaps that's why we didn't have to pay interest on the loan. Anyway, here is historical proof that a band could record something and sell it at a profit. Today, this is very difficult and recordings are mainly considered as promotional vehicles for the live act—which often doesn't pay that well anyway.

And so *Gargoyle* was born and sent out to the shops of Australia. It wasn't a huge hit at the time, but it definitely established the band. I was personally growing more confident and less gargoyle-like on a daily basis. Sydney seemed to be embracing us, and the inner-city world was opening up.

We scored some publicity early. At the time, Clinton Walker was both a rock critic and a groover round town with a bit of a smack habit (which would have gone unnoticed by us). I'm tempted to quote from a story he once wrote to illustrate the sort of person who might appear at our door—so I will.

> In the years between about 1983 and 1986, I had more sex with more women than I've had in all the rest of my life.
>
> Clinton Walker from *Men Love Sex*, a collection of short stories by Aussie masculist authors, Random House 1995

So dear reader, we are getting into confessional territory at last! And these days, Clinton still stands by his prose. How do I know? Because I turned a camera on him recently and asked him a few questions about these happy times.

You know what that is? That's a good opening line. That's what your twenties are for!

So back in the day, we let this man into the house to interview us, taking a break from his busy sex life! What band can resist talking about themselves for half an hour? We felt like artists. And here was Clinton, from darkest Surry Hills, where the heroin-taking thing went on. Things were starting to get interesting, but would he write something good about a band on the more jingly-jangly side of Cleveland Street?

My first real introduction to Sydney had actually been the Surry Hills area, where all the heroin takers gravitated. At the time, I was travelling up from Canberra every weekend to a big share house in Bourke Street, with trucks rumbling past all night and all sorts of dissolute youths lurking in every crevice. There seemed to be about twenty people sleeping in this place and I'm sure they got into a bit of the gear. I could also see their beady eyes focusing on my recently obtained girlfriend. I had to rescue Juliet from this sort of Dickensian hovel in the early phase of our relationship.

Clinton's book *Inner City Sounds* is a good reference book for this era—if you want to go a little deeper into the bands around—especially this smacked-out scene. I'm pretty sure it's still available. Clinton was a little bit of a rock star himself, and looked the part. I think he fancied himself as Australia's Lester Bangs—for those who know of that American rock critic's work and persona.

On opposite page: hand-drawn covers of the *Gargoyle* EP.

Chapter 3 : Lighthouse Keepers

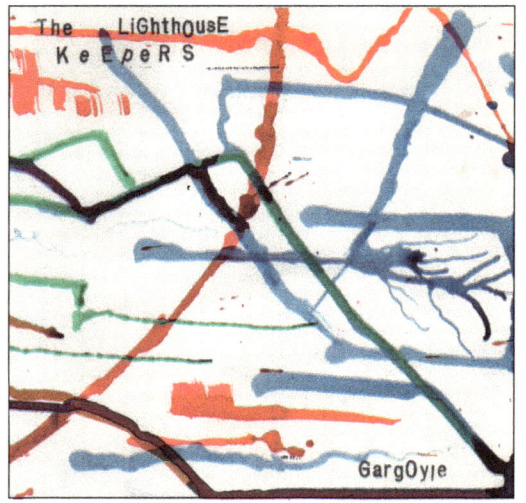
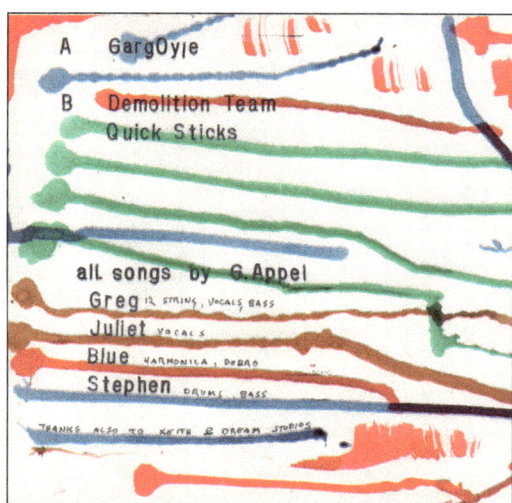

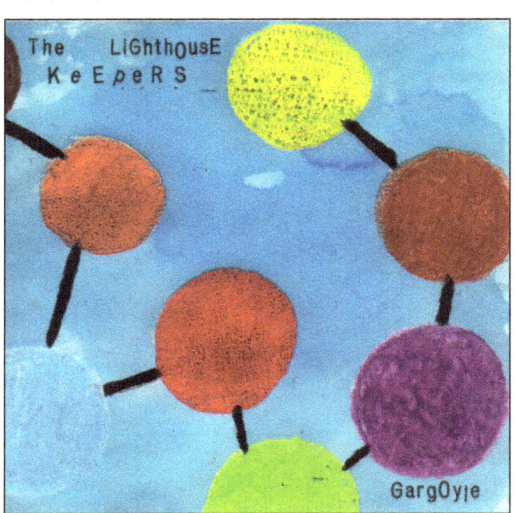

Astrid Spielman (in shades) and Nicole Menzies from the Particles.

What I'm known for now is that Australian post-punk thing. I liked songwriterly, narrative driven stuff… Nick Cave, the Go-Betweens, the Triffids, the Lighthouse Keepers. The scene became increasingly rootsy influenced. I did pursue the songwriters. But I do also feel a bit responsible for propagating shit. Back then, there was a line drawn between Jimmy Barnes and the Celibate Rifles—not to be cruel to the Rifles, but I probably had to side with them. It's championing the underdog. I thought Jimmy Barnes doesn't need my help. Now the Go-Betweens, the Triffids…they don't need my help anymore.

Clinton Walker

I think Clinton is doing me a bit of a favour mentioning the Lighthouse Keepers amongst that hallowed crowd, because yes, we do need his help still. Back to my own impressionistic version of this bygone era.

I also indulged in some lighter drugs and this perhaps adds to the scattered nature of this text. My mind now drifts to the other people around at the time. Weirdly, like Clinton, they will pop back into your life at strange moments. It's not very nice for either party when you run into someone after a long time. You know they're thinking the same thing. But once you get past the gnarled face and battle-hardened expression, it's all good, because you spent some time in this juvenile twilight zone together. Less happily, this begins to occur at funerals. Only recently, I attended a memorial service for Astrid Spielman, the singer from a band called the Particles. It seemed way too early. She and her gang of sisters were a big part of our new world in Sydney. I had already started to write about them in this book, so this was a warning to me. Don't write nasty things about friends or even close acquaintances, as you never know what might happen.

However, I have not changed a word of the text that follows. Astrid had a good sense of humour, as I recall, and would be the last one

Chapter 3 : Lighthouse Keepers

Proof sheet: `pling

to want this to be boring. And, in the spirit of these confessions, it was only at the memorial that I found out about her tryst with Mel Gibson! I think he might have had more sex than Clinton Walker—going from some other bits of information about him that have come to me over the years.

The Particles were our sister band, and a bit of a strange one musically. We frequently supported them at artsy left-wing venues like one called Behind Enemy Lines or Alpha House, which was a big warehouse on King Street, in Newtown. Some of the band also lived there.

As well as playing with us, Hairy also played bass with the Particles. He was, and still is, the sort of musician who can play with a wide range of people. He didn't seem to suffer from the jealousy that racked most other inner-city musicians that I knew. So he was able to lead a double life in seemingly opposite kinds of bands.

The Particles were sort of electro pop but with a feral edge. Really, they only sounded electro because of the drum machine that was their constant companion. From memory, they purchased it after kicking out their original human drummer, Stephen Williams, who ended up playing drums and managing our band. Of course, privately we thought we were far superior.

The drum machine was full of those eighties beats that now sound hip and nostalgic, but at the time seemed sort of artificial... The Lighthouse Keepers (with the possible exception of the more progressive Hairy) viewed this technology with horror. We always wanted to play and record with as few gadgets as possible—just the odd dog or weird piece of percussion. In retrospect, I think that has probably served us well. The music sounds as rough and raggedy now as it did then. But free of audio effects.

To give the Particles credit, this was the period when dance music was being reborn, and perhaps bands like them helped it along the way. Somewhere in Chicago, people were already making house music. For me, dance music was good for a while, starting in the early eighties, but then it became horribly repetitive sometime in the nineties. You really did need drugs to enjoy it. I can't say I've been out clubbing recently, so I wouldn't really know. But doesn't disco come up well? I mean the dance music before this period. Maybe disco didn't really suck. At least, I never wore the badges.

Back then, we were just coming off the end of this badge-wearing era. Aussie punks started to be embarrassed by them. There were all sorts of scenes going on amidst the confusion. The new wave end of punk was doing well in the charts. Bands as varied as the Police and Dexys Midnight Runners were popular. New wave could mean pretty much anything as long as it was young and rude to journalists. It also saw a new breed of journalists—that were rude to the bands.

> Just two weeks ago, I got an email. I quote verbatim: "you are a cunt, what did we ever do to you". That was a bloke Shane Shane from a band called La Femme in Melbourne. I'd written something bad about them 30 years ago... I've had more slaps in the face than I can tell you. I won't say it's water off a duck's

Chapter 3 : Lighthouse Keepers

The Lighthouse Keepers at the Glengarry Hotel.

back...but the worst that used to happen was someone used to take a swing at you.

Clinton Walker,
punk rock critic (sort of)

All this new music was underpinned by a thriving live scene. At one end you had stadium rock—at the other, whatever you call the level below pub rock. There were pubs-slash-venues everywhere in Sydney during the 1980s. That's where we did our socialising, and where we saw all this other music going on. It was just a small step to playing in a band ourselves.

> In 1984, when I first saw the Lighthouse Keepers, there was, of course, no mainstream internet, no Facebook, no mobile phone, no plasma screen; tumbleweeds blew down George Street and King Street on a Sunday. The second phase of new wave was on the wane. The Lighthouse Keepers' style and music seemed quite a contrast to their contemporaries. It was occasionally sombre and spookily atmospheric, songs such as 'Gargoyle,' but for the main there was a jangly, upbeat, exuberant rhythm to the tunes and the lyrics bore a curious hybrid of introspection, wry humour, gloom, tetchiness tinged with tenderness (and vice versa), and joy. They featured some anthemic choruses, to boot.

Annabel Bleach,
Lighthouse Keepers observer, 2012

The great thing about modern technology is that you can write 'as I write' so often. And as I write on my portable device, I'm in one of those old Sydney venues in Chippendale. They didn't have many bands in what was then called the Native Rose. It has since been simplified for the modern attention span to just the Rose. However, I'm pretty sure we played here. We definitely drank a lot here

The Lighthouse Keepers at the Britannia Hotel.

and we often played over the road in the Britannia. We also played further up at the Glengarry Castle or down towards the city at the Lansdowne. There seemed to be venues everywhere in that period.

They are still sort of here, but they are odd versions of their previous selves. I don't think you could sidle up to the bar owner of the Glengarry Castle now and ask if you could play on Sundays for the next four weeks. It would probably disturb the people playing poker machines.

But was it such a great time or just different? What's wrong with today's seven-dollar schooners[3] and a bit of gentrification for a grubby old pub? They were pretty ugly inside, sort of like toilets. I think they were the original design inspiration—harking back to the days of the six o'clock swill. But in the 1980s, we could swill all day and night and sometimes did. Juliet was more of an early opener person. I just tried to keep up…

> I didn't really think about what I wore, like those western-style shirts. But they kind of fitted in with our music.
>
> Juliet Ward,
> Lighthouse Keepers, 2017

The non-fashions from the time have strangely percolated down. For instance, the girl serving alcohol at the Rose just now has a look very reminiscent of Juliet's from back in the eighties, with super dyed black hair and slightly butch working men's clothes. All this seems to be put together in a calculated manner. Then another one has a checked flannelette shirt on, which was one of my old favourites. However, back in 'the day', these clothes were worn for their cheapness, comfort value and, come to think of it, we hardly thought about it.[4] Recently, I was interviewed for a study on the venues in Melbourne and Sydney during this era.

---

3   Sorry—the beers are $8.50 as of early 2015—just got one.

4   And an update from the more recent past—I mentioned my fashion observations at home and my daughter tells me they're called 'boyfriend clothes' now.

Chapter 3 : Lighthouse Keepers

```
E     FEVER
F#    SPRINGTIME
A     I KNOW I HAD A WONDERFUL
F#    TIME
F#    LOVE ME
E     TUMBLING WEEDS
E     THE WANDERER
Gm    I'M IN A BAD MOOD
E     QUICK STICKS
G     GARGOYLE
F#    POWER RING
B     KEEP ME HANGING ON
F#    I WILL LIVE AGAIN
G     THE BEAT
A     FIRE
E     NOT FADE AWAY
     (THAT'S ALRIGHT    F#
      SUMMERTIME        Am
      THAT'S ALRIGHT    F# )
```

Good to be an object for archival research. Actually it is good, as I've spent a lot time listening to other old musos waxing lyrical about their experiences back in the day and it was good to be able to voice my own opinion. The conclusion of this study seemed to be that:

> For better or worse, live music scenes now survive with more performers, performing less often, and in a smaller area.[5]

Sounds about right, but I think we must also take into account the never-ending moaning from musos that echoes down to us from the past. It has always been the same. Never enough places to play, people or money. I should know—I've moaned too.

But talking through all these venues with the young researcher made me remember them all. They were pretty grubby places, atmospheric, yes, but probably toxic. A venue I went to in Melbourne recently had gone out of its way to recreate that ambience. The carpet had a specially cultivated stickiness, from which footwear needed to be peeled. They also seemed to have recreated the overpowering smell of old cigarette smoke—without having any actual smokers in there! Ah, the good old days. That cigarette smell still does it for me, even though I didn't technically smoke. I guess I was smoking by being inside these rooms. Juliet was a real smoker, despite her bad asthma. So it was all part of this heady new lifestyle.

Smoking was also a source of conflict between Juliet and me. I had to take her into hospitals a few times because of her asthma. I remember her lying on the white sheets looking so pale and so fair. The doctors were always telling her to stop, otherwise… My nagging didn't do any good. She just kept on smoking.

But let's breathe in that old tobacco smoke and travel back in time. To see if we can relive a few of those heady days. Cough…

---

5 Sarah Taylor, 'Lost Venues, Long Nights: An Introduction to Historical Maps of Live Music in Sydney and Melbourne', *Cordite Poetry Review*, February 2015.
http://cordite.org.au/essays/lost-venues-long-nights

CHAPTER 4
We've Got a Gig!

Lighthouse Keepers; Tim Palmer on bass, Hairy on drums, Britannia Hotel, Cleveland Street.

It may seem like information overload, but I think it's worth noting the venues and dates as we travel through the next chapter. We definitely weren't a huge act, and didn't even qualify as a leading Sydney independent band like Do-Ré-Mi or the Machinations. But for a few short years, we played around Sydney and the wider beyond in all sorts of venues. From smoky little tiled pubs to suburban beer barns—lots of them. I can only imagine what it was like in a proper hard-working successful band, instead of a lazy inward-looking one, like ours.

The Lighthouse Keepers years represent only a short part of my life, but this period seems to have branded me forever. Who would have known that these self-indulgent activities would shape the future old man? The Lighthouse Keepers are remembered by certain people, amongst a certain demo-

Chapter 4 : We've Got a Gig!

21 NOV 1982	**BRITANNIA HOTEL** [Chippendale/Sydney]
18 DEC 1982	**CREMORNE PARTY** [Cremorne/Sydney] w/ Non Fiction
31 DEC 1982	**ALPHA HOUSE** [King St, Newtown/ Sydney] w/the Particles, Jelly Babies, Wet Taxis, Like Unruly Children

graphic, from a certain period. With great fondness, luckily. Even if they never saw any of our shows, some people are convinced they were there. So they were! Let's re-enter those smoky, beer-drenched venues, where five dollars might even get you a jug.[1]

For a while, Juliet and I lived near from the Britannia Hotel in Cleveland Street. Today, it's a fast food, all-you-can-eat, pokie establishment but in the 1980s, it was still an unrenovated tiled bar, where people could buy beer and get drunk, as they had been doing for many years. There were many of them around the inner city, left over from the days of the six o'clock swill. This was a period during the first half of the last century, when Australians had to drink as fast as they could from 5pm when they knocked off work, to 6pm when the law forced all the pubs to shut. This was meant to make the country more morally upstanding and less drunk. It probably had the opposite effect. There was often a tiled trough surrounding these bars that looked suspiciously like a urinal. Men didn't want to leave the bar for any reason. The laws were relaxed by the sixties, and by the seventies and eighties, they needed new drinkers. Publicans would therefore tolerate bands if it meant a few people came along.

I remember Juliet's dog Chaos was still in the band and barked into a microphone, like he did at the UTS talent quest. The bedraggled audiences loved him and Chaos enjoyed the attention. I don't think he ever really liked me that much—we were competing for the same master. But he was gracious about leaving the band. When we went to an all-human line up—he didn't say a word.

At this point, the band were paid in beers and supplied our own sound system. Other bands like the Triffids and the Wet Taxis came to the Britannia to check us out and enjoy a drink, or ten. The vibe was generally pretty drunken by the end of the multiple sets. Anything could happen. Hairy might perform a drunken bass solo version of 'To Sir, With Love'. He didn't usually sing, but when extremely drunk, he emitted a sort of slurred moan with a hint of beast.

King Street, Newtown, was the starting point for many of our musical adventures. It was pretty much as grimy then as it is now, except a lot cheaper. Even today, you might still see the odd punk walking along the street like an endangered species—occasionally, a whole family of them. Somehow, these

---

1 Dear reader, you don't have to read all these venue dates and locations—let them flow over you in an impressionistic manner.

Camperdown skyline, from Alpha House rooftop. Still from 'Ocean Liner' video clip.

tribes still survive in the gentrified world. But King Street looks the same, and smells the same as it did in the early eighties.

Although I always had mixed feelings about its ambience, I was drawn to it in a kind of unthinking manner. Perhaps it was because I felt I fitted in there, or perhaps I found it so unlike Canberra. But, most likely, it was the cheap rents in the area. I ended up co-making a TV documentary about the street in the nineties. During the filming, I remember an old drunk yelling at us that it was 'Sydney's biggest bottleneck'—and so it remains.

Others remember King Street more fondly. Murray Cook is perhaps better known as the 'red' Wiggle. At this time, he lived in a share house in Newtown, like the rest of us. Nowadays, he still lives in the area in a sort of rock star mansion, filled with expensive-looking guitars. I caught up with him not that long ago…

Newtown was quite different then, I remember when a venue opened on King Street, they had needed a map on the flyer and it said 'plenty of parking'. Back then, everyone went to see bands. If you had a band, it was easy to get a gig, and you didn't have to be that great.

Murray Wiggle, 2017

Alpha House stood at the top of King Street. It dominated the Newtown skyline in a physical sense, as it was the biggest building around. The abandoned interior was full of empty offices, that were home to an ever-changing gang of groovers, drug dealers and exotic humans.

Steven Williams, who would become the Lighthouse Keepers' drummer, ran the first floor as an artsy music venue. He was eventually busted by the licensing police for illegally selling alcohol. He also had the unenviable task of extracting gas and electricity

Chapter 4 : We've Got a Gig!

money from the squatters and trying to organise them. Alpha House also had great views of Sydney from the roof. I used a shot to open the music clip for the Lighthouse Keepers' 'Ocean Liner'...

At the time, Steven managed the Particles, our semi-electronic pals who ruled the building. Astrid, the singer, had a sister named Ingrid, and I remember her singing the praises of a new drug, not just plain old MDA, but one with an additional, magical letter—MDMA. I think the sisters and other members of the Alpha House clique were planning to take some, but the Lighthouse Keepers were possibly too drunk or stoned, or both, to pay enough attention—so didn't get into any of this new substance. Again, the Particles were ahead of their time with their recreational drug use. Soon the whole Western world would be smiling, swapping partners and dancing to drum machines.

1982/83	**21st PARTY** [Bondi/Sydney]
22 JAN 1983	**GLENGARRY CASTLE** [Chippendale/Sydney]

Our drinking territory could be loosely called the 'inner west'. A map of the band's gigs would show a distinct cluster around Chippendale and Newtown, gradually spreading to other suburbs and cities. The Glengarry Castle was a favourite drinking hole, a triangular place on the corner of Abercrombie Street. Full of alcohol-fueled confidence, we offered to play there. In those days, a publican just might say, 'go ahead,' and we did.

Blue would set his little Peavey Backstage amp up on the pinball machine, to play amplified harmonica. Then he had a little showbiz gimmick where he would waltz with Juliet while she sang 'Who's Sorry Now', a teary classic made popular by Connie Francis. The

pay was fifty dollars and a whole lot of beers. The crowds were starting to build in this admittedly small space.

I went into the Glengarry Castle the other day and, like many other venues in Sydney, the poker machines had taken over. This was a result of another change of laws in NSW in 1997. Is there a more boring way to lose money? But can we really blame poker machines for the end of this intense band scene? Or did it just fade away, like everything eventually does?

In truth, I can't remember that much about many of the bands we played with. Just odd image flashes—not always pleasant. The sound of feedback might also take me back to those times. In those days, feedback just meant the noise Angus Young makes at the

30 JAN 1983	**GLENGARRY CASTLE** [Chippendale/Sydney] as Me & You & a boy named Blue ie. was just Ap, Blue & Juliet
6 FEB 1983	**GLENGARRY CASTLE** [Chippendale/Sydney] (Personnel: Ap, Blue, Juliet, Stephen)
13 FEB 1983	**GLENGARRY CASTLE** [Chippendale/Sydney] (Personnel: Ap, Blue, Juliet, Stephen)
19 FEB 1983	**ALPHA HOUSE** [Newtown/Sydney] w/Box of Fish, Lighthouse Keepers, Jelly Babies (Personnel: Ap, Blue, Juliet, Stephen)
3 MAR 1983	**GLENGARRY CASTLE** [Chippendale/Sydney]
5 MAR 1983	**ALPHA HOUSE** [Newtown/Sydney] w/the Particles + Poles Apart
10 MAR 1983	**GLENGARRY CASTLE** [Chippendale/Sydney]
26 MAR 1983	**AUSTRALIAN NATIONAL UNIVERSITY BAR** [Canberra] w/the Particles
28 MAR 1983	**SOUTHERN CROSS HOTEL** [Surry Hills/Sydney] w/the Particles

end of a song. Nowadays, it has a new horrible meaning known to anyone in the creative arts, or government department or corporation or just about any job. Other bands had marine-inspired names, like Box of Fish, while cutesy names like the Jelly Babies were also popular. I'd have to say the Lighthouse Keepers were on the cutting edge of both marine-related and cutesy names—we were still young enough to get away with it. Then there were the politically worthy bands, like Poles Apart, though I'm just guessing they were political, as I cannot remember a thing about them. I was slightly suspicious of overtly political music; it often seemed contrived and berating. Perhaps I was just nervous about its intent—being a white middle-class male.

> **I had photos from around this time showing friends of mine from Newtown dancing at this gig: sort of my seventies friends versus my new eighties musician friends. The two groups didn't really mix, even though they lived in the same inner-city suburbs or even streets. It was a sort of pre-punk/post-punk divide.**
>
> Blue, Lighthouse Keepers, 2017

The Lighthouse Keepers were never at the cutting edge of fashion. Most of us came from the eternally unhip capital of Australia and we'd regularly take the six-hour drive down the partially constructed freeways to Canberra. Back to middle-class living at the parental home for a while. We could eat enough steaks to get our iron levels up, and perhaps I'd steal a few of dad's socks to make my personal Sydney economy work just a little more efficiently.

I guess most bands have a hometown sort of thing going on. That is, if you can appear to be doing okay in a bigger city, you can return home periodically and reap the benefits of a decent crowd and a loving atmosphere. The home crowd would never really know if you were hip or not. It works even better than this if you go overseas, of course. Once we were able to play at Canberra's Uni Bar, we'd made a little step. Again, not a particularly beautiful bar, but a seventies concrete and lino bunker that saw all sorts of bands playing to Canberra's supposed students (many were just drinkers). I'd spent a lot of time feeling sorry for myself back there a couple of years earlier, when we were fresh out of school, grimly clutching plastic cups filled with warm beer.

There are some photos from one of these early trips back to Canberra, showing us proudly holding our new 'Gargoyle' single. It must have been around the time I presented Prince Charles with a copy of this record.

But before you mistake me for a right-wing royalist, my fascination with the royal family is similar to an appreciation of kitsch music. Anyway, Charles had come to Canberra on a post-marriage tour. More to the point, his new wife, Diana, was appearing for the first time as a Princess in the Antipodes. So there was a big crowd in an ugly square in Civic, in the middle of town. Maybe Charles was just a bit easier to access—so I slipped him a copy of 'Gargoyle'.

'I hope it's not punk!' he said as he gave it to the person carrying the basket behind him.

I can't remember what I said in reply to his light-hearted jibe. It wasn't punk, as any 'Gargoyle' lover will know. Punk never quite did its job with the British royals. They have survived remarkably well, though today every good Aussie yobbo loves to turn up 'God Save the Queen' (Sex Pistols version) nice and loud at a barbeque. It's almost as much of a homage to royalty as the real British anthem. The Sex Pistols have stood up pretty well compared to some of the other punk recordings from that time.

As you will recall from the Canberra years chapter, I played a bit of punk myself with

The Lighthouse Keepers. Photo: `pling

7 APR 1983	**GLENGARRY CASTLE** [Chippendale/Sydney]
21 APR 1983	**GLENGARRY CASTLE** [Chippendale/Sydney]
5 MAY 1983	**GLENGARRY CASTLE** Back room [Chippendale/Sydney] This was possibly the first show with Steven Williams on drums and Alex on trumpet (Personnel: Alex, Ap, Blue, Juliet, Stephen, Steven)
14 MAY 1983	**MIDDLE HARBOUR 16' SKIFF CLUB** [The Spit/Sydney] w/the Particles + JFK and the Cuban Crisis
15 MAY 1983	**STRANDED** [Sydney City] w/Soggy Porridge + Safehouse (Personnel: no Stephen)
18 MAY 1983	**STRAWBERRY HILLS HOTEL** [Surry Hills/Sydney] w/the Particles [Strawberry Hills Hotel: previously known as The Southern Cross Hotel]
19 MAY 1983	**GLENGARRY CASTLE** [Chippendale/Sydney]
28 MAY 1983	**AUSTRALIAN NATIONAL UNIVERSITY BAR** [Canberra] w/the Particles

my more badge-loving friends. This small colonial sect wasn't very focused. Some angrier badge wearers might go and kick a few phone boxes at night, but that was about as far as it went, anarchy-wise.

Back in Sydney we ventured further into Surry Hills. The Southern Cross Hotel was renamed as the Strawberry Hills Hotel around this time and we started to draw quite a good crowd here. The back cover of our album and later a 'best of' CD featured a photo from the pub and revealed the magnificence of its decrepitude: peeling walls, a portable television wedged on a small ledge above the stage, a broken trail of gaffer tape. The Strawberry Hills was another relic from the six o'clock swill days. The publican probably turned on the TV for the daytime drinkers so they could watch the greyhounds.[2]

2 'The puppies', as I've heard it called.

I remember standing outside after the gig with friends of the Particles while arguments raged around us about money, who was loading the gear, where was the free beer, etc. There was a lot of ridiculous arguing over what even at the time seemed quite petty, but not usually by the Lighthouse Keepers.

Blue, Lighthouse Keepers, 2017

At this point, we rarely left the inner city, although one time we made it as far as the Middle Harbour Skiff Club, just down the hill from Mosman. Also on the bill were JFK and the Cuban Crisis, led by John Kennedy, possibly best remembered for his 'King Street' song, which was always a bit earnest for me. It was sort of the opposite to how I felt about this legendary street. But I can't be too down

Chapter 4 : We've Got a Gig!

The Lighthouse Keepers. Photo: Darian Turner.

on the song as I've had a few friends in his bands. John's also a friendly guy.

Indeed, there was a delicate relationship with other bands around at the time. They were partly your comrades and partly your enemy. But this kind of unease could easily start to spread within your own band. If things were going well, you tended to get on. At this stage, we were getting plenty of shows, and it felt like fun. Because it was. A drinking game that appeared around this time called 'Beerhunter,' was perfect for bands. Based on a scene from the film *The Deer Hunter*, it combined the tensions that occur in any random group of people, with drinking. Blue learned about it at a venue called Stranded, an upmarket venue downstairs in the Strand Arcade on George Street.

> It was a kind of Russian roulette where you shake up one can of beer in a slab and then put it back mixed among the other beer cans. Before drinking, each can had to be opened next to the drinker's head, so that if it was the shaken one, it would explode all over the drinker.
>
> Blue, Lighthouse Keepers

We played in Canberra whenever we could. The capital might be a middle-class haven: however, there were other, scarier towns *en route*. Collector is a small town near Goulburn and on one trip, the band turned off there to take a collective piss at the local pub. At the male piss trough Blue, being a friendly bloke, got into a conversation with a regular who insisted we all stay for a drink. Blue bought a round for all of us. But this seemed to aggravate the other drinkers, including the lone singer/guitarist who was amplified through a small sound system. Juliet, in particular, was singled out for unwelcome attention. The local drinkers yelled at her and called her a 'pro', as in prostitute. We were jeered out of the pub, led by the singer at the mic. We would always remem-

ber Collector as an unwelcoming place and would shake a fist as we drove past. Just a taste of what was to come on country roads in the future.

Canberrans were far more welcoming. My younger brothers, sister and cousins were of drinking age by this time and were regular attendees. A number of shows featured members of my extended family joining us on stage. On these sweaty nights, we began a tradition of backing vocals bellowed out to the Elvis song 'Suspicious Minds'. Anyone could join in and it could become quite crowded at the microphones. We were into audience participation and I still think it's the key to a good show. People will forgive a lot if they're allowed onto that hallowed space occasionally. And sometimes they could actually sing, like the 'Boy Soprano', a mysterious character who appeared around this time, and disappeared equally mysteriously.

The extended family were very supportive of my creativity. Perhaps it was just an easy event to attend and hone your teenage drinking skills. I have a clear memory of my cousin 'Jum' bellyaching to me about making a music clip for 'Gargoyle'. He envisaged using some giant lips. What? The actual clip I eventually made still stands up well. No lips required, its amateur ambience nicely captures the pleasantly aimless lifestyle which we now enjoyed.

The agro we came across on the road to Canberra was not unusual. The atmosphere of potential violence made life more precarious back then. Australia has become a much less intimidating place. I believe crime statistics would support me on this. Blue's reminiscences certainly do.

> We played the back bar of the Sussex Hotel in Haymarket. I lived not far away in Ultimo and, at the time, Marko Halstead from Tex Deadly and the Dum Dums was living in the house. He came down to see us, but old Stella who ran the place took an immediate dislike to him and tried to throw him out. Stella also ran the Star on the corner of Sussex and Goulburn streets, just opposite the Trades Hall. She was bludgeoned to death by one of her tenants.
>
> Blue, Lighthouse Keepers

Lighthouse Keepers.

Chapter 4 : We've Got a Gig!

Proof sheet photos: Bleddyn Butcher.

Uni bars were a good source of income for us. Student activity officers always defaulted to bands as a way of keeping their clients happy and assumed just about any band would do. Once they booked us, they could cross out a date on their calendars and go back to hanging around their respective uni bars. Unfortunately, students could be very apathetic in their appreciation of the free music served up to them. Occasionally, they would stir, but usually it was like playing to seated zombies eating stuff.

But the excellent flat fees provided by the student activity officers healed any damage to our fragile egos. They inevitably assured us it had been great too. But who cared? We had more shows to play.

The Southern Cross Hotel had changed its name to the Strawberry Hills when the Lighthouse Keepers and the Particles played a run of double bills. It was a solid line-up, and with both bands, we drew a decent crowd. But we wanted to break free from the orbit of these musical atoms and see what happened when we played on our own.

When we eventually did, the Strawberry Hills became one of our best residencies. One night after a show, a record company type

2 JUN 1983	**GLENGARRY CASTLE** [Chippendale/Sydney] Think this was our last Glengarry show?
10 JUN 1983	**SUSSEX HOTEL** [The Haymarket/Sydney]
15 JUN 1983	**SUSSEX HOTEL** [The Haymarket/Sydney]
17 JUN 1983	**MANNING BAR** [Sydney University] w/the Particles
17 JUN 1983	**STRAWBERRY HILLS HOTEL** [Surry Hills/Sydney] w/the Particles
19 JUN 1983	**BRITANNIA HOTEL** [Chippendale/Sydney] w/Mickey Rat[1]
22 JUN 1983	**SUSSEX HOTEL** [The Haymarket/Sydney] w/the Particles Last night at The Sussex: closed down for good the following week
26 JUN 1983	**BRITANNIA HOTEL** [Chippendale/Sydney] w/Mickey Rat
3 JUL 1983	**BRITANNIA HOTEL** [Chippendale/Sydney] w/Mickey Rat
8 JUL 1983	**NEWTOWN RULES CLUB** [Redfern/Sydney] w/the Triffids + The Crystal Set

1 Mickey Rat—geddit? If you don't then think deeply about the famous Disney Mouse.

approached me—a publisher, I think—a mysterious figure with a beard, offering money that could be mine with very little effort. He vanished into the night and I never saw him again. It was the sort of venue where odd things happened.

> The place was packed most times we played there. The mixer mixed the band from the small bottle shop by looking through a window-sized hole in the wall into the band room. Once, a rather large plain-clothes police officer jumped the bottle shop counter and summarily ordered our mixer, John Bassett, to cut the sound. Seems there had been a noise complaint which had really been about a band playing further up the hill on Devonshire Street.
>
> Blue, Lighthouse Keepers, 2017

Even if it had a bit of a silly fruity name, the Strawberry Hills Hotel was a venue that grew in people's minds as time went on. Until it became one of those legendary places where bands cut their teeth in front of wild drunken crowds.

> Whenever I go into that Strawberry Hills back room now, I'm gob smacked by how small it was. So many people crammed in there. It was a pretty big deal filling the Strawberry Hills back then.
>
> Tim Pittman, promoter, 2016

We socialised with other bands from this inner-west rock scene. We first met the Triffids early in the Sydney part of their career. My first memories of them were when the singer/songwriter, David McComb, appeared in our audience. In between sets, we talked about the Lighthouse Keepers' various covers. It was an eclectic group of songs at that point, ranging from country novelty songs, to the Supremes, and more obscure material like 'Little Things' by Bobby Goldsboro. David was a bit of a music nerd and pretty well informed. He was a nice guy, introspective and quite shy. His brother Rob was also in the band. He had a bit of a blond lothario thing going on, and played guitar or violin—often surrounded by a cloud of suspicious smoke. Some of our band might have migrated from Canberra, but the Triffids made the journey to Sydney all the way from Perth.

> The way people in Perth talked about the eastern states was 'over east'. You'd say, 'Na, I'm not going over east this year'. When we got to Sydney, we didn't really socialise much with other bands. it wasn't 'til meeting the Lighthouse Keepers that we thought we'd found kindred spirits—not too rockist or industry-bound.
>
> Rob McComb, the Triffids

There'd be a lot of inward-looking, shy types hanging around these shows. Many of them in bands. As we drank beer, we all started to grow more confident and outward. I sometimes speculate on how these frail egos were inflated, then damaged to greater and lesser

Chapter 4 : We've Got a Gig!

The Lighthouse Keepers. Photo: Robert Fretwell.

degrees according to how big the bands got. People out the front of the bands were especially vulnerable. Both me and Juliet were undergoing change at the same time. We were a couple of shy people being pushed out of the house by unseen forces. An insidious interest in music and the arts can lead you to some strange places. Sometimes, we even went out into the sunshine...

> We had the Sunday afternoon cricket matches. It almost became an institution for visiting bands like the Triffids from Perth. It was an excuse to buy slabs of beer and lie around on the grass. Only Steven Williams took it seriously.
>
> Juliet, Lighthouse Keepers, 2015

10 JUL 1983	**BRITANNIA HOTEL** [Chippendale/Sydney] w/Mickey Rat
23 JUL 1983	**AUSTRALIAN NATIONAL UNIVERSITY BAR** [Canberra] w/the Particles
28 JUL 1983	**BRITANNIA HOTEL** [Chippendale/Sydney]
31 JUL 1983	**BRITANNIA HOTEL** [Chippendale/Sydney] w/Mickey Rat
4 AUG 1983	**WRIGHT COLLEGE** [University of New England/Armidale] w/the Particles + A Disco (+ Alex)
5 AUG 1983	**IMPERIAL HOTEL** [Armidale] w/the Particles (+ Alex)

The Lighthouse Keepers.

We might have been uninterested cricket players, but we were enjoying playing the shows our drummer, Steven Williams, booked. If he hadn't hassled and cajoled all these venues, we'd never have left the crease.[3]

We were an inherently lazy band but, as 1983 progressed, we started to get pretty busy. These weren't always great shows, of course. The Lighthouse Keepers could be very patchy, and maybe half of the shows could be classified as awful. But we kept going. The good ones made up for it.

I saw the Lighthouse Keepers a couple of times. Sometimes, it seemed a little chaotic but I kind of liked that.

Murray Wiggle

I think part of the band's appeal was its rough edges. For instance, we would continually swap instruments, almost randomly. While on some nights this could be charming, other nights it was torturous, as feedback, tuning problems and general onstage fumbling let the audience know we were not professionals. I have to place some blame on the fashion for mixing at the time. Maybe it came down to us via the heavy sounds of Australian pub rock. It was based on drums first, with a big bottom end, meaning the bass frequency was emphasised. There was always some dude at the controls getting the drums as loud as possible, followed by bass and guitars. Last thing was to check the vocals worked. Much feedback followed. Juliet tended not to scream, and this put us at an immediate disadvantage. In retrospect, these shows could have been a lot better with only the vocals amplified.

Put 400 bloody microphones on the drums! It's a PA, I used to say. That's 'P' for personal, not 'D' for drums. PA stands for 'personal address system'. I thought the whole reason they had been invented was so they could hear the vocals over the drums.

Juliet, Lighthouse Keepers

---

3 Pathetic cricket metaphor—sorry.

Chapter 4 : We've Got a Gig!

After doing the rounds of inner Sydney and Canberra, we took our rickety shows further and further afield. Why not try country towns? They had pubs.

As the band spent more time travelling together, we learned a bit more about everyone's past—especially Blue's. I'll let him tell you in his own words as he gets into the spirit of these 'confessions':

> We went up to Armidale by train and I met a former love, Sue Coe, by chance there. This brings me to a methodological/ethical point in this 'story': what to include and what to tacitly censor by omitting from my monologue. So, to know the truth, what do I include? The sex, drugs and rock'n'roll?—we are talking about the rock'n'roll as in the music, but the sex and drugs?
>
> Now I have to think with my theorist's hat on; I wear hats these days. Why wax lyrical about the past? Is it because I'm misty eyed about my lost youthful vigour and sexual prowess or attractiveness to women? As a fat, balding, sixty-year-old with a dodgy ticker and also being in the middle of the book *The Past is a Foreign Country*, I would say yes, but only in part. To me, it is also to bring back an era which really was a foreign country by today's standards. Not a golden past but an era which in practice offered promise, especially based on what was possible for a little band like the Lighthouse Keepers.
>
> For better or worse, the era that I am writing about had opportunities and in part allowed the resources and freedom to construct intense moments of self-fulfilment: sex, drugs and rock'n'roll. As an old bugger, I don't really see that happening today. I see a hypocritical elite looking after themselves in the name of protecting society. It reminds me of the class conscious and ultimately hateful society of my father's time.

> I have a great unease about musicians and artists/celebrities, who in part owe their fame or 'cool' to being, having been, or even thought to have been hard drug users. Impressionable people like to ape role models, and I think we have all done this: we have all been young, impressionable, and trying to establish who we are. In fact, my unfinished PhD and my career as an educator was about this type of learning in adults of all ages and conditions. In the period in question, there was a growing number of the well-intentioned, starry-eyed but impressionable types, who were taking heroin and either didn't survive or whose lives were blighted from then on. And we have all been starry-eyed.

Well, as far as I know, we didn't do drugs, though a lot of people around us did. I didn't even like marijuana after consuming something that left me hallucinating badly for about six hours at uni. It left a lasting paranoia and brought on panic attacks for many years, and even if I didn't smoke, but was in a very smoky environment, the panic would mount 'til I had to just get out of there. The only way I could control this paranoia and panic was to consume massive amounts of alcohol, whole flagons and later casks, or bottles of spirits. And at the very least that is what I and many of my peers did: drink large amounts of alcohol. This was especially so for musicians: to get you on stage, to loosen up for interviews and recording sessions, to calm you down after gigs, etc.

As for sex, there were occasional encounters with women like Sue but, as good as these encounters were, the women would usually get bored because I was usually much more interested in music, playing and the band, or getting hopelessly pissed. What a sicko! I remember looking after Greg and Juliet's house again, but this time Sue was around and we slept in their bed. Chaos was in the house and he leapt on the bed and really enjoyed our performance. Yes, a threesome with a dog, though as a voyeur not a participant!

Blue, Lighthouse Keepers

It is with some alarm that I read about Blue in our bed with this woman and the dog! But at least he's getting back on topic. When I think back, it was true that there were often jingly kinds of women that appeared at the shows, that could be seen listening to Blue afterwards with a slightly glazed look. At the end of the night, both parties would suddenly be absent. With only the vague echo of a wind chime left behind.

Blue, August 1985.

Some of our shows, like 'Rock Against Roxby Downs'[4] suggested that the Lighthouse Keepers were a pretty right-on band. It's true that some of us were at least politically aware, as Blue's writing indicates. And we had a kind of pre-Greens feral look as well—so we weren't out of place at a 'Rock Against Roxby Downs' event. Sometimes I reflect on the musicians' financial lot and wonder if it's fair to keep making them do their thing for free, as we had to here. It was the peak of the Hawkie era and Labor were very much in power. The ALP's three mines uranium policy was what the protest concert was all about. I'm pretty sure it didn't make for any changes.

4   Roxby Downs was an outback uranium mine causing a lot of controversy at the time.

Chapter 4 : We've Got a Gig!

Most bands were more or less 'right-on'. It was a time of mass unemployment, but cheap inner-city housing, and empty pubs needed filling. And the 'youth' politics of the seventies had morphed into something else, but had not yet terminally split into different, and possibly mutually exclusive, communities based on 'lifestyle' choices.

And, yes, I was or had been a hopeless armchair romantic Marxist/Trotskyite, but learnt to shut up and play. I was also a vegetarian until I toured with the band. The Lighthouse Keepers liked a good burger and Greg and Juliet loved Maccas. They were very impressed when we went to Austria and found that you could get a good beer as well as a burger there.

Blue, Lighthouse Keepers

As we tried to spread the joy further afield and travelled the country, we found ourselves at places like the Castanet Club in Newcastle. It was brightly painted inside with a very alternative theatre feel. This was the home of the Castanets, a sort of cabaret act where a few 2JJ regulars like Maynard F# Crabbes and the Sandman got their starts. While we were setting up, the ever observant Blue found a series of postcards from one of the Castanets on the wall.

> It talked about his frolics overseas including the line that he was suffering from piles, which were dubbed the grapes of wrath. Which brings me to another difference of those times, the lack of obvious 'gays' in this story so far. The only obvious gays were the presumed lesbians who worshipped Juliet. Greg had mentioned some students in his communications course writing about their homosexual experiences but that was about it.

Blue, Lighthouse Keepers

Juliet.

7 AUG 1983	**BRITANNIA HOTEL** [Chippendale/Sydney] w/Mickey Rat
8 AUG 1983	**STRAWBERRY HILLS HOTEL** [Surry Hills/Sydney]
13 AUG 1983	**HOPETOUN HOTEL** [Surry Hills/Sydney]
14 AUG 1983	**BRITANNIA HOTEL** [Chippendale/Sydney] w/Mickey Rat
15 AUG 1983	**STRAWBERRY HILLS HOTEL** [Surry Hills/Sydney]
20 AUG 1983	**ROCK AGAINST ROXBY DOWNS** Newtown Rules Club [Redfern/Sydney] w/the Particles, Bapu Mamoos, Mutant Death, Strangelings, Wimmen & Boys, Wrong Kind of Stone Age, Vulgar Beatmen, Funny Stories
22 AUG 1983	**STRAWBERRY HILLS HOTEL** [Surry Hills/Sydney]
27 AUG 1983	**CASTANET CLUB** [Newcastle] w/the Particles

Hairy and Juliet.

It was true that my course had a number of gay students in it. The Sydney Gay Mardi Gras was going strong by then too. So it was all around us. But as far as Juliet being popular with lesbians, I was again oblivious… but I did have a few awkward questions for her recently. Was this true?

People were saying they were gay and openly experimenting to see if they were gay because they felt they were in a safe environment. When I say that, I'm talking about the very small confines of the inner-city area.

Juliet, Lighthouse Keepers, 2017

Rummaging through the baggage of an old relationship, like I had with Juliet, many years after the fact, can be unsettling. I quietly said that it appeared that she was a heterosexual woman… as far as I could tell anyway…

Maybe it suited you to think that… I don't mind what the gender is, as long as they're a good person. I thought I was normal but I've found it's not that common… I think I did actually tell you.

Juliet, Lighthouse Keepers

Maybe she did. A flickering memory of something…long ago. Had I been more focused on all of this—these confessions could have been a lot better—eh, dear reader!

We knew we were doing something different to our parents' generation where we could have lots of sex and there didn't seem to be any risks involved, except tears and people wanting to to get revenge on you and that sort of drama. I thought it was pretty good, although I think I was not very mentally healthy at the time. Isn't every late teenager mentally

Chapter 4 : We've Got a Gig!

unhealthy...possibly? And they've got this fantastic toy-slash-weapon that we didn't really know how to control. So we all had a hell of a lot of fun but we also did some damage to each other.

Juliet, Lighthouse Keepers

I listened to Juliet with mixed emotions. Was she talking about our relationship? A common male trait no doubt—to think everything is about you. But I think back and remember it all as a largely damage-free zone. Neither of us liked conflict, although we both liked to sulk.

Any problems we did have were usually solved by large amounts of alcohol. This was the drug of choice for most of our social group. And this lubricant played a vital part in making Sydney a hotbed of sexual activity—whatever you were into.

Perhaps because of overuse of alcoholic lubricant, these parties would usually end with a few people blubbering in a hallway. By that time, me and Juliet were safely in bed, with the door shut...

The Sydney Trade Union Club has become a bit of a legend and even back then it felt like you'd made it on some level to actually play there. It had real physical levels too, and the biggest bands played on the third floor. It looked like a block of flats, and I think that's what it is now. The stairwell was a kind of purgatory. People would wander the various levels getting drunker and drunker in the smoky gloom. You could still smoke at venues at this stage, of course. The American musician Jonathan Richman always makes me think of smoking, as he came back to Sydney a few times, and on one of these shows he refused to play if people smoked! It sent shock waves through the audience and a lot of them didn't like it. But he was at the front of a movement that would get rid of smoking indoors at places as difficult as France. I can't say now that it isn't good,

29 AUG 1983	**STRAWBERRY HILLS HOTEL** [Surry Hills/Sydney]
3 SEP 1983	**SYDNEY TRADE UNION CLUB** 3rd floor [Surry Hills/Sydney] w/Jonathan Richman + Sekret Sekret
5 SEP 1983	**STRAWBERRY HILLS HOTEL** [Surry Hills/Sydney]
11 SEP 1983	**BRITANNIA HOTEL** [Chippendale/Sydney] w/Mickey Rat
17 SEP 1983	**HOPETOUN HOTEL** [Surry Hills/Sydney]
18 SEP 1983	**BRITANNIA HOTEL** [Chippendale/Sydney] w/Mickey Rat
24 SEP 1983	**HOPETOUN HOTEL*** [Surry Hills/Sydney] w/Dadednyne
* One of the few occasions where the pub decided to short change us despite a decent turnout! $70 in this instance. (Hairy, 2015)	

not coming home stinking of smoke, if I ever happen to go out. Today, smokers have to spend their time in windy alleys (where they network, I've heard). But I'm sure Jonathan Richman didn't try and stop the smoking at the Trade Union Club in 1983. People just wouldn't understand. They might have torn him to pieces on stage.

Bands like the Disney-influenced Mickey Rat thrived in the inner-city pub scene. I'm not sure why they appeared with us so many times. There were a lot of other musicians trying their luck. The Hopetoun Hotel on Bourke Street in Surry Hills was another great little venue. To play there bestowed a small but significant dose of street cred on musicians. Graham Lee was in a band with Paul Kelly at the time. Paul had already had a few ups and downs in his career.

> **I remember driving around with Paul Kelly and we'd go past the Hopetoun Hotel. He said to me, 'I wish we could get a gig there'.**
>
> Graham Lee, the Triffids, 2016

Hairy, the Lighthouse Keepers' multi-instrumentalist, also kept meticulous show records and noted that the Hopetoun Hotel short-changed the band by seventy dollars (haven't heard that expression for a while), which brings to mind the musos' eternal dilemma: can you make your music pay? And for how long?

I suspect many Australian musicians mistakenly believe that, once they get a taste of a subsistence wage, it's possible to have a career in music. Losing seventy dollars might sting at the time, but it was possibly a signal that the music game is not a secure form of employment. Strangely, musicians' fees have barely changed in decades. I've discussed the issue with some hardened old musos and some young ones too: ten dollars per band member is the going rate. Now, of course, there are a range of payments above

and below this industry standard, but it's remained at this paltry amount in the face of steady and persistent inflation. The buying power of the muso, once he or she gets 'the earn' as I've heard it called, can be measured in beers. Just the other day, someone waxed lyrical about the days a schooner cost less than one dollar back in this period. Ten beers will make you a lot drunker than one.

I've heard tell that it is possible to actually make a living in other countries. There are also rumours that some places consider musicians to be artists! My friend, the Jazz pianist Chris Cody, lived in Paris for a long time—and made a living too.

> **France has a system where they actively support artists. If I had tried to make it in Australia as a Jazz musician, I would have ended up begging at the beach.**
>
> Chris Cody, Paris, 2015

Chapter 4 : We've Got a Gig!

Me doing lights at Alpha House. Very drunk. Pre-OH&S.

But in 1983, in Australia, we weren't thinking too hard about the long-term viability of our career choices. Music-making was really an elaborate form of socialising, with a free-flowing osmosis between the performers and the audience.

I think it was at this Mosman show where I met a young man called James. He seemed to come out of nowhere—with no history. I guess that large room did tend to be quite dark. James had a few different surnames, due to his parents' divorce and his mother's stage name. She was an actor on the ABC TV soap opera *Bellbird* at some point, I think. The different names were useful when applying for the dole. Over time, I helped James settle on Cruickshank.

At the time, he was in a band called the Gargoyles. I think they may have been fans. James Cruickshank would go on to be quite a presence in my life. Not so much at that point. But he kept reappearing.

As I stated earlier, the music scene was very diverse. But the diversity of this scene

25 SEP 1983	**INTERVENTION BOOKSHOP** [Haymarket/Sydney] w/Dadednyne
25 SEP 1983	**HUGO STREET PARTY** [Chippendale/Sydney] w/the Particles & Dadednyne
30 SEP 1983	**MOSMAN HOTEL** [Mosman/Sydney] w/the Triffids
13 OCT 1983	**NEWCASTLE UNI ARTS BALL** Shortland Room [Newcastle] w/Waiting for Brasso + Upsidedown House
21 OCT 1983	**SYDNEY TRADE UNION CLUB** 3rd floor [Surry Hills/Sydney] w/John Cooper Clarke, No Night Sweats, Scant Regarde, Funny Stories, The 'X' from Outer Space
4 NOV 1983	**UNIVERSITY OF NEW SOUTH WALES ROUNDHOUSE** [Kensington/Sydney] w/Do-Ré-Mi + Idiom Flesh
12 NOV 1983	**MOSMAN HOTEL** [Mosman/Sydney] w/the Triffids
19 NOV 1983	**CASTANET CLUB** [Newcastle] w/the Particles

was largely amongst white people. The musical influences were largely English and American (both strongly influenced by black American sounds), although inner-city types liked to think they were edgy and could take inspiration from anywhere, including outer space. Sometimes, music was not part of the equation at all. John Cooper Clarke was a sort of Cockney poet that even made it to the mainstream charts (I think). Today's slam poets might refer back to the old master here. I could also see it was a great way of keeping a band economical. No instruments to cart around, and no other people to cause trouble—all income to self. A more likely road to a sustainable career perhaps. I guess that's why there's so many stand-up comedians. But this acceptance of all sorts of creatures meant that a band like ours could find an audience. Blue was guarding our band gear in the goods lift at the front of the Trade Union Club, about to 'lug out' when John Cooper Clark himself appeared—wanting to use the lift.

> John Cooper Clarke was pencil thin, in his trademark tight-fitting suit with dark glasses and long dark hair stuck out like a dandelion puffball. I told him curtly to use the stairs and remember adding something like, 'it'll do you good'.
>
> Blue, Lighthouse Keepers

I don't think anyone consciously was thinking there was a scene happening at the Trade Union Club or Sydney or Australia at that point. On the contrary, I remember people whingeing the whole time. It was always better somewhere else. Like back in old England, where John Cooper Clarke's Cockneys all lived.

> There was a bunch of bands that came out of Australia in that period, but they weren't the same, you couldn't really link them together, each had their own distinctive sound. I guess that's what happens when you come up with it yourself.
>
> 'Evil' Graham Lee, the Triffids, 2015

Chapter 4 : We've Got a Gig!

Punk rock was like the vortex. It was really necessary. Then everyone had to start again. A lot of those Australian post-punk bands got into the roots of things and got a bit country. A lot of them were reading books. We weren't just illiterate cavemen. There were also the different streams synth pop, country swamp bands, ska revival. It was a restart to the whole history of pop. Like you can do anything you want now, that's why it's so post-modern. Gram Parsons was the coolest thing. I remember sitting round with Nick Cave—listening to the first Kris Kristofferson album, a huge influence when he went solo. And the same with the Go-Betweens—we were all into the wrong records. Kris Kristofferson 'Sunday Morning Coming Down'—is that not one of the great records?

Clinton Walker, 2015

With country and roots music on people's radar at the time, Blue, our harmonica and slide player, was in demand. The Lighthouse Keepers often played the old trad Jazz standard 'St James Infirmary Blues' as part of our set, and I remember Dave McComb from the Triffids asking me very politely if he minded if they recorded a version of it. Of course not, it wasn't our song anyway. So Blue was co-opted to record the song with the Triffids.

Afterwards, David asked me to join the Triffids, but I didn't hesitate in saying no. They were to become friends, but I was very loyal to the Lighthouse Keepers and somewhat overawed by it all.

Blue, Lighthouse Keepers

Allegiances were forged and broken quickly in this inner-city world. I didn't remember David McComb asking Blue to join the Triffids 'til I read Blue's ramblings! It could all be quite brutal, even if it was all fairly polite.

Juliet and Greg.

By the end of 1983, the Lighthouse Keepers, with no clear agenda except perhaps a social one, had become part of a wider Sydney scene. I never really liked the expression 'DIY', but music journalists often applied it to Lighthouse Keepers to describe our musical skills. As we developed, the band remained fairly technically inept but, somehow, all the parts came together to make a rickety whole. We made a noise that clunked along, going in odd directions, with a hint of wild country.

What the Lighthouse Keepers took from punk was—if that dickhead can do it—so can I.

Juliet Ward,
Lighthouse Keepers, 2015

CHAPTER 5

Springtime

Juliet. Photo: Darian Turner.

Once we'd tasted the heady heights of selling a few records on our own label, Guthugga Pipeline Records, nothing could stop us. We had to make a second. Our ambitions knew no bounds and we decided to make a whole mini-album. We were no 48-track-studio-coke-snorting eighties cliché (unfortunately). Without having tasted these excesses, we already wanted to get back to the basics and make something real. *The Exploding Lighthouse Keepers* was partly recorded in a bathroom in a rented house in Redfern. For the rest of it, we returned to good old Dream Studios at Bay 5 in Haymarket.

So we launched *The Exploding Lighthouse Keepers*. What better place to release this very apolitical 12-inch 45RPM than a left-wing bookshop? This time, we decided to cut back on labour and didn't create original artworks for every single record. Nevertheless, we still hand-coloured the covers that had pre-printed black and white artwork on them. The mini-album contained 'Springtime', which I'd actually envisaged as a mock love song—you know—ironic and everything. It still sounds like that to me, but people seemed to love it. In fact, it's a great favourite of my son Anders, who has

| 27 NOV 1983 | **BEHIND ENEMY LINES** aka Intervention Bookshop [Haymarket/Sydney] w/the Particles + Wimmen & Boys, *The Exploding Lighthouse Keepers* 12-inch mini-album launch |

Chapter 5 : Springtime

3 DEC 1983	**AUSTRALIAN NATIONAL UNIVERSITY BAR** [Canberra] w/Moonbathers
11 DEC 1983	**STRAWBERRY HILLS HOTEL** [Surry Hills/Sydney]
16 DEC 1983	**MOSMAN HOTEL** [Mosman/Sydney]
17 DEC 1983	**BEHIND ENEMY LINES** aka Intervention Bookshop [Haymarket/Sydney] w/Madroom, the Particles, Wimmen & Boys, Mutant Death + poets
30 DEC 1983	**MOSMAN HOTEL** [Mosman/Sydney] w/the Triffids

AUSTRALIAN TOP 20 CHART 1983

1. AUSTRALIANA ....Austen Tayshus
2. FLASHDANCE... WHAT A FEELING....Irene Cara
3. GLORIA ....Laura Branigan
4. BILLIE JEAN..............................Michael Jackson
5. UP WHERE WE BELONG ....Joe Cocker & Jennifer Warnes
6. TOTAL ECLIPSE OF THE HEART......Bonnie Tyler
7. SAVE YOUR LOVE..................Renee and Renato
8. KARMA CHAMELEON .... Culture Club
9. BEAT IT......................................Michael Jackson
10. EVERY BREATH YOU TAKE................ The Police
11. BOP GIRL... Pat Wilson
12. RECKLESS...............................Australian Crawl
13. I WAS ONLY 19......................................Redgum
14. TWISTING BY THE POOL.................. Dire Straits
15. RAIN ....Dragon
16. 1999 ....Prince
17. GIVE IT UP................KC and the Sunshine Band
18. HEARTBREAKER....................... Dionne Warwick
19. I'M STILL STANDING.........................Elton John
20. ELECTRIC AVENUE ....Eddy Grant

Anders.

a romantic streak. Perhaps a lot of love songs are misfired jokes.[1]

While the Lighthouse Keepers were beginning to make a name for themselves in a very insular scene—it might be interesting to have another look at the Australian 'mainstream' charts and see what was actually popular at the end of 1983.

I can remember just about every one of those songs down to the lead solos. Although the Australian element is pretty awful in there, I would imagine it's a good year for Australian music and also Australian poetry! I was probably actively avoiding the much-sneered-at Top 40—while still listening out of one ear. Mainstream culture was very omnipresent in this era. Elton John had been one of my early favourites, but he was obviously well past it in 1983. Dire Straits' 'Twisting by the Pool' still sounds horrible.

But those songs never seem to go away. The worst were annoying then and remain annoying now. Who would have thought they'd still be following you around the aisles of Woolworths? Not that there aren't a few to like amongst those hits. Michael Jackson, KC and the Sunshine Band, the Police. I was pretty mainstream underneath.

Parallel to this popular stuff were alternative scenes in Sydney and all around the world. Micro-scenes. I include another chart

---

[1] Do I walk around the house playing my old music at all hours for the benefit of my children? No, I heard it enough back in the times you are reading about. But it's still nice that they're interested.

from that year. Directly opposite Alpha House on King Street, Newtown, was a little record shop called Scratches. They put out their own charts that were sometimes reprinted in that hallowed English rock magazine, *New Musical Express*.

Scenes like the one the Scratches charts documents were perceived as anti-mainstream. But it was really just music that sold to a niche audience. Once you got popular, you were mainstream by default.

> Really, there were very few people involved in this scene. But a lot of those people went on to do interesting things. It was quite elite in that sense. There was no expectation of it leading to anything—even though there were accusations that people wanted to be pop stars. But I don't think anyone really thought that putting out an independent record would take them anywhere. There was a lot of resistance to the alternative scene in the mainstream record industry. Eventually they solved the problem by co-opting as many people as they could and minimising the rest.
>
> David Nichols, 2016

Did the Lighthouse Keepers want to be mainstream? I don't think any of us thought about it that much. But we must have had some aspirations: they grew as our audience grew. I enjoyed writing songs, getting them played and seeing what would happen.

In those days, I might write a song before breakfast and then another after it. The morning was always a good time. The late morning—to be exact. You might still have a bit of a hangover, which would loosen up the cogs of creativity. From early on, I made sure they never did become Top 40 songs. I did this by giving each song a title that was totally unrelated to any of the lyrics. This was certain to confuse any potential customers. For example, 'Ocean Liner', 'Love Beacon', 'Wilderbeast' and on and on through my back catalogue. I named the songs like objects or animals.

But to be honest, I think the rickety sounds and raggedy looks of our ensemble also put off those mainstream types. Who would buy our thin music when there was something as well produced and shiny as Michael Jackson's 'Billie Jean' around?

The rock writer Clinton Walker said something to me after a recent reunion show…he'd just realised that the Lighthouse Keepers songs were an entire set of love songs to Juliet. 'Well, der', I'm pretty sure my common law wife said on hearing this. And perhaps he was right—with some caveats.

They are indeed mostly love songs, with the occasional deviation to left field subjects—like worksite management. It was also strange but appropriate that I was writing these words of love and then having them come back at me— right out of the muse's mouth. Neither me or Juliet gave this any thought. She was just a

Chapter 5 : Springtime

The Exploding Lighthouse Keepers cover.

better singer, and the songs worked when she sang them. Even though she was as insular as me, perhaps more so, she was forced into the front person role. She did a great job and developed an onstage presence that was both inward and outward looking. Make sense? Not really. But again, the Lighthouse Keepers' songbook is full of half meanings. We never really thought about putting those lyrics on the inside covers. They were better half heard.

What is love anyway? As the English singer Howard Jones asked in his hit from that year. Love is very much mixed up with lust in your twenties, which has at least something to do with reproduction—and goes all the way back to cells dividing many millions of years ago. I guess I just wrote down what came into my head at the time. So even though I wasn't quite having a Clinton-Walker-of-a-time, sexually, it was good enough to inspire these odes to something beyond—yet of—reproduction.

NYE 1983	**ALPHA HOUSE** [Newtown/Sydney] + Wimmen & Boys + (maybe) Maestros & Dipsos + More or Less

Juliet Ward.

My lyrical touch has perhaps evaded me here.

So on with the shows. The Lighthouse Keepers fearlessly played in the New Year, as the allegedly meaningful 1984 came upon us. It was the title of a George Orwell book we'd all studied about a dystopia, and people were sort of scared. It was like an early version of the Y2K thing, and just like that—nothing happened.

As an aside, Roger Grierson from the Sydney punk band the Thought Criminals (1977–81), whose name was inspired by George Orwell's book, had become a bit of a record industry guy by this time. He was the only person who I ever signed a contract with. It was for the publishing rights to 'Gargoyle' for a few years. He offered me $500 up front or more over a longer term if such and such happened. I took the $500. I'm pretty sure this proved to be the correct choice.

And now I must cross to the muse herself. For Juliet began writing her own dairy from our Australian utopia. No thought police in sight as we kept on playing and drinking and making merry.

Juliet's diary
1984 New Years Eve

We played at Alpha House on the bottom floor where Steve and Lee are now living. We had a bit of a party. By 10:30 the place was still empty but people began to arrive and we started playing around 11. Then we all ran up the wooden stairs to the roof (8 floors!) and watched the fireworks. We played some more later but were all too pissed to be any good. Home to bed about 5am or something.

Juliet's diary is full of friends, houses and drinking. I don't think I could be this social anymore!

Friday 6/1/84

Jane and Jonathon, Ben, Donna, Darian, Alice and Blue all came round to watch the video of 'Bad Mood' on Rock Around the World on telly. Pretty thrilling being on TV. Mum saw it and rang afterwards to say there wasn't enough of me in it.

My video work was developing alongside the band's sound. It definitely had the same ramshackle feel. Since I was a communications student, I could churn out video clips for free as well as pass my course units. The clip for 'Bad Mood' that Juliet is referring to was not my best work. Just a couple of stick figure animations of a band with a few of our friends chroma-keyed on top of it all—dancing self-consciously. It was a lazy exercise in passing a unit of video production. But some of my other clips from that period still work for me. I looked at the clip for 'Gargoyle' just a couple of years ago (while in Paris, of all places). I hadn't seen it for a long time, and I felt pretty good about my student efforts. I wouldn't change a thing. From the dodgy old U-matic video texture, to the awkward scenes of dogs and humans, it captures the moment perfectly. As a director, my work ethos owes something to Ed Wood, the American filmmaker of such cult works as *Plan 9 from Outer Space*. I'm usually pretty happy with the first take and like to arrive on set fully unprepared. But playing my own critic (because I don't think anyone else is going to), I think my best work is contained within these accidental moments.

> We were often at UTS in this period as Greg made a number of videos for the band there. My dog, Bubbalouie, even featured in one which incorporated several songs. Louis Tillett makes a cameo appearance as an aggressive bar fly. This project went towards Greg's degree as did a sound project 'A Sad Tale'. Both projects are linked in their story lines. 'A Sad Tale' came in at around eleven minutes and would end up as the B-side to 'Ocean Liner', the single from *Tales of the Unexpected*.
>
> 'Ocean Liner' was put on the jukebox at the Native Rose Hotel, a favourite watering hole. 'The Bear', Martin the publican, really didn't like 'A Sad Tale', especially its tearful sobbing over-the-top finale. He would pull the plug out of the wall to cut out the 'sadness'.
>
> Blue, Lighthouse Keepers

My clip for 'Ocean Liner' is another one that works well and also features animals and people from our happy life and is popular on YouTube (by Aust indie standards anyway). Barely any of us can handle looking at the camera, except to grimace.

But Juliet looks amazing. The flying cats also predict the internet's lust for feline activity. Our video clips captured the life of relative ease we all enjoyed. Full of unlegendary people and animals.

Most of the 'Ocean Liner' clip is set in a shared terrace in Chippendale. There were outposts like this all over the inner west, with an incestuous rotation of residents. There was a darker edge to all this socialising, especially when drugs and alcohol were introduced into the situation. Similar to any workplace, you would get both your good and your diabolical humans. Mostly people got on, but there could be sudden switches of allegiances. Blue was amongst it all one night in a Redfern share house.

> One time, I witnessed or overheard one of the Particles' hangers-on pressuring a couple of girls to take or buy the drugs he was offering; I assume it was heroin. I had had a brief fling with one of them but I hadn't wanted to continue this. The other one, Donna, our drummer Steven Williams' girlfriend at the time, asked me to have sex with her in front of the friend; not the sex act in front of the friend but the asking. These two women were very close and almost inseparable friends. She said that it was because I was gentle and sweet, which might seem to clash with some other things I've written, but I hope she was right. As much as I liked Donna and she was a good-looking young woman, I really couldn't do this to Steven.
>
> Blue, Lighthouse Keepers

Blue was a popular redhead! Not everyone got out of that scene sane and/or alive. I was somewhat sheltered from this, by having an inner sanctum. Made up of me, Juliet and quite a few animals. But wait—Juliet is about to get a call from the inner-city kingmaker himself!

14 JAN 1984	**REHEARSAL ROOMS** [Newtown/Sydney]

Juliet's diary
Monday 9/1/84

Spent all day in bed.

At about 4pm I got a call from Clinton Walker (SMH) saying he wants to do an article on Lighthouse Keepers in the Metro. I wonder if he actually likes us. We'll find out.

So, dear reader, we've already heard about the rock critic Clinton, but stay with me, we're now telling the same history from multiple perspectives. Post-modern or what.

Juliet's diary
Saturday 14/1/84

Lighthouse Keepers played at the Rehearsal Rooms. A really nice room above a garage station. It wasn't advertised very much so there weren't many people which made me a bit uncomfortable. We played 3 sets and did quite a bit of C&W.[2] I was really a bit too drunk and talked too much. Jane and Jonathon are back together. Afterwards packed all the gear away. I worked very hard carrying heavy gear up and down the stairs. Expending nervous energy, I suppose. I collapsed and went to sleep on the stairs of the stage. Gus and some of his mates were there, made me nervous.

The Gus referred to here is the Gavin that featured in my childhood section. He was still in his mean phase and probably had some angry friends around him. Sometimes they liked to wrestle each other outside bars. Not every show was that much fun. You were a little at the mercy of whoever turned up, and very exposed. On a larger scale, I often wondered why some of the bigger stadium bands weren't shot at more! You rely on the audience to keep you going, but anyone can come to a show. As noted in her dairy, Juliet could sleep at any time and any place. It was not unknown for her to take a nap curled up in a W-bin—these were the gigantic speakers at the bottom of PA systems. This ability to sleep through anything meant that early in our relationship, I was always nervous when she put on a loud record before bedtime. I didn't realise yet that once she was asleep I could quietly lift the needle off the record player. So I often suffered through a whole LP side of Stiff Little Fingers, Patti Smith or Janis Joplin at full volume. I still shudder when I hear any of those artists. But it was all worth it. Perhaps the first few tracks of those albums sit more comfortably in my mind…

Tuesday 17/1/84

Lighthouse Keepers practised in the afternoon. Greg has written 5 more songs so it was very tiring learning them all. He is trying to make me more of an extrovert, I think, by making me scream and sing obscene words. Don't know what's come over him.

I'm not sure what songs Juliet is referring to here, maybe 'Evil Touch'? But perhaps we can already feel a little darkness coming over the whole ambience of our relationship (as if it wasn't always there). My ego was also being gently prodded, even though it was lightly. It could make you keep pushing the boundaries—however delicately. No wonder real rock stars end up rolling around their hotel rooms naked, with chickens or whatever. But then, Juliet's diary does take a sinister turn….

20 JAN 1984	**SYDNEY TRADE UNION CLUB** [Surry Hills/Sydney] w/SPK + Watusi Now + Arms & Legs

2 Country and Western.

Chapter 5 : Springtime

The Lighthouse Keepers.

Juliet's diary
Wednesday 18/1/84

This is the day when things started to get bad. Firstly the plumber arrived at 7:30 am! To fix the gas pipes which are full of water. Then I went to the CES because they had sent me a card implying that they had a job for me. I waited there for 1½ hours to be told that because I had moved I didn't belong to that office anymore—PISS OFF.

Dark times indeed! But these incidents were just omens. The next day she smashed her car on the Sydney Harbour Bridge. Luckily, no animals were harmed.

And there was always a show to make you really depressed. Juliet records a night with SPK—an 'industrial' power-tool-wielding band, up on the top level of the Trade Union Club. In those days, you had to pay your penance as a support band, by lugging those huge W-bin speakers, up the four sets of stairs! The other bands higher up the support act pecking order could also make your life miserable.

Juliet's diary
Friday 20/1/84

Went to the Sydney Trade Union Club about 9:15 and started playing about 10:30 or so. We played well, I think. People were dancing at first but seemed to slow down a bit towards the end. John was mixing out front and some other guy was doing stage sound. Every time I needed some more fold-back or something this guy was gone.

Then some other bloke started waving his arms and telling us to finish up. So we introduced our last song and this guy turned my foldback off. I glared at him and the sound came back while this bloke laughed with his mate. He whistled and yelled in the middle of our song. Turns out he was in Arms & Legs—Ignatius Jones' new band—which were on after us. The nerve!

Later when I was drinking downstairs a bloke came down claiming one of the members of SPK had hit him with a whip. Somebody else said that they had seen a girl who had been hit in the face with a chain. Greg went up there for a while and reported that they had a blow-torch and a chainsaw that they were threatening the audience with. Greg drove home (I don't think he was very sober).

SPK were literally at the cutting edge of music with all their chain-sawing and blow-torching. They were Australians, but had been living overseas and were doing the return tour thing. The Trade Union Club would appear to be the perfect venue for them in Sydney. Possibly the only venue. Being more familiar with left-wing factions and writings than us, Blue knew a bit about where the name SPK came from.

Their name derived from the Spartacist Party, a German Communist party who were active at the end of the First World War and whose leaders, Karl Liebknecht and Rosa Luxemburg were shot while supposedly escaping from the German authorities. They were not a Leninist party: they did not have a tightly organised inner group of party members running the party and revolution. The name was reborn in the 1980s as an alternative to the official far left parties in the West.

Blue, Lighthouse Keepers

Juliet had a car at the time she called Chuffy,[3] recently involved in the accident on Sydney Harbour Bridge. It was a Holden FB station wagon that, when tightly packed, could transport the entire band's gear. It was a complicated procedure and Steven Williams, the drummer, and Blue both had elements of the knowledge required to get it all in.

With painstaking placement, the gear would fit in snugly. However, the lining on the car was being ruined, chiefly by the foot spikes on the bass or kick drum. These were adjustable but in practice never were retracted and so tended to stick through the roof lining as they were being manoeuvred into the back of the car or turned about to fit like pieces in a jigsaw into place with the guitar cases or other equipment. This car had large back fins, but somehow they had become full of water—I remember a very wet summer—and then the car would steam up and you could hear water sloshing around.

Blue, Lighthouse Keepers

And so Clinton Walker's article came out in the *Sydney Morning Herald*. It was titled 'Lighthouse Keepers: the ultimate casual band' and began…

When Stuart Coupe described Perth group the Triffids as 'the epitome of the casual band' he was a little way off the mark. That label is more appropriate to a new, young group called the Lighthouse Keepers. The Lighthouse Keepers is similar to a contemporary jug-band. The band plays pop music to be sure, poignant and simple, but it's made distinct by the clear, light sounds of acoustic guitar, washboard rhythms and strolling bass, smooth harmonica and brass, and a lilting female voice…

from article by Clinton Walker,
Sydney Morning Herald

24 JAN 1984	**STRAWBERRY HILLS HOTEL** [Surry Hills/Sydney]
26 JAN 1984	**MIDDLE HARBOUR 16' SKIFF CLUB** [The Spit/Sydney]

---

3   At this stage, Juliet was young enough to get away with cute car names.

Rock
Lighthouse Keepers: the ultimate casual band

Lighthouse Keepers — back row from left: Blue, Greg, Stephen. Front: Steven, Juliet, and dog Chaos.

WHEN Stuart Coupe, Sun-Herald Rock Beat columnist and author of The New Rock'n'Roll, described Perth group the Triffids as "the epitome of the casual band," he was a little way off the mark. That label is more appropriate to a new, young group called the Lighthouse Keepers.

On the street-level of Sydney rock there's a growing reaction to the current overload of synthesised sounds in contemporary pop. The reaction has not only taken the form of a new wave of guitar-toting rock'n'roll outlaws (epitomised by a group like the Scientists) but also in a push to acoustic music.

Sometime-Saint Chris Bailey goes out solo accompanying himself on acoustic guitar, all-acoustic outfits like No Dance appear, and the Lighthouse Keepers quietly top the independent charts.

The Lighthouse Keepers is similar to a contemporary jug-band. The band plays pop music to be sure, poignant and simple, but it's made distinct by the clear, light sounds of acoustic guitar, washboard rhythms and strolling bass, smooth harmonica and brass, and a lilting female voice.

Lighthouse Keepers' personality is unassuming, innocent and worldly wise at the same time. Its music is an urban folk lament, where "Springtime ... is the season that you left me." But unlike the crying-in-your-beer school of country music, Lighthouse Keepers refuses to wallow in self-pity; although its songs are pervaded by a sense of loss, there is also self-knowledge and a sunny atmosphere that makes for optimism.

"I was a bit worried that the words were miserable or too corny," songwriter/guitarist Greg Appel told me, "but the way to listen to it is not to take it too seriously.

"I think we're a –," he laughs "– a joyful group."

Greg Appel and singer Juliet Ward began their collaboration in 1982, when they arrived in Sydney from Canberra. Picking up Michael "Blue" Dalton (harmonica, slide guitar and vintage music enthusiast). The band won a NSW Institute of Technology talent quest under the name Tex Truck and the Semis, and that was encouragement enough to continue.

Soon after that bassist Stephen O'Neil, also from Canberra, arrived in Sydney to join cult popsters the Particles; he enlisted with Lighthouse Keepers as well. This marked the beginning of a fruitful association between the two groups. Particles' manager, Steven Williams, later joined the Lighthouse Keepers as drummer. It was evident from the onset that Lighthouse Keepers was not at all a rock'n'roll band like all the others in Sydney.

Juliet Ward: "It's like David McComb from the Triffids said, and it's probably the same for us coming from Canberra, you don't get the influences you get in Sydney."

"It's changing all the time too," Appel adds. "I suppose we started off playing country and western – that was partly a joke, but it was also because we didn't want to play heavy sort of stuff. And then, after a while, I realised it was quite pleasant to play. And since then, in the music I've been listening to, I've been going further back into the past, and it's amazing how good it is."

Early last year, Lighthouse Keepers released a debut single, Gargoyle, on its own Guthagga Pipeline label. With a minimum of publicity, Gargoyle became one of the best selling independent records of the year, and Lighthouse Keepers was accumulating more fans at live performances.

"We had a good residency at the Brittania Hotel (in Chippendale) in the afternoons," Juliet Ward said. "We'd play three sets or so, and by the end of it everybody had a few drinks and got up dancing."

On stage, Lighthouse Keepers projects an endearing looseness and playfulness that's utterly engaging.

"It's nice to be musically tight a bit," Appel said, "but we're always swapping instruments. People have just got to put up with that."

"Stephen's sort of the real floating member of the band," Juliet went on. "He always wants to play drums; he gets bored with playing bass, because he plays bass in the Particles as well, and he's a very good guitar player too. So everybody moves around, and nobody gets bored."

Lighthouse Keepers certainly has the ability to sway any tender heart it encounters, but it doesn't impose itself.

As well as re-releasing some early Particles' singles Guthagga Pipeline has also just released The Exploding Lighthouse Keepers, a mini-album only the hardest heart could fail to fall in love with.

Lighthouse Keepers may not hard-sell itself, but that's no reason not to give the band a hearing. Before the band embarks on a national tour next month, Lighthouse Keepers will appear in Sydney tonight at the Trade Union Club, on Tuesday at the Strawberry Hills Hotel and Thursday at the Middle Harbour Skiff Club.

– Clinton Walker

It was basically a pretty positive article, no doubt written quickly in the gaps of his busy, druggy, sexy life. It was a key moment for the Lighthouse Keepers and it felt like we were on a roll.

Juliet's diary

Lighthouse Keepers played at the Strawberry Hills to a record crowd. It was packed. Has a lot to do with Clinton Walker's write up which was fabulous. It was very hot and stuffy. Poor old Barnaby got thrown out this time for being underage. I argued with the bouncers about this for quite a while but they would not budge. So I had to take him back to Alpha House. He was pretty upset, poor sausage.

The Barnaby that Juliet is referring to here is another one who's sadly not around. Her brother was unlucky enough to be born with haemophilia, and doubly unlucky to have blood transfusions in the early era of AIDS. A great kid. I remember him fondly, sitting around their family home with all his medical paraphernalia, making up songs

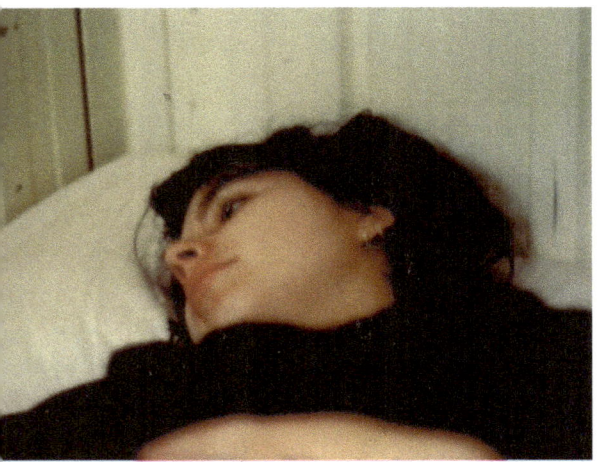

Juliet, Bermagui.

Juliet's talent for falling asleep anywhere, was an excellent way of avoiding carrying anything. Singers are well known for pointing out they only use a microphone and so don't need to carry any more than that (though they don't actually ever carry the mics). But as we all know, the microphone is amplified by a large contraption manned by a scraggly looking dude sitting at the back of the room. Mixers and roadies are a whole other story and often lorded it over the bands they had at their mercy. Especially if they weren't your mixer, as in another band was employing them.

They loved nothing better than giving a large speaker box to an emaciated guitarist. They were often trained in the beer barns, where the aim was to make everything as loud as possible. For some reason, they seemed to attract followers, often in the form of young girls who would bring them drinks and roll up leads after the show. It was a glamorous trade.

about every country in Africa. Some of them were a little repetitive and he was too young to understand the un-PC territory he was getting into, but the result was a formidable set of recordings. Later on, he had a musical career (he was sometimes called Baterz then) with the Bedridden, amongst others. He had an excellent song called '1968'. Which, although it might sound dated now, (in the truest sense of the phrase), was all about trying to get into a venue under-age, by using an older sibling's ID. The lyrics go:

> 2nd of November, 1968
> 2nd of November, 1968

Repeated to doorman, bar staff, etc, etc, demonstrating a knowledge of the birthday on the ID card. I wonder if he may have had some inspiration from that night at the Strawberry Hills Hotel?

Juliet's dairy
Thursday 26/1/84

> Lighthouse Keepers played at the Middle Harbour Skiff Club. Pretty good. About 20 people dancing and sang along to Springtime. Packed all the gear into the truck ready to go to Perth. I didn't do any lugging cos I fell asleep on the table.

Juliet. Photo: Darian Turner.

CHAPTER 6
Wheels Over the Desert

Stephen Williams, the Lighthouse Keepers.

The Lighthouse Keepers were having a great time in Sydney, and at the beginning of 1984, we decided to take our good times interstate and go to Perth. It was very ambitious in a way, as until then, we'd barely got out of the inner west. It was almost all due to our enterprising drummer Steven Williams.

I'm sure that it would have been him, pulling out from King Street, in the first vehicle of our fleet of two. I still have no idea what possessed him to put a bunch of whingeing musicians into a couple of vans and start the long drive, but we'd had one fan letter from Perth, and the Triffids came from there. What the hell! It wasn't just us that made the journey.

Of course, we had to go with our sister band the Particles and a huge gaggle of friends. Fourteen people in total. We even had a chef on board—at least that's what he told us. He was a guy who cooked stuff… sometimes.

> Basically, we kidnapped a French girl called Alice. She just happened to be hanging around at that time. I remember we were all in a bus with the Particles on King Street, ready to go to Perth. Hairy and I promised we would look after her. Of course, we didn't. Often, she was in a back room after a show crying because she didn't have anything to do.
>
> Juliet Ward, Bermagui, 2015

took an old-fashioned percolator and a tiny portable gas stove on tour and I remember serving up coffee to tired drivers in the middle of the Nullarbor. It was partly the diet on the road of fast food and junk food, where the best you could get was a hamburger, that took its toll. I had been a vegetarian and usually cooked at home, hardly ever eating out, before becoming part of the Lighthouse Keepers. Juliet and Greg seemed to exist on McDonald's, Coke and barbeque chips.

Blue

The Lighthouse Keepers were now getting a taste of real touring. The Adelaide shows were good fun, but the real destination was the other side of the country. The Triffids had just released their *Treeless Plain* album, and we couldn't help posing for a mock photo of their album cover. Bloody long way to go for a blurry photo. Juliet records our mood in her dairy as we finally arrived in Perth.

The kidnapped Alice has remained in our lives. She has lived in Australia ever since, more or less, and maintains an incredibly thick French accent. Her sons have even been in my whacky musicals and it's made for a strange bond with France in general.[1]

So, on towards Perth we went. I hadn't quite realised how large and flat Australia really was until this journey. And talk about unchanging vegetation! The scrubby bushes went on and on and on. There is some beauty in monotony, but enough is enough. Euros and Americans just don't quite comprehend the distances Australians travel. Just drive for a couple of days and you'll be at the next town.

> Talking about food, during this time travelling and touring, I had terrible digestion and tended to self-medicate with alcohol, coffee and cigars. I even

Juliet's diary
Tuesday 31/1/84

We arrived at the Old Melbourne, Perth, finally, and there was the usual row over rooms. I think I even threw some heavy objects at Peter (Particles). Some of us started griping about food. I was under the impression that we were to be fed every night out of the band's money and it was Ciaran's job to buy food and cook. He actually spent $100 on muesli and fruit, and we had to give up most of that when we crossed the Vic./S.A. border. We went downstairs for a beer while Astrid from the Particles continued to move people around until she had a room she was happy with.

[1] You might want to refer to the clip for 'A Time of Evil' to see this link with France (I don't know what it's all about either—but nice images).

28 JAN 1984	**CREMORNE HOTEL** (Stop 5) [Adelaide] + the Particles
29 JAN 1984	**AUSTRAL HOTEL** [Adelaide]

Chapter 6 : Wheels Over the Desert

Overlooking the Great Australian Bight.

The Old Melbourne was an atmospheric old pub in the middle of Perth and we were pleasantly surprised to play to a large and appreciative audience. Even though we were on with the Triffids, the crowd knew our set and were on side from the start. We could now challenge the Particles about who should be higher on the bill, but not the Triffids. This was their home town. They were the perfect hosts, and we had a great time in that bright hot summery world. There was a big 'inner-city' scene in Perth. It was cut off from the other cities to some extent and had grown its own musical wildlife—bands like the Scientists and Le Hoodoo Gurus. The Perth people both looked up to and despised 'interstate bands'. But they always put that on the poster if you were from 'over east'.

1 FEB 1984	**OLD MELBOURNE HOTEL** [Perth] w/the Triffids + the Particles

Perth was good. We played cricket with the Triffids and then drank jugs at Steve's Hotel. There was also a bit of tension between the bands over accommodation, as we were living upstairs in the Old Melbourne where the air conditioning was not working: it was rumoured that the Beasts of Bourbon had been there recently and trashed the place. Temperatures in Perth were reaching extreme levels. I think it got to 37°C overnight. I slept out on the roof protected by a sort of overhang from the laundry, but the others sweltered.

We were invited to a party in North Freo, but maybe I went alone because I got a lift back off a couple who informed me that they had supplied one of our hangers-on with enough synthetic morphine for the whole group of fourteen people, as they thought we were all users.

Blue, 2017

Confessions of a Lighthouse Keeper: Greg Appel

Outside Fast Eddies, Perth.

In this period, it seemed that there was a large amount of venues in Perth where bands like ours could play. Though Perth had its beer barns in the suburbs that stretched out along the sunburnt coast, the inner-city scene seemed out of proportion to population. Perhaps I was hallucinating due to the heat. Juliet records the hot electric atmosphere.

Juliet's diary
Saturday 4/2/84

We played at a place called The Charles out in what looked like the Leichhardt of Perth. We went out for the sound check and I got a shock on the lip—not bad—but I did my usual and bawled my eyes out. In the end, I put two rubber mats on the floor and wore Lee's rubber soled shoes. This was the first time we saw the Jam Tarts. They were wonderful and Greg fell in love.

3 FEB 1984	**WHIZ BAH** [Perth] w/the Particles + Diddy Wah Hoodaddys + Jam Tarts
4 FEB 1984	**THE CHARLES HOTEL** [somewhere in Perth] w/Jam Tarts

I now apologise to Juliet, separated from this time and place. I was younger and more obnoxious at this point and probably carried on about the attractive girl who was one of the Jam Tarts. Even though they had a pretty bad name, they did a great line in the Andrews Sisters from the forties and similar material. This was a period that we were fond of, and which indeed found its way into our set sometimes (e.g. 'Big Noise from Winnetka'). The Sophie Gare from the Jam Tarts is now Sophie Elton, as in married to the English comedian Ben Elton, whose best work was very early in his career, and now who we have to suffer for ever more! But I'm sure they're lovely people in person.[2] But back to Perth in the mid-eighties, where we were about to play after the Particles. Meaning we were finally the headline act in Perth.

2 Have to be careful what you say in the biz—you never know who you might meet—actually I do have an idea for a screenplay, it's about a group of English TV producer types on their last legs in the Old Country—they come to Australia—are fawned upon by the local media and decide to give it one more go—not sure what happens next—they accidently make the greatest film in history?

Chapter 6 : Wheels Over the Desert

The Lighthouse Keepers, the Particles and friends on tour.

Juliet's diary
Sunday 5/2/84

We played at the Captain Stirling in the afternoon. This time, the Lighthouse Keepers played second.

I particularly like the Stoned Crow at Freo where the Lighthouse Keepers played solo gigs. If you trod on a particular part of the stage, the drum kit almost collapsed. This gig, however, caused ructions between the two bands, as the Particles thought they should get a cut of the take.

Blue, 2017

Juliet's diary
Wednesday 8/2/84

Underground. The Particles were angry about us playing by ourselves on Tuesday and wanted half the money. Bugger that.

The war with the Particles had now reached its nadir, as Juliet records. Yet being young people, we could quickly forget about the dramas of who went on last and who had the best room in the hotel. The very next day, one of the Particles is apparently dancing to the Lighthouse Keepers. All was forgiven.

Thursday 9/2/84

Lighthouse Keepers and Particles played at the Red Parrot with the Triffids. I decided to walk to the sound check in bare feet, which was stupid, as I had to sprint all the way and I still scalded my feet. The Red Parrot is a huge ex-warehouse with a few thousand lights on the roof and a few glitter balls. We played first and about three people danced, one of which was Peter Particle. The Triffids were wonderful. They were followed by some ballet dancers. Doors Ajar were a bit corny. You know lots of pouting and sticking out bottoms.

The Triffids came back to the hotel with us and we sat on the roof, where Blue had made his bed. We sang songs and drank 'til the early hours.

5 FEB 1984	**CAPTAIN STIRLING** [somewhere in Perth] w/the Particles
7 FEB 1984	**STONED CROW** [Fremantle]
8 FEB 1984	**UNDERGROUND** [somewhere in Perth] w/the Particles
9 FEB 1984	**RED PARROT** [East Perth] w/the Triffids + the Particles + ballet troup + Doors Ajar

Karen Bayley, our Perth fan, and Lee looking coy.

It was a very successful trip to Perth and we finished off with another show by ourselves. The Stoned Crow in Fremantle might not have been the biggest venue around, but it was packed full of adoring fans. Perhaps I should have been jealous when Juliet was given a mass of roses by a group of men. But I remained smug and self-satisfied. There were always the hazards of the tour bus to bring us back to earth.

One of the Particles' friends had wired up a sound system in the band bus, but this hadn't been used much as I think there was a squabble about the music. We had forgotten about the wiring which snaked across the floor linked directly to the bus's battery, and with all our treading on it the wires had become stripped. One day parked outside the Old Melbourne, we all boarded the bus and as the last of us got on board the bus filled with smoke. Everyone scrambled to get off, while Steven, realising what had happened, tried to disconnect the wires from the battery. Steven was rather critical of our panicked stampede.

Blue

We boarded the repaired bus and waved goodbye to Perth. We were on a bit of a high after the recent run of great shows, but not for long. We were only well loved in the inner part of Perth and maybe Fremantle. Western Australia is a gigantic state full of tough nuggety people—who knew what sort of music they were into? It probably wasn't indie wimp...

10 FEB 1984	**WHIZ BAH** [Perth]
11 FEB 1984	**OLD MELBOURNE** [Perth]
12 FEB 1984	**CAPTAIN STIRLING** [somewhere in Perth]
14 FEB 1984	**STONED CROW** [Fremantle]

16 FEB 1984	**NORSEMAN HOTEL** [Norseman] w/the Particles

Chapter 6 : Wheels Over the Desert

The Lighthouse Keepers in Perth.

Juliet's diary
Thursday 16/2/84

We left Perth and stopped in Kalgoorlie for some guitar strings. It's a bloody awful town, where girls aren't allowed to go to the loo.

We arrived in Norseman on Thurs. afternoon and started setting up after a beer. We had a little discussion with the publican about not letting any 'coons' in. Lee was a bit upset because she had already invited a lot of people, including Aboriginals.

It was a pretty awful night. All the men in Norseman are miners about 6 feet across the shoulders. I heard that the three only unmarried girls were at the gig. I think that explains why anyone came at all.

At Norseman, Hairy came into the dining room in what looked like a shift dress. It was very hot but I think it was a dare concocted by the Particles. He usually wore eye-liner and I think he was wearing a beret but it seemed to send the miners off. They were all along one side of a big table facing us. I could hear their muttering, 'is that a man or a woman?' and they seemed to get particularly interested when the real women in the bands came in.

Blue

The Norseman Hotel stands out as a particularly scary show. We doubled the town's population of women when we arrived. Steven Williams had thought it would be a good way of getting some accommodation paid for and some food. We didn't sleep well that night with the menacing sound of hotted-up cars circling the hotel.

Greg, Juliet, Blue: Ceduna.

Juliet's diary
Friday 17/2/84 & Saturday 18/2/84

After the inevitable running out of petrol halfway across the Nullarbor, we had to park outside a petrol station 'til it opened, so I went to sleep. I slept like a log until Ceduna. We stayed and played at this spiffing motel, with air conditioning, colour TVs, showers and stuff. We even got a proper feed; T-bone steaks and heaps of salad. The Particles played first, deciding that it was such a hick town. We knew we'd go down better and we did.

18 FEB 1984	**CEDUNA COMMUNITY HOTEL** [Ceduna] w/the Particles
20 FEB 1984	**CREMORNE HOTEL** (Stop 5) [Unley/Adelaide] w/the Particles
21 FEB 1984	**AUSTRAL HOTEL** (Stop 5) [Unley/Adelaide] w/the Particles
22 FEB 1984	**SEAVIEW BALLROOM** [St Kilda/Melbourne] w/the Particles

There are some shows that remain in your memory for a good reason. This would be one of them. We had the Yin and Yang of the rock experience crossing back over the Nullarbor Plain. The Norseman show had been truly terrifying and I'm sure we all didn't want to play another country town in our life. But a combination of factors led to the Ceduna show being one of the best Lighthouse Keepers shows ever.

The key factor was my cousin Bruce and his wife, Rebecca. They were residents of this town. Bruce had followed his dreams, born during our holidays along the NSW South Coast near Canberra, and become a marine biologist. This had sent him to some strange outposts of marine interest, like this little town on the South Australian edge of the Nullarbor. They'd lived there a little while, and had gathered a reasonable circle of like-minded friends. But something, almost magical, happened in that seventies-styled motel bar. It made even the hard-core locals get up and get into it.

Even way up the back, where the old men sat on stools all day, there was all sorts of dancing going on. A flickering memory of Australian creatures being interpreted through dance comes back to me. We could play just about anything and cause a roar of approval.

> We went over big in Ceduna. The audience did not want to go, even after we had played every song we knew, so Hairy eventually set his guitar up against the amp and let it feed back.
>
> Blue

**Juliet's diary
Sunday 19/2/84**

Back to Adelaide. I'm starting to get a bit impatient to get home.

Here endeth Juliet's diary. We played a couple of shows in Adelaide, a place that felt a little like Canberra to us. Slightly spooky, just the way we liked it. And we seemed to find a like-minded audience too, as I recall.

Then on to Melbourne—with no small town-dates on the way. Perhaps we had learned our lesson. Recently, Graham Lee from the Triffids told me about Melbourne band the Moodists playing in a country town in the stretch between Adelaide and Melbourne.

> The Moodists did have a bit of a hard edge. They were playing in this little South Australian town—did a set and Steve Miller was called into the hotel manager's office. The manager said, 'what was that?' Steve said, 'rock and roll'. The manager says, 'No, mate, that was shit! Get out of here!' And they had to leave.
>
> Graham Lee, 2016

Rock and roll indeed! We were now playing in some of the classic venues of the era once we got to Melbourne. The Seaview Ballroom was well known to the punky Melbourne types. But I don't think they ever fully accepted our feral ways in this city. It was all about dirty suits there—but no thongs. It seemed very different to Sydney. We had a sort of core following but never quite cracked the town. It's a difficult place, I've learned over time, though there are moments when the audience will get on board and give you a half smile.

The Particles and The Lighthouse Keepers tour bus.

But then again, we never even attempted to try any of the suburban venues in Melbourne. I remember James Reyne[3] telling me many years later that Melbourne was divided into two parts during the eighties: Nick Cave ruled a ring around the centre, but James's old band Australian Crawl ruled the rest. This was all the suburban venues in that vast flat city—and a much bigger area, he hastened to add. Not many bands could cross this formidable barrier, and we certainly never tried.

Occasionally on a tram, you'd get a feel for the Melbourne yobbo, and they were quite a fearsome species. The Sydney ones were a bit more boiled and brain-addled I think, because of the climate. Not that there weren't some scary yobbos all over Australia at the time. I remember a Canberra band had a song 'Land of the Boons' which said it all (in fact, that may have been the only lyric).[4]

In Melbourne, the hotel of choice for visiting bands attempting to win the hearts of the inner ring crowd was the Prince of Wales. Indeed, it was just a block from the Seaview Ballroom in St Kilda. It had an odour and ambience that was quite attractive. You could play and live there as part of a richly rewarding 24-hour cycle.

You might not get a huge crowd at the Prince of Wales bar downstairs, but you'd feel like a proper rock star when you trudged back to your room down the red carpets that smelt faintly of vomit. It was like the hotel in *The Shining*—except with living spooky people (at least, I think they were). I remember many pizzas, late nights watching drivel on TV, and every one of the Carlton family of beers available at all times. I still think that if you put Carlton Draught in a green bottle and called it 'Sweet Stinging Bee' or similar, it would be very popu-

25 FEB 1984	**PRINCE OF WALES** [St Kilda/Melbourne]
2 MAR 1984	**MANNING BAR** [Sydney University] w/the Particles + Wimmen & Boys
3 MAR 1984	**SYDNEY TRADE UNION CLUB** 2nd floor [Surry Hills/Sydney]

3   When I worked with him on *DIG TV* ABC2. *note Aussie celebrity name drop.
4   News to hand 2020 – the band was called The Liquidator and this song's chorus included the lyric (repeated several times): 'HR/HQ'.

Chapter 6 : Wheels Over the Desert

lar with the beer snobs of the world. Obviously, it's big with the footy crowd regardless.

Back in Sydney, we kept on plugging away. I've since realised that we did very little compared to those bands that were up and down the Hume Highway every week. But still, we were lazy people and this felt like work. Good work, mind you. Sometimes, people ask me how I did a university degree at the same time through all this. I tell them it wasn't very hard. My course was also 'pass/fail', leaving me no option but to put in the least effort possible. Which I did, leaving plenty of time for self-indulgence. Which brings us back to the Sydney Trade Union Club.

This previously mentioned venue had nothing to do with any trade union that I could tell, but it did have a lot to do with bourgeois indulgence. I'd at least learned this word from my communications degree, although I did have trouble pronouncing it and had an awkward moment in one tutorial. I pronounced it 'borgeese'—like the fowl...

Anyway, back to the Trade Union Club. A credible source has told me that the guy who ran the club paid off the police to keep it running. I'm sure it's true. Sydney was still a very criminal kind of place in that period. Crime has always been very close to the music industry, though I never personally had to deal with it. Occasionally we'd get 'ripped off', and our drummer Stephen Williams might shout at a scary-looking man, but that just seemed to be the way it was.

As a slight detour to our tribulations on Australia's rock circuit, I relate a family anecdote. My own uncle Tim Bristow, from my father's side, was part of this criminal world and still working a bit up at Kings Cross during this era. When I met him later on in life in his Newport home, he was getting old, but he had been a much-feared gangster from the sixties forward. He seemed to have a story about just about any politician that you could think of. Definitely Hawkie, Wran and Askin. People that crossed him always had 'bad luck'. I remember he kept talking about bodies under the tennis court that we could see behind us in his backyard. Then he took us down to the Newport shops and walked around all the takeaway shops getting free dim sims. It all felt slightly silly, especially when we watched

The Particles family and friends: Ingrid, Peter, Astrid and Darian.

some Patrick Swayze films with his young 'girlfriend' and my own—who were of similar age. Uncle Tim's girlfriend was a big fan of Patrick, but Tim didn't seem to mind.

10 MAR 1984	**SYDNEY TRADE UNION CLUB** 2nd floor [Surry Hills/Sydney]
17 MAR 1984	**SYDNEY TRADE UNION CLUB** 2nd floor [Surry Hills/Sydney]
21 MAR 1984	**WAR AND PEACE HOTEL** [Parramatta/Sydney] w/Champions
22 MAR 1984	**MOSMAN HOTEL** [Sydney] w/the Triffids
24 MAR 1984	**SYDNEY TRADE UNION CLUB** 2nd floor [Surry Hills/Sydney]
31 MAR 1984	**SYDNEY TRADE UNION CLUB** 2nd floor [Surry Hills/Sydney]
7 APR 1984	**HAROLD PARK HOTEL** [Glebe/Sydney]
8 APR 1984	**SYDNEY TRADE UNION CLUB** 3rd floor [Surry Hills/Sydney] w/Violent Femmes + Lighthouse Keepers + Flying Doctor

My brother Steve was with me on another of these fact-finding missions, when Uncle Tim made us go diving with him. He kept pointing right out to sea as we parked his Mercedes at the beach. Steve and I looked at each other nervously when he talked about wrestling sharks. We then timidly followed Uncle Tim's flippers out to sea and watched him dive deep below, sticking his hands bravely into any crevice that he came across. We were glad to get back to dry land and tuck into the free Chinese food. Such is the life of a stand-over man. But back at the Trade Union Club, we were oblivious to any of the backroom activities that kept our industry afloat.

> **We got a Trade Union Club residency every week on the second floor. Having to play for so long… we got quite good. I remember you got down on your knee and put a ring-pull on my finger there… I'm sorry I didn't take you seriously.**
>
> Juliet, 2015

This is from an interview I did recently with Juliet. I had actually forgotten this until she mentioned it. I'd proposed to her with a ring-pull from a beer can at the Trade Union Club! Even though it was a joke, I think it's clear our relationship must have been going strong at that point and we were enjoying playing, drinking and generally having fun. Later on, I wrote a song called 'I Met My Wife at the Trade Union Club'. The best thing about it was the title.

The Violent Femmes, who we supported at the Trade Union Club, are one of those bands

13 APR 1984	**STRAWBERRY HILLS HOTEL** [Surry Hills/Sydney]
14 APR 1984	**HAROLD PARK HOTEL** [Glebe/Sydney]
15 APR 1984	**BEHIND ENEMY LINES** aka Intervention Bookshop [Haymarket/Sydney] – just Lighthouse Keepers

Chapter 6 : Wheels Over the Desert

who've broken out of their time and become a bit of a retro radio mainstay. They were great fun. The little fellow who sang came out on stage with a woman on each arm, as I remember. Their music was definitely a better match for us than the power-tool-wielding SPK.

And so time passed in a fairly happy blur of Sydney inner-west activity... but Melbourne kept calling. It was taken for granted that once a band got going, you were obliged to go up and down the Hume Highway as many times as you possibly could. You would often see the hired Tarago vans of other bands coming in the opposite direction—an anonymous (but familiar) gaggle of sickly-looking young people dressed in the requisite black. Perhaps eating a ham, cheese and tomato toasted sandwich, definitely swilling beer for the entire journey. You might even attempt a show in Sydney on a Friday night, set out after it and attempt Melbourne on a Saturday evening. This would make for a really cranky, odorous group of musicians and lay the groundwork for an unmemorable show. There were various levels of bands, in a highly stratified class system. Generally, everybody hated everybody else. But the hate would be less intense if you were on the same level. Coming from the same city was also kind of a positive. You might even be friendly with the bands just below you on the bill. There were also musicians that had a go at the supposedly lucrative job of managing venues. I'm pretty sure 'Bongo' Starkie from Skyhooks managed 'the Club' (or one of these clubs we played in). It goes without saying, most of us loathed Skyhooks.

I've learned since that AC/DC didn't like them much either. We did have a soft spot for AC/DC though, and Juliet had a couple of albums which she occasionally pulled out from under Patti Smith's *Horses*, or other such difficult works. These bands were the older generation, and the true rockers, really. When the Hume Highway used to be far more deadly, and the crowds bigger, uglier and meaner. And without them, there would never have been a golden age for bands to whine about. Indeed, my whole career seems just to have been at the wrong end of the golden age of something...

Blue has his own diary of the times, and he records his memories of this Melbourne tour in 1984. Blue is quite an evocative writer, as you now know, but if he rambles on too much, I'll edit him. If only we were able to do that occasionally during those long drives! It was a long stream-of-conscious oral history that dipped into Australia's left-wing past and whatever happened to him yesterday on the way to the shops.

19 APR 1984	**THE CLUB** [Melbourne]	
21 APR 1984	**SEAVIEW BALLROOM** [St Kilda/Melbourne] w/the Cockroaches + Gas Babies	
22 APR 1984	**THERAPY** [Melbourne]	
23 APR 1984	**VENETIAN ROOM** [Melbourne]	

**Easter '84 Melbourne Tour
by Michael 'Blue' Dalton (A diary
written soon after the fact)**

My memory is going a bit hazy these days, (we are recording and my mind tends to get a few kangaroos in the top paddock on such occasions), on what happened and when.

There are things we should have thought about twice when visiting Melbourne. For instance, playing The Club in Collingwood, on the Thursday before Good Friday in 1984. A truly miserable booking, we had taken a ridiculous time to travel from Sydney to Melbourne. It was something like

26 APR 1984	**MOSMAN HOTEL** w/Second Language
28 APR 1984	**SYDNEY TRADE UNION CLUB** 3rd Floor [Surry Hills/Sydney] w/the Particles, Pop Up Toasters, Dadednyne, Madroom
26 MAY 1984	**SYDNEY TRADE UNION CLUB** [Surry Hills/Sydney] w/the Triffids
1 JUN 1984	**PLAYERS PADDINGTON GREEN HOTEL** [Paddington/Sydney]
2 JUN 1984	**CARMENS AT MIRANDA** [Miranda/Sydney]
8 JUN 1984	**SYDNEY TRADE UNION CLUB** 3rd Floor [Surry Hills/Sydney]
9 JUN 1984	**CARINGBAH INN** [Caringbah/Sydney]
11 JUN 1984	**KINGSHEAD INN** [South Hurstville/Sydney]
14 JUN 1984	**UNIVERSITY OF NEW SOUTH WALES SQUAREHOUSE** [Kensington/Sydney]
15 JUN 1984	**THE GRIFFIN CENTRE** [Canberra] maybe self-support or possibly with Falling Joys
16 JUN 1984	**QUEANBEYAN LEAGUES CLUB** Oval Room [Queanbeyan]

20 hours, when we ran out of petrol at around 6am. Juliet and Greg had to hitch for fuel. When we got there the support band didn't show. We started late and finished early, due to the licensing laws for Good Friday. On the following days we played a venue called Therapy in North Melbourne. Therapy was a nightclub somewhat similar to the Underground in Perth, North Perth. Both venues were a maze of rooms, with corridors designed like tunnels or railway carriages or whatever. Both venues were up-market, and belonged to those clique cool venues, which refused entry to those who didn't look 'their sort of people'. However, at Therapy, we were told to start late, then later finally, only one set. We did do two sets, although the staff tried to stop us—they were having a private party in the bar in an adjoining room. At the end of the night, we were asked for an encore, and we had to play out on the street, as we weren't allowed inside. I think we played at the Seaview Ballroom, supporting the Cockroaches, which went down very well. We then had to get back to Sydney to play on Anzac Day or the night before. So we set off down the road in what we called the Barge, a Bedford-issue Holden van that reeked of fuel. We'd rented it from rent-a-wreck and for most it was plain sailing on the freeway from Barry's road to Seymour, but then tragedy struck!! We slowed down at the first town, Euroa, which was 100 or so kilometres from Melbourne. This name will be forever etched in my mind, along with Jonucci's the RACV representative. Our 'Barge' slowed, and then refused to start. Oh, Cursed Earth, Oh, Joyless Day! Little did we realise the fate we would have to endure. It eventually became apparent

Chapter 6 : Wheels Over the Desert

that the barge would take some time to get going and, as the next day was a working day between the Easter weekend and Anzac Day, we thought nothing much of going to the pub for refreshments. As dusk settled early on that cold autumn day, the gnarled and toothless cronies of Euroa assembled in the bar. Hunched over their beers, they gazed at us young 'uns, who by now were laughing and listening to a cassette in the corner.

News from the Jonucci's was we would have to spend the night in Euroa. Steven Williams still going strong from his negotiations with Jonucci, managed to get rooms at the pub without damaging our bank balance too much. The rest of our crew, cold and hungry, slowly climbed the stairs to our rooms, and to the communal TV. We saw a lot of TV and each other in the hotel over the next THREE DAYS! We did get out of Euroa on the next day, yet the Barge only made it as far as Benalla, the next town on the road. I bought myself a bottle of cheap port and numbed my brain, while we coasted back to Euroa. We were woken by a boy scout playing the Last Post at the Anzac Day dawn service out front of the memorial hall next door to the pub. I blearily raised the curtain, and peered at the ragged line of old codgers and young scouts and guides standing to attention. I have heard the Last Post many times but this was bad.

Blue, Lighthouse Keepers

20, 22 & 23 JUN 1984	**SMIGGINS HOLES HOTEL** [Queanbeyan] This was a short residency at the famous ski resort
29 JUN 1984	**MOSMAN HOTEL** [Mosman/Sydney]
30 JUN 1984	**SYDNEY TRADE UNION CLUB** [Surry Hills/Sydney] w/Wet Taxis + Altar Ego
20 JUL 1984	**BLAST FURNACE** (back of Clarendon Hotel) [Newcastle]
25 JUL 1984	**STRAWBERRY HILLS HOTEL** [Surry Hills/Sydney] w/Just A Drummer
27 JUL 1984	**METROPOLE HOTEL** [Fitzroy/Melbourne] w/the Shindiggers + [maybe The Bol Weevils]
28 JUL 1984	**THE SEAVIEW BALLROOM** [St Kilda/Melbourne] w/Scrgh Museum + Pilot to Bambadier
1 AUG 1984	**HAROLD PARK HOTEL** [Glebe/Sydney]
2 AUG 1984	**UNIVERSITY OF NEW SOUTH WALES**: Library Lawns [Kensington/Sydney] maybe self-support
3 AUG 1984	**SYDNEY TRADE UNION CLUB**: 2nd Floor [Surry Hills/Sydney]
6 AUG 1984	**WOLLONGONG UNIVERSITY** [Wollongong] Think this may have been supporting Sekret Sekret
9 AUG 1984	**HAROLD PARK HOTEL** [Glebe/Sydney]
10 AUG 1984	**SYDNEY TRADE UNION CLUB** 2nd Floor [Surry Hills/Sydney]
24 AUG 1984	**SYDNEY TRADE UNION CLUB** 2nd Floor [Surry Hills/Sydney]

Steven Williams and Juliet, Bunbury; about to play a particularly unpleasant show.

Tales of the road as told by Blue. But now back to me, in the less distant past. I don't remember much of this, but it obviously left deep scars on Blue. The Hume Highway is now, of course, a dual carriageway all the way—more or less. I don't really miss the windy old roads full of agro trucks that much. However, Jonucci's Victorian bit of the highway looks pretty much the same now, if you drive past. Just be careful and check the temperature and oil regularly when driving near Euroa.

The shows kept mounting up and we seemed to be playing every second night. I don't think it would be possible for a band of our level, playing mainly original songs, to do this anymore. Amazingly, we were almost making a living from music at this point.

Not that all shows were equal. A lot of them were forgettable or memorable for the wrong reasons. I remember the Queanbeyan Leagues Club as being a particularly small crowd in a very large room. Queanbeyan hadn't been gentrified at all then—it was a concretey old RSL and I guess we never played there again. You've got to have a hit to do this sort of place. But if Steven Williams was able to bluff his way through the bookings officers in Queanbeyan, then why not give Smiggins Holes a go? They love music up in the mountains. The skiers were probably pretty pissed off about having us there for the après thing. Three nights of it too!

We were asked back to continue the very successful residency at the Sydney Trade Union Club, and were kept busy there, as we'd do three sets a night. It was at this point that we decided to record the only al-

31 AUG 1984	**SYDNEY TRADE UNION CLUB** 2nd Floor [Surry Hills/Sydney]

bum the Lighthouse Keepers were to make, *Tales of the Unexpected*. The title was taken from a favourite late night TV show—of the B variety.

We'd had a few meetings with the enigmatic Martin Jennings, from Hot Records, a character who had arrived in Sydney with a background in the British record industry that stretched back to the Beatles days. He thought Sydney could be the next Liverpool, and maybe he wasn't completely mad. He was also inspired by frequent puffing on joints. He'd even worked at Apple Records in some junior role, and had witnessed the tail end of the swinging sixties in London firsthand. Hot Records already had our friends the Triffids and the Wet Taxis, as well as the much admired Laughing Clowns, along with a pretty good collection of Sydney bands. Why wouldn't we go with them? Especially after listening to Martin wax lyrical of an evening. He ruminated on music and the artistic life from under clouds of smoke. Martin also had open relationships with lady friends that accompanied him in different cities of the world. This cat was a swinger!

So a verbal deal was done. And we ended up doing about a week of late-night recording sessions at Paradise Studios, in Kings Cross. This was a big studio for us, but by doing it after hours we could save a lot of money. We were young enough then to do without sleep for a while. It felt like things were starting to happen. Paradise Studios was owned by Billy Field, who had a retro-sounding hit with 'Bad Habits'. I think he put the money from that into this fairly modern 24-track studio. He never appeared at the sessions, but the studio always had a faint smell of eighties fairy dust.[5]

I was coming up with a lot of songs at this stage, and I wanted to record everything. So

Inside the Paradise Studios, Kings Cross.

we did as much as we could, and put a lot of things down fairly live. I think it helped the recordings in some ways. The playing isn't brilliant, and you wouldn't know it was the height of the eighties, where INXS were just down the road at Rhinoceros Studios spending a week on a bass drum sound... but it captured the feel of the band. It could have been sonically better, and Juliet's vocals were often buried but nevertheless, I still like it. Out of these sessions came 'Ocean Liner', which is probably our best-known track these days. It was, as usual, a love song, but through the mists of time, I can now hear darker things happening here. Isn't all love doomed in a way? Love is often about self, along with all the lust. Somewhere along the way, the two selves will not be one.

But neither me or Juliet pondered the lyrical content. We both just wanted to have a good time all the time.[6] I think that was the motivation of a lot of musicians, and it was definitely the agenda for all those on the stage and in the audience on the second floor of the Trade Union Club. This album sounds like a good night there to me. Probably because we had our residency at the same time we were

---

5 Our engineer David Price, who had a bit of a blond Dracula thing going, could also have been behind this.

6 Yes, I am quoting directly from *Spinal Tap*.

The Lighthouse Keepers in party mode.

recording *Tales of the Unexpected*. Many harsh dawns were seen as we opened the doors of Paradise (accidental poetry, hey?).

> Recording *Tales of the Unexpected* was a bit of an ordeal. I definitely felt overawed and out of place as it was very imposing and I was to play and record bass on quite a few songs. Keith Hale was to have helped us transition from his studio to a larger more commercial set up. However, on the night we were to go into record for the first session, Keith said he wasn't coming. We were using an engineer who came included with the studio, David Price, again another unknown. The assistant engineer queried whether we were ready for a big studio, too. He was someone who knew one of Hairy's friends and I suppose knew something of the band. We had a lot of songs to record as Greg was in a very prolific writing stage. Juliet didn't want to leave him by himself for any length of time as he would then have written a song or two which meant she'd have to learn them. We also had more players: John Papanis, who lived above Keith at Bay 5 and played in Non Fiction, played banjo on 'No Reason' and mandolin on 'Wheels Across the Desert'. Alex Hamilton was again on trumpet, joined by Glad S. Bag on trombone and her brother Beat Boy on baritone sax. Hairy was also playing his sax—a marching band sax in the key of C. Juliet's brother Barnaby added sound effects such as barking, and Lee Vergona, Steven's then girlfriend added spoken word.
>
> Blue, 2017

[6 OCT 1984   **PARTY AT 197** [Chippendale/Sydney]]

Chapter 6 : Wheels Over the Desert

The artwork for *Tales of the Unexpected* was an original piece by Hairy our multi-instrumentalist. Hairy also designed some band posters. These were printed and stuck up all over inner-city Sydney, especially wrapped around telegraph poles with sticky tape. Art was a source of conflict between Hairy and the drummer/manager Steven. Steven wanted clearly worded and informative posters, while Hairy wanted arty ones. However, even though this tension hovered over the band, we partied on.

> I think we only played the once at no. 197 Abercrombie Street. Myself, Hairy, Alice and maybe Ben Donaldson lived there though there was often a continual stream of visitors, mainly to watch some daytime serial. The party was after a prolonged series of recording sessions for *Tales of the Unexpected*. The police came fairly early but, though they advised us to turn down they also pointed out that as it was changeover of their shift, we would be undisturbed for a few hours before the next patrol arrived. When this next patrol arrived, they cut the power, which blacked the house out, and ordered us to disperse.
>
> Blue, 2017

26 OCT 1984	**STRAWBERRY HILLS HOTEL** [Surry Hills/Sydney]
7 NOV 1984	**ST GEORGE SAILING CLUB** [Kogarah/Sydney] w/the Cockroaches
9 NOV 1984	**CHEVRON** [Kings Cross/Sydney] w/Wet Taxis + The Change + Benders
11 NOV 1984	**CLARENDON PARTY** (back of Clarendon Hotel) [Newcastle] Not sure this date is correct ie may have been 1st Nov 1984
14 NOV 1984	**STRAWBERRY HILLS HOTEL** [Surry Hills/Sydney]
16 NOV 1984	**MANZIL ROOM** [Kings Cross/Sydney] w/Tin Gods of Promise
17 NOV 1984	**AUSTRALIAN NATIONAL UNIVERSITY BAR** [Canberra]
21 NOV 1984	**STRAWBERRY HILLS HOTEL** [Surry Hills/Sydney]
5 DEC 1984	**MIRANDA HOTEL** [Mirandah/Sydney]
7 DEC 1984	**NEWTOWN LEAGUES CLUB** [Enmore/Sydney]
8 DEC 1984	**CARINGBAH INN** [Caringbah/Sydney] w/the Go-Betweens
12 DEC 1984	**OPHIR TAVERN** [Orange] Orange!
15 DEC 1984	**CLARENDON PARTY** (back of Clarendon Hotel) [Newcastle]
16 DEC 1984	**CLARENDON PARTY** (back of Clarendon Hotel) [Newcastle]
20 DEC 1984	**BONDI PAVILION** [Bondi/Sydney] w/Laughing Clowns (was the Clowns' 'Just Because I Like' single launch
21 DEC 1984	**MOSMAN HOTEL** [Mosman/Sydney]
22 DEC 1984	**SYDNEY COVE TAVERN** [Sydney] w/the Cockroaches + Lighthouse Keepers + Swinging Tees + Guy Delandro Band

The band was getting a bit more ambitious now. We were attempting to conquer the suburbs by playing out at Miranda, in the Sutherland Shire. As usual it was difficult. We were no AC/DC and I remember crumbling a bit. I've met quite a few people from 'the Shire' now, but back then it seemed like a different country. You'd get some in the audience who were sympathetic, but a whole lot who were pretty oblivious—if not hostile. You have to deal with this to make any sort of living from music in Australia. Bands like Hunters and Collectors started out arty and ended up in blue singlets. The Go-Betweens and the Triffids fled the country except for annual kitty-replenishing tours. 'Love it or leave it', as they say on those unfriendly car stickers.

1984 had been a great year for the band. We saw a lot of the country.

As the Christmas party season kicked in, we found ourselves playing with the Cockroaches. These guys were a soul cover band that eventually morphed into the Wiggles. Similar territory was covered by the Dynamic Hepnotics. Yes, they both sounded white, because they were, but I loved these kinds of cover bands. I'd never heard James Brown when I first saw the Dynamic Hepnotics, back in Canberra. I'd only seen a picture of him on one of those bubble gum cards you collected, to swap at school. He looked very different from all the Peter Framptons, etc. These cover bands could be a lot of fun compared with some of the more po-faced, inward-looking outfits that stalked Sydney's inner city. It was this very variety that made our music scene the vibrant thing that it was. It was a diverse world—from heavy masculist guitar bands, to the squeaks and bleeps of the early electronic musicians. Diverse in a white people way perhaps…

Now I might as well give you an update on the popular music of this year again. We are at the end of 1984. The year that didn't really take an Orwellian turn. The good times kept coming. But was there a hint of the trouble to come in the music industry that could be detected in these charts? The quality of the Top 40 was starting to waver. 'Footloose' by Kenny Loggins, for example, remains annoying, while 'Come Said the Boy' by Mondo Rock was definitely a sign that difficult times were ahead. It's just plain horrible. The Eurogliders just happened to be managed by my common law father-in-law at the time although, he does his best to defend them, but they don't sound like very nice people, the same goes for this inspirational song. The music industry dudes and foxes at the INXS launch party might be snorting coke at this point, but little did they know what destruction the arrival of the internet would bring! Not long now… (sort of).

Of course, there is also some fantastic music in this Top 20. George Michael and Frankie Goes to Hollywood 'Relax' and 'Two Tribes'. This is where high-end production from that period really works well. The British had some producers like Trevor Horn, who worked on the Frankie songs, who did amazing things with the sound technology of the time. I just don't think this was ever achieved in Australia. The whole big

AUSTRALIAN TOP 20 CHART 1984

1. **DANCING IN THE DARK**.........Bruce Springsteen
2. **IT'S JUST NOT CRICKET**..........The Twelfth Man
3. **GHOSTBUSTERS**............................Ray Parker Jr
4. **CARELESS WHISPER**.................George Michael
5. **WAKE ME UP BEFORE YOU GO GO**.........Wham!
6. **I JUST CALLED TO SAY I LOVE YOU**.........Stevie Wonder
7. **FOOTLOOSE**................................Kenny Loggins
8. **HELLO**...Lionel Richie
9. **GIRLS JUST WANT TO HAVE FUN**..Cyndi Lauper
10. **ISLANDS IN THE STREAM**.........Kenny Rogers & Dolly Parton
11. **LOVE IS A BATTLEFIELD**.................Pat Benatar
12. **ORIGINAL SIN**..INXS
13. **COME SAID THE BOY**.....................Mondo Rock
14. **WHEN DOVES CRY**...................................Prince
15. **HEAVEN (MUST BE THERE)**.............Eurogliders
16. **RELAX**......................Frankie Goes to Hollywood
17. **THRILLER**................................Michael Jackson
18. **99 LUFTBALLONS**......................................Nena
19. **CALLING YOUR NAME**...........................Marilyn
20. **TWO TRIBES**.............Frankie Goes to Hollywood

2 JAN 1985	**CLARENDON HOTEL** [Newcastle] Unconfirmed
5 JAN 1985	**PARAGON HOTEL** [Circular Quay/Sydney] Party
5 JAN 1985	**CHEVRON HOTEL** [Kings Cross/Sydney]
11 JAN 1985	**MOSMAN HOTEL** [Mosman/Sydney] w/5th Corruption
12 JAN 1985	**SYDNEY COVE TAVERN** [Circular Quay/Sydney] w/the Go-Betweens + The Crystal Set + Tribe
13 JAN 1985	**STRAWBERRY HILLS HOTEL** [Strawberry Hills/Sydney]
15 JAN 1985	**AMAROO HOTEL** [Dubbo]
16 JAN 1985	**NEW OCCIDENTAL HOTEL** [Cobar]
17 JAN 1985	**NEW OCCIDENTAL HOTEL** [Cobar]
18 JAN 1985	**ALMA SPORTING CLUB** [Broken Hill]
19 JAN 1985	**LARK & TINAS** [Adelaide] w/Zero Hour
20 JAN 1985	**THE ASTRAL HOTEL** [Adelaide]

production thing did cause havoc in the local industry, though. Everyone was trying to do it—barely any Australian records from this period came out unscathed. There are some notable exceptions, but I'm struggling to think of them. A few by Mental as Anything? The Hoodoo Gurus? One INXS song…possibly something from Midnight Oil…

I'm sure there were many. I'm just a bitter old muso. So let's keep moving into the mid-eighties. 1985. If nothing else, we were playing a lot.

Out to Cobar, in central NSW for two big nights. I can't be too hard on cover bands because I'm sure we would have dug deeply into our songbook of covers here. You had to pull out 'Hit the Road Jack' at this kind of place. Even this wasn't always enough to appease the cranky faces.

Juliet, Blue and Greg in Cobar.

Cobar was surrounded by a bushfire on a 40km wide front, so the stifling summer heat was added to by the smell of smoke and a purplish haze. Eventually, the army was called out to contain the fire. (While I am writing this, the gay couple in the next bedroom are having sex. Well, I assume from their conversations that that is what they do. I can hear, 'oh, ohh, ohhh'...)

Back to Cobar, the bar manager stalked around behind the band muttering and vaguely threatening us. It seemed that a rival establishment in the centre of town had heard of our coming, so had booked in a band from Adelaide and hijacked our audience. The club we were playing was on the outskirts of town. I was told this by the club manager at the end of the night; he seemed to be more sanguine about the whole matter. These experiences weren't taken as setbacks: we seemed to live in an eternal present where it was always sunny.

Blue, 2017

The Lighthouse Keepers now had a solid enough following in Adelaide. It was a bit like Perth. There was a good feral base from which to work. They were pre-ferals actually. No one had come up with that word yet. These people were very supportive and at times people might have mistaken me for one of them. But really, my raggedy clothes and unkempt look was due to pure laziness and economics. Myself and Juliet were eager consumers of Coke (as in cola), barbeque chips and a whole lot of other

20 JAN 1985	**THE TIVOLI** [Adelaide] w/Tu Tu Z
23 JAN 1985	**UNO ARIBA** (Anglers Club) [Melbourne]
24 JAN 1985	**PRINCE OF WALES HOTEL** [St Kilda/Melbourne] w/Clear As Day + Captain Coco
25 JAN 1985	**CENTRAL CLUB** [Melbourne] w/Painters & Dockers + Weddings Parties Anything
26 JAN 1985	**AUSTRALIAN NATIONAL UNIVERSITY BAR** [Canberra] w/the Go-Betweens
30 JAN 1985	**HIP HOP CLUB** [Sydney]
31 JAN 1985	**YUGAL SOCCER CLUB** [The Haymarket/Sydney] w/the Fifth Corruption + Maestros & Dipsos
10 FEB 1985	**PHOENICIAN CLUB** [Glebe/Sydney] w/Ruby My Dear

Chapter 6 : Wheels Over the Desert

Juliet.

unferal indulgences. Juliet also smoked heavily and had a fetish for cars and such things. Ferals somehow merged with Greenies at some point and created a scary hybrid that is still alive today. These kind are very right-on—you must tread extremely lightly in all conversations with them. Not that I don't love diversity, trees and whales. But on we go.

The Hip Hop Club was part of Sydney's early dance scene when things were crossing over into the heterosexual world. You went down some stairs into a basement off Oxford Street. This was the beginning of raves and all that palaver. It was probably slightly out of date already. The world's fashions used to come to Australia ten years late in the fifties and sixties, but things had sped up a bit by the eighties. I did like some of that early dance music, and feel that hip-hop's best moments were early on. Did the music get truly repetitive or did I just get old?

Getting old does, however, bring some perspective to this period. I think back to the

16 FEB 1985	**HYDRO MAJESTIC** [Medlow Bath]
21 FEB 1985	**MOSMAN HOTEL** [Mosman/Sydney] w/Spectres Revenge
24 FEB 1985	**NORTH SYDNEY LEAGUES CLUB** [North Sydney] w/the Triffids
25 FEB 1985	**WOLLONGONG UNIVERSITY** (under the figs) [Wollongong]/just Lighthouse Keepers
27 FEB 1985	**GRANVILLE SOUTH HIGH SCHOOL** [Granville South] + wild disco!
28 FEB 1985	**STRAWBERRY HILLS HOTEL** [Strawberry Hills]
1 MAR 1985	**AUSTRALIAN NATIONAL UNIVERSITY BAR** [Canberra] w/Falling Joys & the Crystal Set
9 MAR 1985	**NEW YORK TAVERN** [Newcastle]
10 MAR 1985	**HOPETOUN HOTEL** [Surry Hills]
15 MAR 1985	**MOSMAN HOTEL** [Mosman]/just Lighthouse Keepers or perhaps with the Fifth Corruption
16 MAR 1985	**SYDNEY COVE TAVERN** [Circular Quay/Sydney] w/Hoi Poli + Samurai Trash + Jump Inc
20 MAR 1985	**HOPETOUN HOTEL** [Surry Hills/Sydney]
30 MAR 1985	**HAROLD PARK HOTEL** [Glebe/Sydney]
4 APR 1985	**CHEVRON HOTEL** [Kings Cross/Sydney] w/Coloured Stone
10 APR 1985	**PICADILLY HOTEL** [Kings Cross/Sydney] w/Lunar Circus
12 APR 1985	**AUSTRALIAN NATIONAL UNIVERSITY BAR** [Canberra] w/the Gadflys
13 APR 1985	**BALMORAL 12' SKIFF CLUB** [Balmoral/Sydney]
17 APR 1985	**STRAWBERRY HILLS HOTEL** [Strawberry Hills/Sydney]
19 APR 1985	**BONDI PAVILION THEATRE** [Bondi Beach/Sydney] w/Just A Drummer

Phoenician Club—a huge firetrap on Broadway in Sydney. These days I'd be looking around nervously for the exits and plotting my escape. It didn't cross my mind at the time. Today we live in a world of fluro jackets, witches' hats and Occupational Health & Safety that would not allow this venue to exist. And so it doesn't. The thing about OH&S is you can't really argue with it, so it has created an enormous industry of... yeah, what do they do exactly?

We ramped up our activities further towards the middle of 1985. The mission was to get to the old country. Martin Jennings from Hot Records encouraged us. They were going to put our album *Tales of the Unexpected* out in the UK and Europe. We wanted to try and save enough money from these shows to get there. It's hard to believe that this was even a possibility. I do remember that we eventually went to my father and asked for a $5,000 loan to cover the tour. It even got paid back. The Lighthouse Keepers live show records are becoming more sketchy as we get more busy.

A few memories of 1985: a diary of sorts by Hairy

This year a past member of the band and Juliet's long-term furry companion Chaos was run over on Cleveland Street. It was certainly a year in which a lot more than usual happened. Two more journeys took us through Cobar, Nyngan, Adelaide again, and we did our first visit to Brisbane. We also had a small bus we could almost call our own and as a result had been to Byron Bay, and Tamworth. We could afford to go to Perth again.

1985 also saw Glad S. Bag and Beat Boy from Just A Drummer respectively playing trombone and baritone sax with us. They also featured on the single we recorded in April titled 'Seven Years' c/w 'Ode to Nothing'. Dave Baby (also a member of J.A.D.) helped produce and meanwhile Wadey (also a member of J.A.D.) was helping us out with lighting duties at live shows.

The Lighthouse Keepers. Photo: Darian Turner

Chapter 6 : Wheels Over the Desert

The single 'Ode to Nothing/Seven Years' would be our last official recording. It was a very pleasant way to sign off, and sounds well recorded—even now. Nick Mainsbridge was the engineer at the small studio in Sydney's northern suburbs. He was quite a glamorous character with a long skinny body and thick black hair. Like the guy at school who buys a car very young, walks by himself and gets girls (I have no idea how early Nick purchased a car). Again, I've run into him in later life—living in a Sydney south coast suburb up the road. He is now a kind of techno-audiophile hermit, inclined to philosophise about mathematics and coding. He remembers recording the Lighthouse Keepers' last single.

> I just loved the overall sound. Everyone concentrates on Juliet's voice, it is unique but there's something about the unusual treatment of the songs. If you look at the instrumentation—it should be boring as batshit blues stuff. But somehow it didn't sound like that... I don't want to compare them to the Beatles, that's just totally wrong. But... there's a bunch of English lads trying to do black American music and failing utterly and I think it was a similar thing with the Lighthouse Keepers—oh, is this how you do it? That naivety.
>
> Nick Mainsbridge, 2017

Nick would also be our live mixer in the UK.

28 APR 1985	**SOMEWHERE**
30 APR 1985	**SOMEWHERE**
5 MAY 1985	**AUSTRALIAN NATIONAL UNIVERSITY BAR** [Canberra] + Madroom
31 MAY 1985	**AUSTRALIAN NATIONAL UNIVERSITY BAR** [Canberra] w/Just A Drummer
1 JUNE 1985	**FLOYDS** [Phillip, ACT]
19 JUNE 1985	**HIP HOP CLUB** [Darlinghurst]
13 JUL 1985	**MACS 409 CLUB** [aka Sensoria aka OP-SHOP] Brisbane + Mop and the Dropouts + another band [billed as another band!][from flyer]
14 JUL 1985	**MACS 409 CLUB** [aka Sensoria aka OP-SHOP?] Brisbane + Let's Go Naked
AUG 1985	**THE TOTE** (Melbourne)
8 AUG 1985	**AUSTRALIAN NATIONAL UNIVERSITY BAR** [Canberra] billed as 'For the last time in the ACT'.

CHAPTER 7
Torture Road

I recall reading an article about David Bowie when he was touring Australia sometime around this period. He was quoted as saying, 'Australia is a great place for driving.' It stuck in my mind for some reason and often comes back to me when driving those enormous distances that Australians do, just to get from A to B. But it's also hard to work out what he meant by that exactly. Was he giving the country a backhanded insult? Or did he really enjoy the mind-numbing drives that are an integral part of the Australian dream. He must have been in the middle of his rather hideous 'Let's Dance' phase at the time. The film clip is set in an outback pub—somewhere near Bourke. So perhaps he did drive there from Sydney and so experienced those mesmerising country highways—probably with a little medicinal help as per the times.

Chapter 7 : Torture Road

Me at ceremonial pouring of water from the Pacific Ocean to the Indian Ocean.

So let us dance too—and head out across the vast spaces of the Australian continent. Though I imagine you're getting sick of all this driving. But sit there and shut up. We'll be going to Europe this time!

It's interesting that everyone in the band were writing diaries and recording this momentous history taking place. We were filled with self-importance. It was only the poor manager-cum-drummer Steven Williams who didn't seem to have the time to loll about and put pen to paper. Here is Steven Williams's only contribution to the Lighthouse Keepers archives—tapped out on an old-school typewriter which seemed to be part of his managerial thing. He types from the comfort of his cheap Sydney rental accommodation, which also served as his office—just round the corner from Eveleigh Street in Redfern.

Off to Europe (Aug 1985)

At the moment I'm sitting in my kitchen typing this. I really should have done it about 4 weeks ago but with the rigors of work etc I managed to leave it till the last minute. This is my last night at home. Tomorrow we all go away to far off places like Canberra, Wagga, Port Pirie, Kalgoorlie, Vienna, London etc. People are chatting in the lounge-room., so if my writings seem somewhat disjointed it's probably because I'm eavesdropping.

Now what about the band when I joined? My first impressions of Hairy were that he did seem to be rather shy. Blue did talk to me an awful lot and gave me the impression that he was highly knowledgeable. In fact, he recently told me that he thrashed the pants off a local team of young hopefuls at a game of Trivial Pursuit. Juliet's first words are now obscure but she impressed upon me that she really enjoyed a beer. Greg was importantly polite on first impressions. You know, 'No worries, sounds alright to me...'

I've got to clean the kitchen and prepare for the near future.

Regards,
Steven Williams.

And so Steven went back to his domestic duties and the unrewarding task of getting an independent band off to Europe. But I think his little character descriptions are quite timely in the context of this book. In case you want a reminder as to who the hell these people are. So I'll describe him—in his own style. Steven was a no-nonsense salt-of-the-earth type—muscly too.

I now turn to my own diary as we begin the tour to end all tours. I wrote this 'Roadhouse

Guide' from inside the tour bus, and at last it comes in handy. I always had a feeling it was an important document.

The full title was 'Eating Guide To Roadhouses Of The World' by G. Appel, culinary expert. I was ahead of my time. The celebrity chef and TV cooking show phenomena was a long way off and something that I never saw coming—along with bottled water! I will correct a lot of the atrocious spelling for you. I began by rating our roadhouse meals from one to ten.

It beginneth in South Australia...

Writing the first pages of *Eating Guide To Roadhouses Of The World*, by Greg Appel.

Day about 8 (late morning)
the day before today being the 16th of August of a Friday in the year 1985

I had some chips at AMPOL CRYSTAL BROOK and found them to be quite excellent by general consensus from other members of my party. The cups of Tea were the normal Lipton Tea bad job. However on arrival at Port Pirie that smells like a toilet—I vomited the lot up. Nothing to do with the quality of the food however and it came up and out—with no sticking to the sides etc.

But right now, almost recovered, I am testing my stomach with a bacon and egg roll and a cappuccino from 'GOBBLE 'N' GO' WHYALLA. Not bad actually and not many telltale signs of regurgitation. Many entertaining hand crafted burgers etc. adorn the walls. Reasonably grumpy service—so we know we are getting value. I give it an 8 but Juliet goes for the 6. The other members of the team seem a little less satisfied than me. Steven even gives it a 5 basing his mark on wholesomeness and value. So there it is, not having time to sample all the meals available (the Little John or Nick's special) I can't give a complete opinion but I'd say—slightly recommended but don't go more than 100 miles out of your way (distances are big around this area).

The girl in the shops asked us if we are from a radio show as I write, being afraid of a bad review (might get some free food). She said that Port Lincoln is nice but the people are horrible—our next food stop!

But first BP FRANKLIN HARBOUR ROADHOUSE unfortunately I only feel capable of a cup of tea, as Blue just said—at least the cups of tea are getting cheaper—only 60c. But the petrol is getting more expensive. I feel

Chapter 7 : Torture Road

I overheard a comment as to negative coffee ratings and no soup was available. The toilets passable, scenery a few trees, a bit of water and some nicely placed silos.

This epic tour is entering a bizarre stage as we encounter some of South Australia's remote stretches and towns where people are a bit more inbred. Last night someone yelled out to poor battling Juliet to show them her muck hole. But after a few million miles and a few weeks in our bus you become oblivious to this sort of thing.

Driving across Australia gives you an idea of how big it is. A few hundred roadhouses wide.

Dear reader, is this getting too much for you? I'm sorry about all the takeaway foodie jargon, and in-jokes. But I think you should come along for the ride. My writing from inside the tour bus is a little impressionistic and extremely self-indulgent, but it tells a story. Not always a happy one. We had been warned about Port Lincoln.

Port Lincoln.

Day 17th Aug, Saturday

THE TASMAN HOTEL PORT LINCOLN, although not strictly classifiable as a Roadhouse still had foodware that definitely takes it into a classifiable zoneage. In fact the food was pretty pathetic considering the attempt at spiffiness. Definitely in the low fives, staff pleasantness alternated between darkly rude to cheeringly nice and this served to keep our morale low due to the coping with schizophrenia. I had a veal zonogal (or something equally fake exotic) and it was digestible at best. I held it down with some trouble. Blue and Lee had lobsters that they were not at all keen on. Hairy's ungourmet-like tongue was heard to say the taste was subtle. However the garlic prawns proved to be quite good.

My eating team and I then set about our part-time occupations that include entertaining the people of Port Lincoln with our music après dinner digesting time. We were meant to play four sets, but the lights and electricity suddenly went out at the commencement of the third when someone ran into the power station. I could not help but feel a surge of joy as I realised the power was out for the night. The candles came out and everyone looked so much more beautiful and became so much friendlier in the atmosphere. I cannot help thinking electricity is the root of all evil. I wonder if there will be a baby boom in Port Lincoln in 9 months. The crowd to gourmet appreciation rating was about the same as the food but better than the inhabitants of Port Pirie, what uncandlelike people they were!

Juliet.

Blue on the beach in Sri Lanka.

Greg, Hairy and Juliet in Sri Lanka.

If you look at a road map of Australia, you'll see there is a pretty obvious route from Sydney to Perth. This is the route we took (yet again). I rated the food all the way on this leg of the journey, but I will spare you the details. Suffice to say, not a lot of our meals got higher than five out of ten. Thank goodness my Roadhouse dairy turned away from rating food pretty quickly. After we played Perth, we flew to Europe via Sri Lanka.

It must be the 7th—nearly the 8th September

Well, here we are in Sri Lanka about to go. It's not a bad spot, not where we were anyway (Ranvelli Beach Resort). It was hot—still is—but the hotel had a nice fan in the roof and a cool sea breeze blowing in the door. How I wish I was there instead of at the airport, a bad roadhouse. They served us nice food, traditional Aussie breakfast and curries at night. On the beach we were immediately assaulted by many people trying to sell us things. The first thing the locals will do is try to extract money from you, but after this they are very friendly and speak English with a nice accent. I sampled some local herb for the guide, and found it reasonable—but not worth upsetting my moral guardians Blue and Juliet. Who thought I was about to be shot (there are many soldier types). But basically we lazed around drinking beer and taking photos of each other (for the photo edition).

I'd been to Europe when I was eighteen, and on my own. This would be an entirely different experience. Number one, I had a girlfriend with me all the way, and then

11 SEPT 1985	**THE TITANIC**,	Vienna
12 SEPT 1985	**THE TITANIC**,	Vienna
15 SEPT 1985	**STADT WERK STADT**,	Linz

The modest charm of the Lighthouse Keepers

Vienna's Titanic the starting point for European tour

With neo-hippiedom the flavour of the month in England, Sydney band the Lighthouse Keepers seem to have timed their British visit well; the band's waifish appearance and free-for-all approach to music-making is sure to appeal to neo-hippy sensibilities.

But more than that, it's hard to see a limit to the Lighthouse Keepers' potential. Songwriter Greg Appel is a rapidly burgeoning talent, and the band's style, swapping and changing instruments amongst themselves as well as with guests, lends his elusive pop songs a spirited earthiness, humour and freshness. And if they are sometimes somewhat sloppy, that can only be counted as one of their charms.

"We can still be sloppy, but we're not as bad as we were," laughed Steven Williams, the band's drummer/organizer, on the eve of their departure from Australia. "As far as Greg's songs go, we're yet to see the best."

Although the Lighthouse Keepers have always seemed to maintain a low profile, their debut album of late last year, *Tales of the Unexpected*, was a critical success. With a new single, "Ode to Nothing"/"Seven Years," on the market, the band plus friends played a farewell Sydney gig at the Graphic Arts Club, which attracted 900 eager punters. From there, they worked their way to Perth, whence they left for Vienna to begin a European tour, which will wind up in England.

"We didn't originally plan to do it that way," explained Williams, "but we met a person who runs a venue in Vienna. The first show is at a place called the Titanic."

Hoping that this will not be prophetic, the band will be promoting the European release of *Tales of the Unexpected* through Europe and the U.K. for a couple of months before returning to Australia for Christmas. Their ambitions are characteristically modest.

"I think we'll do okay," says Williams. "We always wanted to go anyway. If we can just play, have a bit of a holiday, maybe record something, I'll consider that a success."

Certainly the trip will provide the Lighthouse Keepers with a new stimulus.

"It'll push us along. For the first LP, the production could've been better, but what was good about it was that it sounded like the Lighthouse Keepers. We want to retain the rough edges; it's more honest, anyway. But the next album will be much better."

Clinton Walker

The Lighthouse Keepers: European tour kicked off in Vienna

---

there was the band, along with a few close friends, as usual. I was the opposite of lonely in this tightly packed tour party. For all its claustrophobic elements, it was a much better way to see Europe than backpacking as a solitary male. People could be amazingly welcoming, and often let the whole band and entourage sleep on their floors. They would rope in their extended families to feed and transport us around. In retrospect, we couldn't really complain—but we did.

16/9/85. A Tuesday, I think

This pen does not work very well and I just bought it today—bad roadhouse value over here. I think they call them gasthaus(es). Well, another day another malaria tablet. Things have been gripping enough for me not to write in this filthy roadhouse guide. Meals have come and gone. I've even traversed the distance between Vienna & Linz and stopped at a roadhouse (Not bad goulash soup but the service was slow and fairly grumpy) and I've had some fine stuffings, last night a notable example. I ate my Cordon Bleu and then Juliet's whatever as well, lots of large ales, and then some local herbs to top it off. A fine effort in gluttony. We enjoyed Vienna a lot despite losing money at the 'Titanic', very aptly named—and the organisation was absolutely non-existent so we spent a day rushing about getting amps and stuff. It sounded a bit weird—but the second night was more encouraging than the first. We did a lot of walking in Vienna and my joints are aching.

We played the 'Stadt Werk Stadt' in Linz, where I am now. A decidedly peculiar place populated by dwarves and men in dresses and '60s rejects. There was no power and we had to get a large extension lead for everything. Candles were the go. But it was quite exciting and the people made some peculiar noises, sort of singing and strange yips and yahoos. A person called Stephan has

Window shopping, Vienna.

Window shopping, Vienna.

Greg, Juliet and Blue on the streets of Europe.

helped us a lot and here we are staying at Brigitte Steiner-Schober's house, who is sitting across the table from me holding forth so I'd better look interested.

I realise this may be getting a little too detailed for some people now, with the entry of Brigitte Steiner-Schober, *et al.* However, I think it illustrates the mood of the one European tour we managed to complete and the way the band lived on the road. But read on—Blue gets even more detailed and gives us a hint of his sexy past—in the real hippy days when the pill had just been invented and sexually transmitted diseases were very treatable.

Brigitte was interested in me, but I was a bit shy about getting involved possibly because Lee and Juliet seemed to be encouraging it. I was sitting at the table in the kitchen and she would appear in revealing attire along with giggling or egging on from Juliet and Lee. Left to our own devices something could have happened, but it was a bit public.

Brigitte put us up in her flat which she shared with two others in the old part of town. We slept on the floor. I think Hairy and I slept in the same bed on the floor with Brigitte. We used her tiny bathroom, as we hadn't had much opportunity to wash. Steven was shaving at the sink, so I decided to jump in the shower. Steven was not impressed. He said something like 'when in Rome ...' criticising me for acting like a 'Continental'. The others were shocked when Brigitte and the others were watching a film on TV with Geraldine Chapman, when Geraldine masturbated on screen.

This was a strange part of the Lighthouse Keepers and their world. I was only a few years older but sometimes, it felt like I was from a different generation. I was not particularly

Chapter 7 : Torture Road

wild or socially libertarian—in fact I didn't think that I was adventurous at all—but I'd had different experiences to them. And sometimes I had to keep quiet about them.

Food wise, we went to Nordsee, a German and Austrian fish restaurant franchise, but Juliet and Greg went to McDonald's where they marvelled that you could get beer.

Blue, Lighthouse Keepers

In Linz, we were treated very well. Brigitte's parents turned on a real Austrian meal for us. Blue had some intense drunken discussions with them. They had lived under the Russians from 1945–55. Brigitte's father showed us his Nazi card proclaiming his Aryan status going back five generations.

Blue, Juliet and Greg, Europe.

> There was some type of election coming up and the local slogan was 'Linz the third-cleanest industrial town in Austria' or something similar. There was a connection between Austria and Australia besides a couple of letters: Bob Hawke had championed the 'Austrian economic miracle' as a model for Australia. This was a type of state-controlled or at least highly regulated capitalism, though it seemed that almost everyone worked for the post office or the railways. However, Bob and Paul seemed to go out of their way in dismantling government enterprises as inimical to the 'free market'.

Blue, Lighthouse Keepers

Economic history aside, it all felt very exotic and 'sound of music' in this mountainous country. We were literally singing for our suppers, and they were very good ones. I would still rate the meal with Brigitte's parents as a '10'. An Austrian goulash followed by sugar coated dumplings which had ricotta in the pastry and an apricot inside.

Hairy, self portrait, Europe.

CHAPTER 8

Bad Mood

In September of that 1985, we also got a great, if small, review of our album in the scary UK music paper, *New Musical Express* (NME). If ever there was a time to try our luck in London, this was it. And so we left our new-found friends in Austria and travelled to England. Australia has changed demographically since these days but back then, the UK was still the old country for many. The place where Prince Charles waited patiently for his turn on the throne, no doubt listening to 'Gargoyle' over and over. A place Australians still have a love–hate relationship with, and vice versa. Though sometimes I think the English hate may be greater than their love.

There were plenty of other Australian bands that were drawn to the UK scene at this time. I recently talked to Graham Lee and Rob McComb from the Triffids about this London era.

All the Australian bands went over there because they couldn't do anything in the pub rock scene. And the Lighthouse Keepers were the same.

Rob McComb, the Triffids

> **THE LIGHTHOUSE KEEPERS**
> **Tales Of The Unexpected**
> (*Hot*)
>
> THE LIGHTHOUSE Keepers, materialising like beacons on the horizon, are here to change our lives. Their first LP, just released, makes for a refreshing change, a reinvigorating face of "pop". They are the perfect group with the perfect pop songs, songs about heartfelt passions with simple intelligble lyrics, able to convey the same gut-wrenching emotions as any affected litterant.
>
> Every Lighthouse Keepers song is a spectral affair, each with its own distinguishing mark, be it the countryesque pedal steel sound on 'Wheels Over The Desert', or the new-found horn section of 'We've Got A Gig'. They veer from the anguished, tender and soulful, to the flippant, joyful, and sometimes completely banal. But they all maintain that endearing quality of honest-to-God feelings.
>
> 'LipSnipeGroin' outshines the other masterpieces of songwriter Greg Appel with its forlorn, woeful apologies for what could have been, delicately accompanied with the most catching of melodies.
>
> These people know what they are about, they know how to touch us lesser mortals right at the heart. Pure genius.
>
> **Jane Wilkes**

Crossing the Channel to Rotterdam, with the Triffids.

ing to sell the freshly recorded album *Born Sandy Devotional* to the record companies in London. I clearly remember Dave McComb giving me a cassette of the mix one night after we had arrived. All my muso jealousy washed away once I played it. Here was one of our kind making a real record! It sounded so professional, yet retained that ethereal thing we were all clutching at.

> That same cassette was given to every major label in London. None of them signed us. We do have suspicions that we could have got a deal for Born Sandy if Martin wasn't trying to get a deal for us...he was trying to get a deal for everyone–you remember the Hot Records night in London?
>
> Graham Lee, the Triffids, 2016

I'm sure that there were English bands that were doing things like the Triffids, but we didn't see them. Everyone we saw seemed to be copying something.

'Evil' Graham Lee, the Triffids

Martin Jennings from Hot Records had encouraged us to go to London. The Triffids had been there for a while and were try-

Graham is referring to a line-up of Hot Records bands that played together in London at the Hammersmith Clarendon. The Triffids felt he was spreading himself

too thin by not focusing on them enough. Oblivious to any of this, we'd planned our trip around the show. Nick Mainsbridge, who we already worked with, was the Triffids' mixer at the time and living in London. Playing live was a constant battle against the technology and the often unhelpful dudes that controlled the mixing desks. We wanted to get that good sound that the Triffids seemed to have live and so we got Nick to mix some of our shows in Europe. They would turn out to be the best…and the worst.

> I hated live mixing and this was a good example of why. It was a Hot Records night in a sort of a cave. There were posters with three bands and twelve bands turned up and then they only played for twenty minutes. They'd spray-painted concrete all along the back of the stage in a curve at the back, which looks okay but if you're a sound mixer, it's your worst nightmare, because the sound from the foldback bounces directly off the back wall into the microphone and you have uncontrollable feedback. It was a disaster—I ended up pointing the foldback wedges at the audience and the band couldn't hear themselves. There were twelve people there or something. It was the worst gig in the world—I felt sorry for the Lighthouse Keepers.
>
> Nick Mainsbridge,
> Audio guru, 2017

I recorded the night in my Roadhouse Guide soon afterwards.

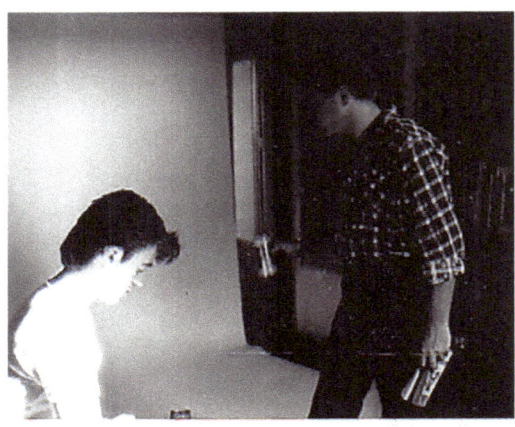

Chapter 8 : Bad Mood

> **20 SEPT 1985 HAMMERSMITH CLARENDON**
> [Hammersmith] Hot Records Night
> w/the Triffids, Gaspar Lawall, The
> Benders & Lawson Square Infirmary

Saturday, 21/9/85

Played on Friday night after VW and Plane from Austria. We played at the Hammersmith Clarendon—a large dirty echoey hall. We played under duress of snapping strings and electronic failure, for all of half an hour, but it seemed to go down alright. We were supporting the Triffids with some other bands from the notorious Hot Records. There was a big brawl upstairs afterwards but luckily I was guzzling amber fluid downstairs and just spied someone flying through a plate glass window. It didn't seem to worry people that much however. So I suppose it's just a natural occurrence.

Pink Floyd have their moments.

My roadhouse guide doesn't dwell on the show but you get the idea with the strings breaking during our set. Afterwards, Martin Jennings told me we'd pretty much blown it in the UK. Jane Wilkes, who'd given us the nice little review in *NME*, was one of the few people in the audience. She wrote a review of the live show. She had completely changed her mind about the Lighthouse Keepers' talents. We were awful and did cover songs as well!

Oh, well—our journey continued. We all stayed at different places in London. My old friend from the punk days in Canberra, Andy Hall, had moved out of share accommodation and was now living in a much larger flat with his future wife—perfect for me and Juliet to inveigle a room for six weeks or so.

Tuesday, 25/9/85

At present I'm ensconced in a room, windows to my left, funky music to the front, walls and stuff to my right and a chair behind me. The guide is on a wooden table which has other objects such as my camera, some records, matches, an empty cup, some wet socks, a wallet, a bigger wallet thing with important bits of paper in it, a big saxa salt, some silk cut cigarettes, some pills, a trivial pursuit dice, a bow, an empty whisky bottle, and two bits of metal that a chap called Pete got when he pulled some letters off something from a previous job. A postcard I just wrote + some grot.

Yes, I'm at Andy Halls' house and no one else is here. Juliet is out in the sticks somewhere. Writing this is taking up valuable time when I could be noting the sights of London—we've been here for a few days.

Thursday, 3/10/85

We've been basically lazing about avoiding each other and I've enjoyed not playing in the band a lot. What a horrible thought and how creepy I am. Gone out to a few pubs and a good party where a Welshman in a suit explained life and how to get on with people. Got quite drunk and Juliet and I went to another party at 'the Thresher' when we got back but they wouldn't let me in and called me a 'drifter' and threw Juliet out because their pounding chances were down. (Oh I've sampled 'Wimpys' (horrible) and Wendy's (good but expensive))

The Gasthaus, Passau.

I was beginning to realise the English weren't all as friendly as Prince Charles. Australian's can't pretend they don't have any class consciousness. For me, having doctors for parents had occasionally been awkward growing up in Australia but compared to the British, it was nothing. In the UK, it's all very regional and complicated and boring. The upper class get themselves twisted in knots about it all. To them, Australians sit somewhere between Colchester and Ireland. Indeed, the working class and regional British are a lot easier to get on with. However, with my food critics hat on, I had to say the curries in London were outstanding. In this way, the colonial heritage has worked favourably for the British.

4 OCT 1985	**LEEDS UNIVERSITY** w/the Triffids
9 OCT 1985	**DINGWALLS**, London w/the Nomads
11 OCT 1985	**ROTTERDAM** Pandora's Box w/the Triffids, Shock Headed Peters, Woodentops, etc.
11 OCT 1985	**NEW MERLINS CAVE** London w/the Triffids

Thursday, 17/10/85

Had some good Indian food from the takeaways at Clapham South Station. But Leeds was fairly much a disaster area for the band, it looked like it too with smoke machines in full swing. The Triffids played well, however, and we had a jolly trip with Calhuach[1] to give a section of joy. I certainly wish we could play a bit better more often. Dingwalls on a Wednesday with the Nomads from Scandinavia was quite bearable, however, then we got a surprise initiation to Rotterdam to a festival with about 50 bands to replace Jesus and Mary Chain.

I do remember this Rotterdam show clearly. It was definitely the biggest audience we played to in Europe and was a great success. We'd got lucky in getting Jesus and Mary Chain's prime slot at the festival. Not a totally compatible band perhaps. So at the start of the show, there was a bit on an exodus of crowd, but also an influx. We went down a treat and everyone was happy. We got to taste a bit of the rock star lifestyle too, backstage. The Triffids were playing this same festival and were already hardened partakers.

1 Another period code word for marijuana.

Chapter 8 : Bad Mood

> The more you're on tour, the more you like to create your own world.
>
> Rob McComb, the Triffids, 2016

In my memory, Rob McComb, the guitarist, and Graham Lee, the pedal steel guitar player (along with Martyn Casey the bass player), were always the last of the Triffids to leave the band room. They kept going as late as anyone would stay up with them. Rob McComb was enjoying the liberal Dutch laws regarding his favourite vice and Graham sat backstage and steadily entered the twilight zone of extreme intoxication. Along with a few of us. On stage, Nick Mainsbridge mixed us again, and was so enamored with Holland that he went back there to live for a while.

Coming from Australia, it was incredible to drive up to security and find they were nice people, they would offer you drinks, make sure you're warm enough. In Australia they were—'what do you want—a compressor? Fuck, mate, can't you make it sound good?' That really made me appreciate what it was like to live in a country where people appreciate the arts, it's quite a different experience.

It was the best show you can imagine! they had an information booth that doubled up as a shepherd machine. So there was a guy herding sheep through the gig. Nick Cave was playing, Nico, the Triffids, Echo and the Bunnymen. It was massive and the equipment was great. The Lighthouse Keepers come on—and these Dutch guys were saying, 'who are these guys?'...there was sort of this tornado of energy that spread around the festival.

> Nick Mainsbridge, 2017

It was times like these that you thought, maybe, just maybe, you could have a career as a musician. Then it was back to the UK and the reality that we weren't actually huge

Lemmy, Italy.

international rock stars. In fact, I was beginning to have a sneaking suspicion that me and Juliet had overstayed our welcome after week five at Andy's flat in London. So I got busy with the household chores.

Roadhouse Guide, Thursday, 17/10/85

The last couple of weeks have involved a lot of painting here at Andy and Clare's house, and I have let fly with a brush because I'm so well mannered and always do the dishes and stuff.

Right—this is getting boring. Suffice to say we played incredibly badly at New Merlin's Cave on Tuesday where we were triple-booked and I have noted during the ferry crossing that the Triffids are consuming a lot of the weed and devil water which could also possibly be said for my own sorry band.

And back in London, we would never make it to the cover of *NME* like the Triffids. While my muso disease might have made me a little jealous of their success, it's all relative. London can be a cold, unfriendly place and we didn't have to stay there very long at all. The Triffids found it difficult surviving in the old country—but they kept going back for more. Year after year.

From '84 to '89, we went to London every year for three to six months or longer. And hanging around there with no money is not much fun.

Rob McComb, the Triffids, 2016

Indeed, their album *Born Sandy Devotional* seemed to me to be nostalgic for Australia—if in a backhanded sort of way. From a small grim bedroom in someone else's house, watching the thin drizzle falling on grey streets, Australia can seem very pleasant. Even though London contains so much history, so much music, so much everything, you have to be in the right mode to enjoy it. That is—rich or famous.

Sometimes, Australians themselves seem better when they're out of the country. The accents may be a bit harsh, the thongs a bit much, but the people can seem sort of real. And even though it's a bit pathetic, they will cluster to-

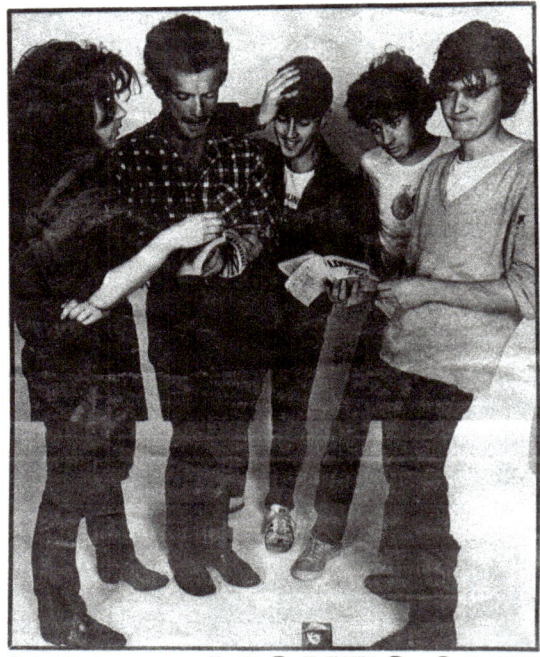

Ralph Traitor gets dazzled by **The Lighthouse Keepers. Bleddyn Butcher** flicks the switch

LIGHTS OUT

IRONIC? POSSIBLY. That the next Australian Lighthouse Keepers 45 is titled 'Ode To Nothing', I mean. Here they are, with a glaring capacity for surprising the living daylights into you, and half of it is knowing, after one play of the hot album 'Tales Of The Unexpected', that these natural beams can create an ode to *anything*.

It makes perfect sense, of course. The Lighthouse Keepers have gatecrashed Austria (which is just two letters away from Australia, their home, anyhow) on a recommendation from someone in a pub. And the Austrians like it.

And now they're here. Or rather, *we're* here. The Lighthouse Keepers must move in a rarified slipstream just parallel to the norm; how else can their beautiful music know so much about us without the slightest trace of mediocrity or cynicism? Why come at all?

"Steve Williams, our drummer, is quite ambitious. He's really the driving force in the band," explains Juliet Ward, "and one of his first ideas when he joined was to go to England. I think he wanted to be in a band so he could go to England."

Since their formation during late 1982 The Lighthouse Keepers have grown from a wholly independent unit into . . . a wholly independent unit, actually, but with a record company they don't run out of a back room themselves.

'Gargoyle', the debut single, launched a thousand shippers and now the days of endless sleeve-folding and nights of dodging missiles in dank Australian watering holes are fewer.

Apart from being based in the same city, Sydney, on the same continent, Australia, The Lighthouse Keepers have little in common with the purist rock action of the likes of the Screaming Tribesmen and their noble breed.

"We started as a country and western band," Michael 'Blue' Dalton, slide guitar Keeper, elucidates in his softspoken way, "and we still play in little country towns in Australia. In some places they like to take the piss out of you because you're a city slicker and they don't want your ego to get too big."

'The Lighthouse Keepers play a melodic pop song that is also a blues song, a soul song and a country song', quips Triffid David McComb in the band's press release, and his observation is true. But it also sounds like a *jazz* song.

"Perhaps vaguely jazz. I don't think we're quite good enough to play that . . ." smiles Greg self-deprecatingly. "Traditional jazz perhaps, but . . . "

Greg does have outlets besides music, however. Witness the idiosyncratic poetry and pen exposition on the insert of 'Tales'. This is, in fact, the first instalment of a Lighthouse Keepers Annual.

"We've got a book we're putting together. It's like the insert but goes on for 40 pages! Meaningless, probably, to anyone else," he laughs.

Says Blue: "The last time we were in the studio we started writing just to get away from music, because we knew we were doing this scrapbook thing. I wrote pages and pages of waffle and the others wrote bits."

Having long ago dissolved their label, Guthugga Pipeline Records, The Lighthouse Keepers now expect to record a new Hot album. Their first, 'Tales Of The Unexpected', which notched up a six-month residence in the Australian independent charts, is now a year old. Yet the group harbour no illusions about their real benefactor's identity. It is beer – as crucial to their functioning as the nameless influences this heartbroken reporter will never uncover.

Juliet: "The whole industry in Austria – and Australia – is based on drink. In Australia some pub owners'll come up and say you're shit after the first set or two. But at the end of the night they're saying, I don't know how you did it! Your music changed! They just got drunk, it has nothing to do with the music."

The Lighthouse Keepers aren't really that naive. They're working for The Lighthouse Keepers. It may have its drawbacks but, on hearing songs as special as 'Ocean Liner' or 'Wheels Over The Desert', one knows these could never be candidates for pity.

On the contrary, admiring The Lighthouse Keepers is only the beginning.

Juliet at Virgin Megastore, London.

Chapter 8 : Bad Mood

Proof sheet photos: Darian Turner.

gether. That's what happened with some of the bands from around that time that decided to move to London. They didn't necessarily have much in common, and probably wouldn't have said hello to each other in the inner-city bars back home, but here they'd be forced together. Huddling close to protect against the cold and the fickle English rock critics.

A few Australian rock critics made the journey to the old country as well. Clinton Walker did his time in Aussie muso accom somewhere around Camden.

> There was a group of Australians in London. If you could get over your distaste for their music, you got on. The English were scared of us wild colonials. I think part of the reason that the Birthday Party became so revered is that people were terrified. I can say this about Australian musicians in relation to the English and American ones: we were wild. Those British boys all wanted to get on the cover of magazines and the Americans were a bit the same. Even INXS seemed wild to the Americans! But hanging out with the Birthday Party in those times—I didn't know anyone in the Australian scene who wasn't a major risk taker. For us Australians when you go around the world—you're off the leash.
>
> Clinton Walker, 2017

Maybe rock critics should declare a conflict of interest when sharing accommodation and drugs with the musicians they are writing about? Clinton has sometimes regaled me with a story about Nick Cave eating his sizzling bacon while he was out of the room in these junkie London days. At least that's how it registered in my memory. So when I hear Nick Cave's music, I always think of him snaffling down Clinton's bacon. Just when he was real hungry an' everything. There would have been heavy drizzle that cold night, I'm sure, while the Australian

Chapter 8 : Bad Mood

exiles lolled about, watching *EastEnders* or something... burned teaspoons lying amongst the Foster's cans. But history has alternative versions, dunit? When I asked him about this legendary event, he claimed my memory was incorrect.

> It's one of those stories that become icon stories. It is absolutely true that I was in a house full of junkies and I knew that no one was going to cook anything. I had a bag of potatoes I'd just bought and was going to bake them in the oven and I say to myself, 'I'm going to eat something tonight'. So I put them down and go to the bathroom and do my ablutions. I come out and Nick Cave's in the kitchen already cooking my potatoes. We might have kicked him out at some point after that...
>
> Clinton Walker, 2017

Potatoes! That just doesn't cut it as a major crime against humanity. Bacon added so much more to the story, and I'm sticking with that version. But I'm sure it was still painful for Clinton at the time.

However, the Antipodean scene had another side to it—perhaps their choice of recreational sport reveals that Australia did have some class differentiation. Lindy Morrison from the Go-Betweens was part of this 'milieu'.

> We played regular tennis. With Tracy Thorn. Robert [Foster] and I played a lot. We used to play with all sorts of musicians, like the Triffids. There were tennis matches that were very serious. Robert used to beat me regularly and I was a sulky loser. There was an Australian band called Tiny Town who played with us—but I don't think anyone from the Birthday Party or the Bad Seeds ever made it to the tennis courts.
>
> Lindy Morrison, 2017

A lot of these people had spent some time in private schools just like me, and it was inevitable that they were familiar with tennis, whether or not they chose to reject their background. Meanwhile, the Lighthouse Keepers were starting to think about the bright sunshine back in Bermagui more and more frequently.

> In Europe, we'd all eat together, sleep together in the same room... not many bands can put up with that for long.'
>
> Juliet, Lighthouse Keepers, Bermagui, 2015

But obviously, there are some bands that can put up with it. It's all part of the deal. Long distances from warm and comfortable homes can make or break Australian acts. I guess it has a Darwinist effect, and any band starting to gain traction with overseas audiences survived a stage longer, then ego pumping, money, drugs, sex, etc, took them to the next level. And on it goes. Perhaps Australians felt a bit weighed down by their recent colonial history and awkward suburban culture. But I don't think anyone 'over there' really cared that much. And for those foreign musicians that made the ridiculously long trip the other way—to Australia—the indifference could be overwhelming.

> When overseas acts get to Australia, I find not a lot of them know a lot about anything here. Henry Rollins knows a bit and has now got obsessive, but for the greater part, they don't know anything about Australia, not just records—anything at all.
>
> Tim Pittman, promoter (of both local and overseas acts for many years)

Perhaps it's a direct result of drawing a mental blank when it comes to Australia that overseas artists tend to err on the side of excess if they actually make the trip. I've come across examples many times in my studies for documentaries on rock history. From Joe Cocker getting busted, to one of the Eagles spending a week in a Melbourne brothel.

But let me take you back to Europe in 1985 to get to the end of the Lighthouse Keepers' attempt to make a name for themselves in the wider world. Here I continue my roadhouse guide, rarely commenting on the meals, but still paying close attention to the ambience of my surroundings. We ended up back in Austria, perhaps drawn by the lure of the cooking.

Hairy in a phonebox, London.

Blue, Zurich.

Chapter 8 : Bad Mood

Sunday, 27/10/85, in Linz, Austria

It's getting cold, I feel ill and I'm just coming to terms with the meaninglessness of my existence (I've just read Steppenwolf). All this travel is beginning to take its toll on my health as I don't have the ability to become an alcoholic. Last night Brigitte's parents cooked us dinner and it was fine, waited on us, hand and foot and gave us the wine. But after the trip from England via plane and train, I am getting run down, but it doesn't matter as I'm lying down now on a mattress quietly drinking some herbal mixture that is bound to put an end to all my woes. And my poor Casio (keyboard) got lost on the plane. How I hope it is not forever. I long to feel its touch once again. The keys not too hard to press down, not too easy, but just right.[2]

The sky outside is dark and misty and still and it is some sort of a holiday with celebrations for soldiers. It is quite good to leave England although I enjoyed my stay there. And would you believe it—we even played well on our last show in England at Riverside Studios where again we were replacing a band (cult industrial funk from Sheffield). Martin Jennings was in the habit of driving us home after shows and in this way I got to know him a bit better. Especially since he was so generous with the green leafed matter. After Riverside he came back to Andy and Clare's where we proceeded to indulge and ended up with a very intense conversation about Martin's sexual set-up, which, in Clare's eyes, was a girl in every port. But best of all was the apple Clare brought home from work where a worm pops out if you talk too loud—hours of entertainment. But I'm back in Austria again, far away from worms and apples.

We were broke now, always staying on people's floors and often hungry and cranky. Blue remembers the last European shows.

At some point, we played at an ex-slaughterhouse/abattoir at Wels, not far from Linz. We had the luxury of a long sound check, so we learnt a new song, a cover of Aretha Franklin's 'I Never Loved a Man'. Juliet got stuck into me for fumbling around with the bass— she was playing it to me on keyboards. She later apologised, saying that she wanted to take it out on someone and I usually didn't bite back. It seems that the claustrophobic atmosphere of touring tended to magnify the relationship pressures on the couples in the band.

Blue, Lighthouse Keepers

Blue probably sensed that me and Juliet were not getting along as well as we had. I can't clearly remember how things began to slip. But being the only couple in the band put us at the top of a hierarchical power structure, especially being the singer and songwriter. This was beginning to fracture too. It must have been difficult for the others in the band because, really, everyone contributed to the sound and songs. It was a rickety band, and taking away any element would make it fall apart.

We couldn't have done the European tour without all the periphery people either. There were characters like a German called Lemmy who hung around, feeding us, and organising shows so we could get a little money to eat.

2 NOV 1985	**VIENNA U4**
7 NOV 1985	**CARPI**
12 NOV 1985	**NÜRNBERG**
13 NOV 1985	**HAMBURG**

---

2 Happy ending to this. it actually came back to me months later via lost baggage—still got it in the cupboard.

Roadhouse Guide, Tuesday, the 19th of November

In a way, we've grown to rely on people's good will. Without them we'd be eating baked beans on a caravan floor. We stayed on another hapless souls' floor in Vienna and I don't even know their names now, and never have, I think. The Italian end of our embargo came about as a result of Lemmy and Monica, his Italian girlfriend. They've been extremely good to us. Apart from organising the Passau touchdown with accommodation included they've gotten us out of financial deep waters and people to stay with in Italy. I've become so tired that I barely grunt a gratis to the kind souls who take us in.

The world has become reduced to the number and size of mattresses, the amount of coal with fireplace available, and if a separate partition can be found for the purposes of sexual gratification. The smallest movement by another member of our family requires a lengthy chain reaction ending in some evil comment or pathetic utterance.

To me the world seems a little overcrowded in these parts. It's probably just a difference in coping mechanisms that make life bearable. We are in one of the richer areas of Italy but still it seems crowded and a bit grubby, a lot grubby, in fact.

Coming over the alps it was very picturesque, unable to be captured on my Konica C-35, and from Austria to Italy a complete change. Lemmy has been a good guide, as he speaks fluent English as well as Italian & German and a few others. Being a non-drinker and vegetarian at present,

Chapter 8 : Bad Mood

Switzerland.

he has always been full of energy, and always impressive with life force and helpfulness. However, we've probably used up these people and the others we've gathered around through our charm and intelligence, and it's time to wing our way home. I pray for no air pockets and I've got a Walkman to cut down on background noise—I'm fully satiated, in other words.

That was pretty much the end of things for the band. The poverty, hunger, claustrophobia and general effort required was just too much for us. And as I described in the opening chapter, we topped it all off with an old-fashioned stage fight in Hamburg. As a side note, I met up with this energetic and generous Lemmy not too long ago—at St George Leagues club in Sydney of all places. I was also saying hello to Steven Williams and Blue from the Lighthouse Keepers in this classy establishment—who I hadn't seen for some time. Lemmy's life had not always been easy, with some long periods of unemployment. He also showed me some recent online footage of him with a comb-over—he was playing the sidekick of an Italian comedian in an ad for a gambling site. Life doesn't always reward intelligence and energy. Oh, well. He was certainly drinking that day. Then he disappeared to see his first Australian rugby league game. I gave it a miss. Like I heard one English commentator say, I prefer a round ball.

Back to Australia in late 1985. We flew to Perth and began the long trip to Sydney. We didn't keep records of all the shows anymore, as I think we'd all had a gutful. My 'Road House Guide' stops abruptly. I didn't seem to care what I ate on the way back to Sydney.

What I do remember from the shows in Perth was our promoter, Neil Wedd, asking if someone called Paul Kelly could support us one night. He wasn't yet rebounding with the 'St Kilda to Kings Cross' stuff. Sure—we let him open for us, never knowing that soon he would become Sir Paul Kelly to Australians of a certain age in the next century.

Another time machine trip forward to an encounter with him in this knighted phase. I was working on a project for the Sydney Opera House around 2012 where a whole lot of artists

26 NOV 1985	**RED PARROT** [Northbridge/Perth]
28 NOV 1985	**ROCKWELLS** [Perth] w/Rabbits Wedding
26 JAN 1986	**HAROLD PARK HOTEL** [Glebe/Sydney] w/Big Waddi
1 MAR 1986	**JAGGERS LOCAL INN** [Ryde/Sydney] w/the Go-Betweens
6 MAR 1986	**TIVOLI** [Sydney]
7 MAR 1986	**ANU BAR** [Canberra] w/Secret Seven

were doing bits from Nick Cave's[3] 'Ship Song'. Waiting to film the great man, I sat in a recording studio deep in the bowels of the Opera House. I put the camera down for the moment. Then one of the sound engineers started acting strangely with me. He was sort of fawning and obsequious. I realised the problem.

'Hang on there... I'm not who you think I am!,' I said.

He should have known better. He was quite a groovy sound dude and even though me and Paul Kelly have the same haircut... well, he should have known the difference. I did get a taste of being Paul for a moment, and it wasn't that pleasant, but I guess I could have gotten used to it.

The other look-alike that I get even more frequently is Rob Sitch, the comedian and whatever guy. I've had people run across the street to meet me. We do work in parallel worlds in the fickle arts and entertainment industries but, sadly, he's like a successful version of me. My lot seems to be the cut-price Rob Sitch, or on some days Paul Kelly. But do those two get mistaken for each other? What's going on people?

Dear reader, am I confusing you as well? With all these different shifts in time and location? Let's go back to the good old mid-eighties. We decided that enough was enough with the Lighthouse Keepers once we got back from our only attempt at an overseas tour. All that was left was to finish off with a bang. We did a few last shows in Canberra and Brisbane, but the main event was a final show in Sydney.

Steven Williams had reached his management zenith. With the band splitting up, he concocted the perfect show for a farewell. It was Good Friday—at that point you weren't allowed to buy takeaway alcohol on this sacred day, and so drinkers had to go to a licensed premises. The stars aligned for the band with a massive queue out the front of the Graphic Arts Club. I can still remember the show. That was what it must feel like for successful bands. A loving audience, an inability to do wrong, with every song seeming to come from a higher place... even for a rinky little indie band.

I believe Halley's Comet was in the skies around this time. A period of change was upon us. The end of some truly wonderful times. The end of the Lighthouse Keepers, and also of me and Juliet as a couple. My memory could be wrong, but I don't think me or Juliet returned to our rented house that night. We headed out separately. It would never be the same. The darkness began to press down just a little harder on me.

7 MAR 1986	**ANU BAR** or **REFECTORY** [Canberra]
21 MAR 1986	**QUEENSLAND INSTITUTE OF TECHNOLOGY REFECTORY** [Brisbane] + Let's Go Naked + I Am Vertical... Advertised as our final Brisbane show ever!
28 MAR 1986	Lighthouse Keepers end it all! @ **THE GRAPHIC ARTS CLUB** [Chippendale/Sydney] Lighthouse Keepers + Jam Tarts + the Nansing Quartet + Secret Seven Last show with original lineup

3   Yes, the bacon gobbler!

Chapter 8 : Bad Mood

> I just remember I was talking and you were silent and then you were talking to other people and that was irritating.
>
> Juliet, Lighthouse Keepers, 2017

Over the years, I began to realise that Juliet has a completely different set of memories about our time together. Sometimes, it can seem quite harsh. Then sometimes, I can see a faint flicker in her eyes. Whatever our different versions, we were together for six years and that is a long time at that age. We never quite made it to seven years... the title of our last recorded single.

The Lighthouse Keepers have reformed for events and a short tour over the years, and I do know we both look back on the band with fondness. As for the rest of the band, I remember Blue telling me that he'd 'crash tackled' Juliet at a Sydney beach not long after the band split. I guess his emotions got the better of him. He relocated to Italy for many years. Hairy kept on playing music with the Cannanes and gradually became thoroughly reliable on stage by learning to drink *after* the show. Steven Williams kept his hand in band management for a while, but found repairing sewing machines a more lucrative business. He now sells spas on the Gold Coast.

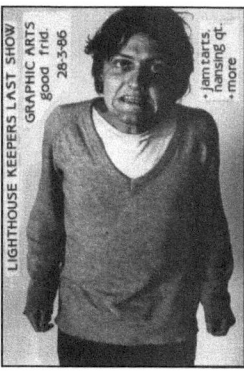

Poster photos: Bleddyn Butcher.

The Lighthouse Keepers, Strawberry Hills Hotel.

Some may say that we generation Jonesers, some of us Generation X-ers, are now at the age of the reunion, clinging to the wreckage of our youth. That the reunion is our version of easy-listening-good-times 2WS. But I'd say the frequency of the reunion is all down to Facebook. Rarely does a day pass on that cyber bulletin board without news of a band from one's heyday reforming. I am not one to gossip but I have heard that a rock against reunions page has been established.

Annabel Bleach, Lighthouse Keepers observer, speaking at an Lighthouse Keepers reunion show, 2012

Yes, you can overdo the reunion thing, and a band has to be careful not to destroy what was good about the past. Even though we were not a big act by any standards, we did affect a few people's lives—even on the other side of the continent. Some of them have come in and out of my life. I originally met Fran Bussey when she disapproved of my courting her good friend, who has since become the mother of our two long and attractive children. Like many from that time, Fran got into the band scene and could never quite let go. These days she's stopped snarling at me.

The best thing was when I got a tape in Perth when I was sixteen, it had one side Lighthouse Keepers and one side Particles, I heard it and thought ...well if they can play stuff like that, then I can do it. It changed my life.

Fran Bussey, 2015

CHAPTER 9
A Time of Evil

The Widdershins. Photo: Steve Appel.

I think being in a semi-successful band can have some damaging effects. In some ways, I feel blessed that we never became bigger—I kid you not. I look at my peers at the time who did a bit better. With just a little more success, you get a few too many sycophants, glamorous girlfriends come a little too easily (not that bad), the people hanging around you are happy to give you some of their medicine. Your head gets bigger. You write ever more cryptic, turgid ballads, 'til there's no way out.

Or perhaps I'm writing about myself. I probably had a slightly inflated opinion of my own talents during this period. I wasn't famous, but I did have a few fans. I never got heavily into drugs either, but I probably would have if someone had offered me something a bit better than speed, which just felt like too many cups of coffee. I was never attracted to heroin, as I've already stated, and cocaine did not appear in front of me that often. A little ecstasy, of course, some trusty prescription pharmaceuticals, a fair bit of

The Widdershins.

marijuana but, again, I was lucky not to do any more damage to myself than I did. But it did give me a taste of what could happen. It wasn't all unpleasant. Indeed, it's quite nice to have your ego pumped and your body's cravings pretty much catered for.

But as the person out the front of our band, I feel Juliet went a bit further down that track than me, and I asked her about it in that strange interview we did recently in the very hut in the Bermagui wilderness in which we had started playing music together.

> I'm like a few other singers that I know, Dave McComb included, that were depressed to the point of suicide after some gigs. You're doing this thing and people just love you, then they go home.
>
> Juliet Ward, Bermagui, 2015

> Dave [McComb] took it very seriously—sometimes, he felt it was a huge load to carry these five people around... I remember once at a show somewhere—he yelled out, 'tonight I cut my forehead on the microphone,' and some woman yelled out, 'bleed for us, Dave!' and I thought, 'I'm in the wrong business'.
>
> 'Evil' Graham Lee, the Triffids, 2016

> The vocalists or main person tend to be the ones who have the most damage. I think that's because without them, the band wouldn't exist. They carry them on their shoulders.
>
> Lindy Morrison, the Go-Betweens, 2016

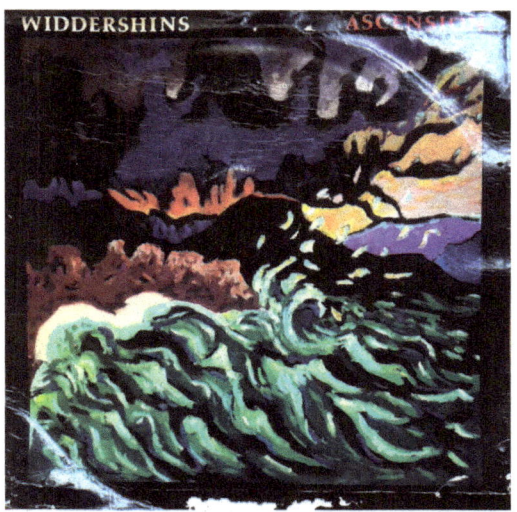

The Widdershins' album, *Ascension*.

Growing egos aside, it was as if all that tour bus time and cramped living at the end of the Lighthouse Keepers had got to me and Juliet—we both seemed to need our space. So much so that I suddenly realised we'd broken up. I found out when Juliet told me! The exact details of her delivery elude me now, but it was all pretty messy. I had my own part to play in it and really should have seen it coming. I was devastated, however. I'd never felt anything remotely like it at any point in my life before. I remember many phone calls to various people (always women, actually) from inside ugly phone boxes so that no one could hear my pitiful whining. One of the women was my mother, who at one point suddenly switched into a weird voice. I realised she'd turned on her 'Lifeline' voice and was counseling me as she did in one of her many volunteer roles. This creepy realisation probably helped start me on the road to recovery a little quicker.

This took ages: luckily, there were other kindly women out there. I remember one saying to me that perhaps I'd never had anything bad happen to me in my life—and this was why I was falling apart. Possibly true. This person may be reading the text with trepidation, as it all led to a tempestuous relationship, thoroughly documented in just about every song on *Ascension* by the Widdershins. But have no fear—all good.

Perhaps foolishly, considering all this, me and Juliet decided to form the Widdershins almost straight after the Lighthouse Keepers. Around this time, Juliet also began to dabble in the black arts, as in witchcraft! An indication of this comes from the name the Widdershins. It's got something to do with witches—I'm not quite sure what. Juliet and me were now pretty much separated, although there was a grey area for a while, and I could not help noticing there were some odd trinkets gathering on her dressing table. We had different groups of friends now—and hers wore long black coats and big boots.

> I felt powerless at the time. I was surrounded by rock and roll men and I was also expecting my brother to die anytime soon. Magic and witchcraft gave me some comfort. Maybe I was just being a dick... but all my life I'd been interested in death... I still feel that people talk like they're not going to die. I loved that [witchcraft] talked about nature, not dancing around in the moonlight naked. But I liked that it was about women and paying attention to the planet... and I think women were able to talk to me more easily than men.
>
> Juliet Ward, Lighthouse Keepers, Bermagui, 2015

Juliet was answering a question I'd put to her about witchcraft, drugs and lesbianism. I could sense there were a few males ogling her during the time we were in bands—but I was completely oblivious to her female fans. The conversation then got into awkward territory for mature people. An interviewer must always leave these difficult questions to the end of the interview. And it didn't go for much longer.

There were all sorts of people involved in the little world I'm writing about, and it's been good

The Widdershins. Photo: Steve Appel.

Juliet and chicken.

asking them a few prickly questions as part of this writing process. Fran Bussey[1] was one of the people who ended up in our social web. She left Perth around this time to come over east and see what it was all about in Sydney.

> I think I came just as everything was petering out, so you may not want to interview me...
>
> I saw the Widdershins and went to a party where Juliet was—she was pretty scary! She was cool but slightly spooky. I remember she had this crazy Bohemian set-up with all these chooks and stuff. I just felt very much like a little child amongst all these people. It was all a bit humourless, or a type of humour that I didn't get.
>
> Fran Bussey, 2016

There was a gang of people that Juliet hung around with at the time that called themselves 'the Crolucks', the spelling of which I am totally unsure. They were a group of Wet Taxi people. If memory serves me well, they

1   Let's call her a musician/academic.

Chapter 9 : A Time of Evil

THE WIDDERSHINS

A S LOU REED WOULD PUT IT, THE Widdershins are growing up in public. Forming out of the ashes of Sydney legends the Lighthouse Keepers, and containing the band's singer Juliet Ward, and songwriter/guitarist Greg Appel, the Widdershins were guaranteed an immediate, and expectant, audience, and one that couldn't help but compare them to past glories. "You tend to get romantic about the past, and you forget that half of it was shithouse," says Appel of the constant comparisons, refusing to let old ghosts haunt him.

He is obviously more interested in the present, and the future, and offers that the Widdershins are "Technically more competent than the Lighthouse Keepers, but not that that's necessarily a good thing in itself." Those responsible for this increased proficiency are Barry Turnbull (bass), Peter Timmerman (drums), and James Cruikshank (guitar and keyboards) and their abilities helps to explain the excellent acoustic-flavoured rock that is their recent single "Now You Know" b/w "Dishwashing Liquid".

It is one of those rare records that is able to embody both the looseness and spontaneity of the Widdershins live. They are considering releasing two albums in the upcoming months. One being a "collection of acoustic songs recorded in my house, and the other being a more serious, properly produced record. I really want that album to be more ambitious than we were in the last band."

While it may sound bold, the thing that makes this proposal plausible is the abundance of strong, perceptive Appel-penned songs that populate the Widdershins' live set. ∎

— *John O'Donnell*

The Widdershins; from the Lighthouse Keepers, better songs and consistent performances

---

always seemed to be standing around flaming 44-gallon drums in the requisite long coats. Louis Tillett, the singer from this band, was the prime exponent of the look.

> **I still don't know if they were joking. All children have a make-up world and these people kept it going a bit longer. You can play the game properly when you've got a bit of money as a young adult.**
>
> **Juliet, Lighthouse Keepers**

But to have money, you also had to have a job. I think being a known rock star can make you virtually unemployable. In that way, I was lucky to be an unknown rock star and able to hold down a job. Sometimes the two would combine, like the classic struggling-musician-job of the time in inner Sydney, delivering *On The Street*. I would fill the back of my white HK Holden with these free music papers and drop bundles of them at various venues and shops around town. This car was enhanced with mags, a spider-encased gearstick and a small, thick steering wheel—as befitted my social status at the time. Old Red Fox from Canberra would have felt at home in it himself.

I drove my yobbo car with irony, of course. Just like we all ironically started calling our male friends 'mate'. But these ironies can quickly become confused. I also started to write a bit more at this time, and I will generously let you read through a whole short story. It will give you an idea of where my head was at around then—a darker, more self-indulgent place than during the Lighthouse Keepers' time.[2] *The Bottle Man* still reads well… I think.

---

2   Actually we were a pretty self-indulgent band, come to think of it.

'Bottle Man' by G. Appel, circa 1986

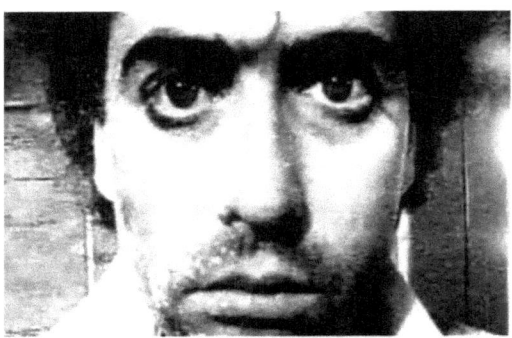

My eyes open, containing a few drops of teary liquid. I am in the bottle man's body again. Most days I wake with watery goggles. I am a miserable wretch and a dirty hound. I have no way of justifying my existence, except that I exist for no reason. I am playing my own small part in human history. I am the man of the future and I am the first to change. I am as worthy as any great mind, or astronaut, or fast runner. Except that I am a cowardly, snivelling little bugger.

And today is my big day. Dole form day. Pushing it to the limit, I get out of bed at 11.30. Got to get moving. If I don't do it today, then it will have to be done tomorrow. This would throw me in a big way. I have spent the last week preparing myself in mind, body and soul.

The powers of bureaucracy are the forces of evil (except for the $200 they give me every couple of weeks). They are hindering the future. In the quagmire of offices and semi-intelligences they have nearly broken the bottle man. But I have risen to the occasion and my life is once again on a level path to non-existence and mineral consciousness.

Yes. When they brought in the personal appearance at Social Security, before the start of The Midday Show, it threw me. I had my life worked out, a routine I had worked on day and

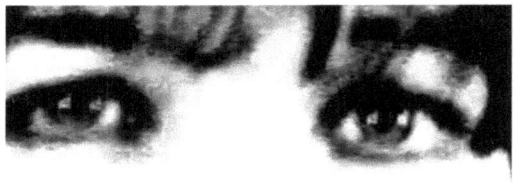

Images from the short film, *Bottle Man*.
Cinematography: Paul Clarke.

Chapter 9 : A Time of Evil

night, refining it and purifying it. Suddenly I was thrown into orbit. I had my human contact level down to an all-time historic low. I was living in a vast city of the future; I ate food. I had a working-condition black and white TV. And I lived in my own dirty little box.

The morning light is cutting through my self-constructed paper venetian blinds. I wipe away the tears with a leaf from the pile I keep near my mattress. I hurriedly put on one of my vast selection of dirty-hound coats. I close my homemade adobe mud cupboard and shift into gear. The morning light is about to become afternoon light. As the sun reaches its zenith, as Ray Martin enters make-up, as the tuna is emptied from tin to display chamber, I make my way out into the harsh world of reality.

My schedule is tight. I learned many years ago not to rely on public transport. Apart from the terrifying experience of stopping a bus, fumbling around for money, saying something to the angry being who has to ice-break through traffic all day, lie about destinations, sit next to people… the list is endless and horrific… a machine cannot be relied upon for precise timing. By walking at a swift scuttle, however, I can make the office in 15 minutes.

People move out of the way. The dirty-hound coat and greasy hair make sure of that. I look neither to the left or to the right. My head is down, back is sloped forward for speed;

I am a dog on a mission. In the unlikely event of anyone calling to me (Fuck off, you ugly bugger. Oi, you! Piss off. etc…) I wouldn't falter. I must get my form in, nothing else matters.

Long ago, in another era, all I had to do was to get to the post office on the day of reckoning. I could amble along at a leisurely pace. A stamp, an envelope and a creative mind were all I needed to get by. Then someone, or perhaps a think tank from the cream of the public service, decided that if dirty hounds weren't up in the morning, they wouldn't be out looking for the work they couldn't have. So maybe if they got them up one morning every two weeks they wouldn't sleep so much. This would lead to a decline in across-the-board laziness, and eventually everyone would be gainfully employed.

This sort of logic has filled countless square metres of office space in their own department, with people thinking up similar schemes and an army of minions to put this into paperwork. But I took it as a challenge. My life is geared to the refinement of the soul, and through this my mind and body, and eventually the future. Nothing will stop me.

Even if they were to take it all from me; my security, my sustenance and my reason for being, I would not be stopped. I have read a few books on eating bark, weeds and lizards. I have tried it out, and even though not a particularly pleasant way to live, it's a possibility. I have my box, my TV and my ever-expanding mind.

My mind is expanding like the original gathering of the matters. Expanding yet densifying through complete non-use. It is only a matter of time before I bang. And then? Who knows? My matter will form an alternative universe. In it there will exist consciousness with no form, minerals, gases, and maybe a few vegetables. With my consciousness redirected over such a space I know I will find peace. Who could not with such an overwhelming feeling of significance? A feeling of massive size and power; a vast swirling, frothing, hissing, magnificence.

And you can share it with me. As taxpayers, every one of you has a share in my fulfilment. And when I am an extra-dimensional entity you will be too, for underneath my dirty-hound coat I am a human. So the small percentage of your income that ends up in my box is part of everyone who has ever stalked the face of the earth's future. And all I ask of you is your coffee break once a year, or no sauce on your sausage roll once a week, or not to flush the toilet once a day.

My friends, my fellow beings, my mirrors in shape and lovers in spirit, this is what we have been working towards. Our time on this planet has been characterised by waves of achievement, and I am riding the crest of one. Let me surf it.

These are the sort of things that the bottle man is working on. Although my physical appearance is on the lower end of the ladder of achievement, my internal mechanics are shining and greased for action.

These are the sorts of things that occupy the mind of the gruesome figure that drifts past you in the street. To some I am invisible, and to many I am the source of anger. I am sensitive to my position in the scheme of things. Although it angers you, to feel your small change trickle out of your pocket, over the concrete and up my trouser leg, I am not ungrateful. I can turn the smallest piece of copper into a vast lump of psychological gold. Everything that is yours will be returned to you in time.

I feed on your ignorance and disgust (lucky for me). The vibrations of despair and mediocrity are channelled into my box, through my body and into my psyche. What do they turn into? I have no earthly means of conveying my work, except perhaps a tiny flash-bulb of our potential. The potential that I am shaping and varnishing, grooming and caressing. My gift to you. For it is you who (reluctantly) feed me and clothe me. You are my mothers, although I know a few men will bristle at the idea, and I am your devoted son.

A flash. I enter the DSS in overdrive, avoiding the eyes that are avoiding the other eyes. Which of us is the winner in the desperate straits competition? There are all sorts of entrants:

Chapter 9 : A Time of Evil

the old diehard three-day-growth-don't-care-anymores, the young and wide-eyed, gathering the free money with open arms, the bitter failed artists living in garrets, and even ones who can't find a job. All of them, some admittedly more than others, working on the grand regeneration scheme.

And, of course, there are the type on the other side of the counter. Employed only because we are unemployed, with free-form osmosis between the two. Some of them have crossed the counter's huge conceptual barrier many times. I have seen one hurdle the wall, after taking a long run-up, during one especially nasty ordeal over a counter cheque with an ex-brickie's labourer.

A bolt of horror wrecks my body as I look at the official clock. What could have gone wrong with my carefully refined scheme of entrance? Is my Digi-robot out of sync with world time? How could an automated time-keeper of the future be wrong? The ad in People beckoned to me; 'crystal set precision in android body of the future a bargain to buy and a guaranteed beautiful little bugger.'

The girl who wields the stamp is beginning to move from her position at the form receiving dock. She has already closed her stamp pad! She is in an incredible position of power. She focuses on my harrowed form. She knows the magnitude of her position. Her expression is of resigned superiority. Our eyes contact, a very rare moment for me.

I feel a little moisture adding gloss to my pathetic countenance. Still she is a granite boulder, the concrete she works beneath has entered her spirit. This vision of minerals reminds me of my work. I must bring some of my inner powers out into this world of blue carpets and green laminex. My eyes light with a volcanic glare, the water turns into steam. She tries to avert her mascaraed slits. She can't—as the gaze is held, the concrete turns to sand. She questions her motives, why is she doing this? the true nature of the monster she is an organ of, looms in her mind. She feels my psyche caressing hers (I'm beginning to get a bit of swelling in my physical housing). She receives a flicker of my work, just as you are. She is renewed with hope for the future of the species. Her own work in turn takes on a new light.

She is making the world a better and fairer place in her own little way. She is Robin Hood, she is re-cutting the cake so everyone can at least have a mouthful. She senses a new dimension to her own potential. I feel her inner self surge through her mantle and touch me. She is all around and inside me. I feel inspired and divine. The dole form slips through my fingers, circling around me, brushing roughly against me under my coat, and through the air onto the counter. The stamp goes down.

I love her… and I love you…

Amanda and me.

The touching end to this story takes me back to the ugly old Harold Park Hotel. A music venue at the time, beside the racetrack in Glebe. It was here I first saw a young woman with a bit of a look. It was like a sixties flashback, and it was only the eighties. Later I would find out Amanda had a legitimate flower child upbringing in Western Australia. Perhaps this gave her license to wear floppy hats and kooky gear. However, I'm really taken back in time, because she would go on to play the part of the bureaucratic stamping girl in the film version of *The Bottle Man* (1995).

This rather long, short story does highlight the federal government's generosity towards struggling artists at the time. Even though the annoying lead character is finding that the regime is becoming more difficult. As we have learned in the preceding chapters, many musicians and assorted artisans were using this money as a kind of arts grant. Sometimes I wonder if that system may indeed work better than actual arts grants.

For who is to know or judge which artists deserve a grant? Why not just spray the money out there a bit? It's like doing English or art at high school. They are interesting subjects, but there's always some dodgy teacher casting judgment. How else can you mark these subjects? I have no solution, sorry.

But try living like the Bottle Man now, and you'll have great difficulty. He'd have to move back home with his mum! Even though the story is on the light side, like much of my material, it is a story about a search for some sort of meaning in life. This feeling has never quite left me, unfortunately. I imagine it is a common affliction. Despite all the gadgets and data at our fingertips today, the search goes on. More confused than ever. I guess it's a search that's been going on for quite some time for many spiritual seekers. I just find it difficult to embrace emptiness as a warm cuddly thing. Hopefully I'll get there.

My *Bottle Man* story was printed inside the Widdershins' mini-album *Bottle Man's Wife*. To me, that mini-album was the band's best

Chapter 9 : A Time of Evil

work. The Widdershins don't quite resound with people like the Lighthouse Keepers, but they are still a somewhat known quantity (to a certain circle). They were a great band of musicians that came together pretty quickly after the end of the Lighthouse Keepers. Two were from John Kennedy's Love Gone Wrong—Peter Timmerman on drums, Barry Turnbull on bass, and James Cruickshank played guitar and keyboards.

James had appeared out of nowhere—playing every instrument very well—behind his back. Dave Claringbold—who'd worked with the Lighthouse Keepers, was our producer and guided us into some interesting recording situations. Like for the mini-album, *Bottle Man's Wife*—some of it was recorded in the dim echoey all-male house I lived in briefly. This can be seen in the clip for 'March of the Green Men' from these recording sessions. It's appropriately captioned 'Failed Men's Refuge'.

James Cruickshank from the Widdershins and Blue from the now disbanded Lighthouse Keepers also lived there.

> I shared a house with Greg and James who were now in the Widdershins. Greg played everything on a twelve-string guitar. I occasionally picked it up and tried to play it but it had a very difficult action. I thought that was something about twelve strings: a difficult

James Cruickshank.

> action. James also played a twelve-string but the action on his guitar was very easy, though I was still a crap twelve-string player. Greg's playing and songwriting ability left me very much in awe.
>
> Blue, 2017

I've left Blue's compliments to my twelve-string playing here for all to see, but the truth is that James was the natural, and I left all the frilly stuff to him. The Widdershins were a twin twelve-string guitar act, with James handling most of the pouts and moves. I only spent a brief period in that group house world. Inside this huge cold house were four large bedrooms, where the various males would shuffle around. Myself, James and Blue were joined by a guy called Ricky, who got completely wiped out on marijuana most

The Widdershins. Photo: Steve Appel.

evenings, but especially on Monday to watch his favourite show—*Four Corners* on the ABC.

Another resident for a while was a grouchy cartoonist. You may have seen his 'funnies' in various publications over time. I find political cartoons a bit simplistic, like political satire in general, but these also had a grim aura about them that no big nose could make amusing.

The telephone[3] was in the hallway next to his room, where the cartoonist worked on his funnies. Therefore, he had to answer its loud demanding ring. Not many of the calls were for him, and we would often get a shout from the hall, 'Hey, enigma heads!', meaning a call for me or James. Hopefully, there was salvation at the other end of the phone. Just like the title of the Widdershins' mini-album—Bottle Man did need a wife.

The real happy end to *The Bottle Man* story is that along with a friend, Paul Clarke, I made a short film of the saga several years later. It was a Tropfest finalist in a great year that saw *Two Hands* director Gregor Jordan win. And even though we didn't get first prize, our film went down a treat and won something or other. I played the part of Bottle Man, of course. It's now on YouTube, like a lot of these clips. And you can see my present-day common law wife, the same Amanda Peacock I saw in the Harold Park Hotel, playing the part of the social security clerk. On that very day, she is also pregnant with our daughter Zelie. My days of group house living would not last long.

---

3 No one under 30 is going to understand this section. The key to it is that we didn't all have personal mobile phones and had to take calls on an old-fashioned ringing non-transportable house phone.

Chapter 9 : A Time of Evil

The Widdershins.

I'm sure all of us became happier people once we'd moved away from this all-male household. The smiling head of Ricky—the *Four Corners* fan—popped up from below the stage at a Lighthouse Keepers reunion not so long ago. He did seem a better adjusted human being and didn't mention current affairs once. I think the cartoonist is still drawing funnies, and I apologise in advance if I run into him again. Just trying to make the book funny. We'll get to James Cruickshank later. This enigma head would become a real rock star. His enigmatic ways, and his head, would get a chance to blossom on much bigger stages than mine ever did.

> I saw a musician one time—it happened in pantomime....I saw from a balcony at a party after a gig across the way. He had this most beautiful girlfriend. I could see this all happening through a window. No sound. They were having this conversation. Waving hands, I could tell he was making a decision. He wanted to go and score. She turned away. Oh, man, bad decision. The wrong decision. He was leaving her to go out and score.
>
> Clinton Walker, 2016

CHAPTER 10
March of the Green Men

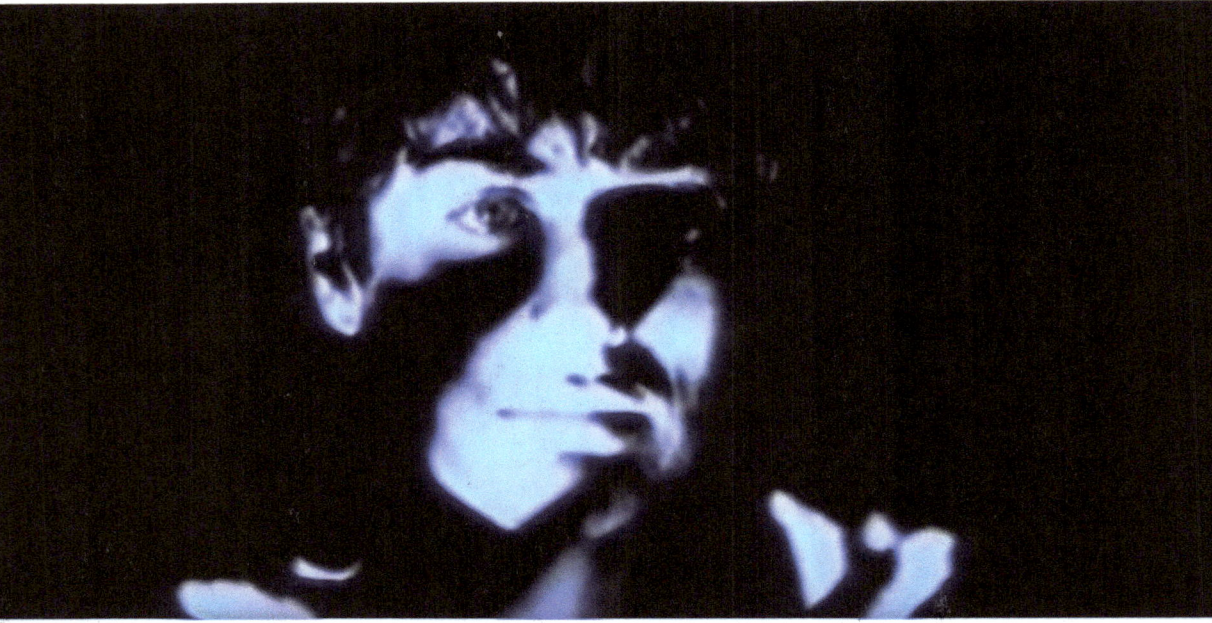

The Widdershins song 'March of the Green Men' is one of the few of my works that have been covered by other bands (The Crystal Set did do a version of 'Gargoyle', as I recall). But somehow, the song 'Green Men' resonated with kind of post-punk punks. I think it was covered in Wagga and somewhere else too. In case you're unfamiliar with this work, it's a bit of a male-to-female whine based around a minimalist Chicago bluesy thing. The lyrics take the full leap into projectile vomiting—in a romantic way, as per usual. It was one of my more extreme songs, and not really characteristic of my more mellow songbook.

On this one, I took lead vocals. Like most of the songs I sang in these bands, it is a novelty song. I did have a slight taste of fame with this one. Although not a hit at all, I remember there was a whole lot of girls who came with cameras—to just one of our shows at the Hopetoun Hotel in Surry Hills. I was wondering what they were up to, as they stood there looking bored for most of the set. But when I sang my novelty song, they sprang into action, there were flashes going off all the way through—

Chapter 10 : March of the Green Men

paparazzi style. It was quite weird and it never happened again. I don't think they liked the other songs.

But I was never going to be a front man. It's too scary—and, let's face it, I couldn't sing very well. Juliet had to handle the spotlight and the Widdershins marched on, 'til we could march no more. The band broke up, time passed, and I didn't see her that much. But people often asked me what happened to her.

> I got really sick of Sydney. What started off as fun started to become really fucked. I think Sydney broke me. I couldn't handle how mean people were to each other. Just going to buy milk seemed like you were living in a jungle. I went to the Blue Mountains to lick my wounds, like a lot of similar people—a lot of no-hopers. None of us worked, it was too far to commute.
>
> Juliet, 2015

But as I wander the country in the present day, looking for clues to the past and trying to make sense of this narrative, I come across some eye-witness accounts of this period that are hard to pass by.

As well as Jewish and English, I have some Danish ancestry. In a way, these ancestors have returned to my family—in a very literal way. One of them came all the way from Denmark and eventually had children with my sister. We have the living results of that union that liven the mood of every family occasion. Bjarne is a fairly distant relative that became a close relative. The first time I nearly met him, he came to the door of the very group house in Toxteth Road, Glebe, that provides the backdrop for the 'March of the Green Men' clip. My father had given Bjarne the address. He was with two other Danes—classic Scandinavian backpackers: heavy tans, sandals, with necks, arms and ankles adorned with trinkets they had picked up in the tropics. Bjarne takes up the story in his still-strong Danish accent.

Bjarne, a little later on, in a classic baby-balancing pose in Denmark. The baby is my nephew, Simon, now much bigger.

We had walked from Central all the way to Glebe, to Toxic Street [sic]. It was forty degrees and we were sweating like a pig [sic]. And when we got there, James [Cruickshank] opened the door and said, 'Oh, you finally made it!' And then he walked away and left us standing outside the door. And so Morten and I looked at each other and said, 'Maybe we should go in?' So we walked in the house, and found the kitchen and made ourselves a cup of tea. No one else was there. The next day, Juliet drove us to Canberra because we were meant to have Christmas there and we had never met anyone. Juliet picked us up in Greg's old Kingswood.[1] It only had two gears, second and fourth. And the first thing Juliet did was to stop at the pub and get herself a bottle of whisky in a paper bag, and put it between her legs, taking a sip every now and then as she drove 130km/h to Canberra. In the back, her

---
1 I think it was actually a Holden Premier—but who cares?

Greg at ABC Archives.

dog, Wolfgang Amadeus Mozart, was sitting between my friend Morten and his girlfriend Bente. It was a big massive St Bernard. Morten hated dogs and it sat all the way there with its tongue hanging out. Juliet was playing the Doors really loud, the window was rolled down and every time I looked around, the big dog's head was just sitting there licking Morten and Bente in the face. Juliet tried to talk to us but the music was so loud. Now and then I had to help her change gears.

Bjarne Kragh, 2016

That is an eye-witness account of Juliet Ward and James Cruickshank from the Widdershins, from a credible Danish source. Apparently around this period, I also told Bjarne that, 'anything that comes out of a can is good for you'. I've never been able to live that annoying statement down. But it does give an insight into my personality at the time. Even today, I sometimes see a niece in the background scribbling down something I've said. They might call them Gregisms. I think 'clangers' is another appropriate term. My grandmother was good at them too.[2]

Anyway, back to the late eighties. But now we are going into a more sinister area of the arts—television. Back then, people might sing about television being the drug of a nation, and it was true. But it doesn't compare with the internet/smart device vortex nowadays, does it? TV was quite a mild drug in comparison. I imagine concerned parents now demand their children watch TV more often. I was drawn to the intoxicating lights of this cathode ray tube. I wanted to be one of the people administering the drug rather than just receiving it. It would be much a less pleasant experience than playing in a band—but better paying.

It was around the time that the Lighthouse Keepers were morphing into the Widdershins that I found myself employed at ABC TV. As with most of my work and creative experiences, I entered the ABC as it passed its golden age. I was employed inside the famously ugly group of buildings at Gore Hill, where ABC Sydney had its TV studios at the time. Inside, the staff frittered away their lives. It could have been the middle of its golden age for all I know, but the overall impression was whingeing from beginning to end. Not to say they weren't good times. I spent twelve years there on staff and at least have a bit of superannuation to show for it. Of course, the ones who stayed on (if they survived the perpetual culls), have so much super they'll be on permanent cruises once they exit, but such is life's rich tapestry.

As far as TV went back then, the ABC was thought of as lowly paid and a sort of boring bludge compared to whatever went on in the commercial world. Strangely, ABC staff have now turned out to be amongst the best paid in TV and some have actually hung on to their jobs. There's a very strange atmosphere there these days; most of the 'creative' staff are long gone or are thoroughly neutered, and the main people are HR and supposedly cutting-edge New Media or oddly named managerial positions. But I'm beginning to whinge like one of them. That's because I was one.

'But how did I get to work at the ABC?,' stu-

---

2 'All men are boys.' 'You can live too long.' (This sort of thing and a few better left in the past.)

dents have sometimes asked me, with wide eyes. It was through human links and a bit of good luck. The one thing my NSW Institute of Technology BA in Arts communications had given me was a group of friends who, despite the course, ended up working in 'the Industry'. To start with, they were often in very peripheral roles, like cutting up newspapers, or driving drunken journalists around. And it was as an ABC driver that I found my way in. Justin Pooley, a good drinking buddy, and one of the few males at our Institute course, had snared this excellent job. I think it was a spin-off position from newspaper cutting.

He wanted to travel to the UK and live in squalor—just like I'd done at 18. Perhaps stupidly, he gave me his job. It was an absolute classic—a car, very good money for a musician, and only the occasional responsibility. Once in a while, I got called on the car radio by the Chief of Staff in the newsroom. The only danger was if you were in the surf or something and didn't hear the call. But excuses were readily at hand—like you were delivering a package. Indeed, this was quite possibly true in the 'confessions of' way. I do remember coming in one day and complaining to Steve, the other driver, of a sore back. He was an older, Dutch lurk-maestro about to retire with his own large package (of the payout variety). He looked at me and stated loudly, "you've got shagger's back". I realised it was actually true! It was at a rather fleeting stage of life when I was licking my wounds after some romantic dramas. Enough for the back problem to be easily diagnosed by Steve, who had his own horrible stories of willing ladies from days gone by.

This feels like the point in many male memoirs where the author goes into graphic details of female conquests. I remember reading a second-hand copy of the autobiography by Bill Wyman, bass player of the Rolling Stones. There was a section where Bill was really overdoing himself, leaving Mick and Keith (who

Widdershins pouting competition – James Cruickshank the winner, upper right. Photo: Tony Mott.

were occasionally faithful to their girlfriends) in the dust. Someone had written, 'you fuckwit,' in the margin. Then again, sex is one of life's joys, and I'll try to return to the subject where I can.

In retrospect, I would love that ABC job back but, unfortunately, it no longer exists. As have many of the other positions I have lurked in. How do drunken journalists get back from their lunches now, I ask? But the reason this job was abolished was perhaps the next driver. He took over from Steve once he retired with the previously mentioned package.

James Cruickshank, who is probably best known as the Cruel Sea keyboard/guitar guy, was at the time a bit of a follower of mine. He followed me like you do on Twitter, but in real life. A little too closely at times. He was not only in the Widdershins with myself and Juliet, but I lived with him for a little while, and he went everywhere I went. Sad perhaps—but true. He moved on to Tex Perkins after me—a harsher

James Cruickshank.

master perhaps, but a more musically successful relationship resulted. Tex and the Cruel Sea had a national hit with 'The Honeymoon is Over' in 1993.

> Sometimes I think I'm just in that lucky one per cent who make it. Like the Widdershins broke up, Barry Turnbull was playing bass with the Cruel Sea at the time. They wanted an organ player—I could do a bit of Booker T...
>
> James Cruickshank, 2015

James was indeed lucky, like Gladstone Gander. You don't remember that relatively obscure Disney character? He was basically a lucky duck. Ken Gormly, the bass player from the Cruel Sea backs me up on this.

> That guy had the luck of the gods upon him. You couldn't kill him with an axe. He crawled out of two horrendous car wrecks (the second infamously bringing half of Sydney to a standstill, making the six o'clock news and front pages). Back then he always managed to crawl out of the wreckage of his own life, brilliantly blundering and dancing through danger and disaster and even slipping straight through the tax office unscathed. And he had great teeth!
>
> Ken Gormly, Cruel Sea, 2017

Ken has many stories about James, but the one he told me about the Cruel Sea in their heyday, waiting to catch a light plane in northern Australia says it all.

> The band on the tarmac with all our gear, weather looking ominous, on our way to a gig in a remote mining town in the Simpson Desert, staring at two tiny planes (one of which would crash into Spencer Gulf only months later), gripped with a primal fear and sense of foreboding, each of us jockeying to be on James's plane and guaranteed safety. Tournaments of Scissors, Paper, Rock turned to bickering and desperate pleading. I played my children card and secured a place on the lifeboat. I felt a mixture of sadness and relief as I watched the others embarking to their fate. I gave James the window seat, clicked my seatbelt and had a little snooze.
>
> Ken Gormly, Cruel Sea, 2017

But back in the 1980s, I needed James just like he needed me. Anyway, once old Steve retired, I was able to get him in as the other ABC TV driver. Lucky break for him.

He followed my lead and took it further, by treating his vehicle as his own. The car was barely ever at the ABC, full of instruments, and ladies. James was very popular in that department and had a sly-puppy way of getting rid of them that somehow didn't appear callous. It culminated in a night when we took the ABC car to the infamous Sydney Trade Union Club and came outside, super drunk, to see it horribly vandalised. We knew we may have gone too far.

James decided he'd sneak the car back to base, as it was the weekend. So he snuck it through the ABC gates and we came in on

Monday and acted horrified by the condition we found it in. Somehow, we didn't get fired, not that it was possible under the incredibly benevolent conditions that ABC employees enjoyed at the time. But it wasn't long after that the positions were made redundant. James left with a small package[3] and I was forced to apply for another job as copy boy.

I actually was rejected first time round, by a stuck-up fuckwit—let's call him Bob Northerly—just in case there's any legal problems with me telling the truth. You've heard and seen him on the news. Typical newshound. The biggest story is themselves. I remember he had the hide to complain about me having bare feet in the ABC building. Man, we had only just left the seventies—that cat was straight. A lot of the journos were like that, but don't get me started. There were a few nice ones. A few.

My next position after I sort of failed to hold down the copy boy position was in TV Archives. Here I felt much more at home. Copy boys didn't do much except dump newspapers loudly in the middle of the newsroom for the journos in the morning.[4] But you had to do your job with an aura of concern for the journalists' world and might occasionally have to appear interested in what they found in the papers. Not so in Archives. They were an odd bunch of people who just wanted a lurky job—well, that's how it appeared to me—a few gay people, lots of women and the odd basket case. But in no way did you have to appear interested in the archival footage you were fetching for ABC staff. We held everyone in equal contempt. The aim was to have fun at the taxpayers' expense, doing minimum work. To anyone who entered Archives, we were always busy, and what they requested was always difficult to

Cindy at ABC News library.

find. As soon as they left the room, we were balancing rulers on our noses.

My period in Archives brought me back into the newsroom in a round-about way. I worked in the News library with a lovely woman called Cindy, who looked exactly like her name. She had an aura of no nonsense that helped make our lives a lot easier. I was able to keep being a muso by night and it was here I started writing a script called *Van Park*. I also became more involved with people there who didn't want to make news stories and were keen to create something a little more interesting. Cindy kept the wolves at bay, and had plenty of time for important phone calls to her mates.

The News library was a little booth away from the main newsroom. It was also a great test of the journalists' humanity, that is to treat their archivist underlings like human beings. In that room, they were alone with us. They were in charge, and no one could witness their behaviour. Our job was to get tapes for them out of sliding metal cabinets. Complex work, yes, but those journalists didn't just want any old footage, they wanted video that no one else had seen, of cinema quality, that was going to make their masterful current af-

---

3   No more sexual innuendos, please.
4   No, there didn't seem to be copy girls, even though this was post feminism—they were PAs, Producers Assistants or similar jobs.

fairs exposés look as good as them. More importantly, they wanted it right now. Sadly, I'd say 80 per cent failed the humanity test. Yes, they were under a little pressure sometimes—it's hard turning *Sydney Morning Herald* stories into visual pieces. However, my feelings began to darken towards those champions of freedom. When I hear that journalists are facing difficulties in the new media world, a part of me is not that concerned. If only they'd been a little more polite. Cindy feels the same somewhere out there, I'm sure. But perhaps beheading is going a bit too far.

Beginning from my time in TV Archives, I have seen a lot of changes in the video editing process. Peeping in at the vaguely glowing creatures behind the windows in the editing rooms at Gore Hill, I got to know all the different visual mediums since the dawn of ABC time. Around the corner from the newsroom, where other programs were made was 'videotape'. It was a long corridor with the look and feel of the reptile section at a zoo. Inside, the creatures sat at different varieties of editing machinery. It was the age of videotape, children—yes, very big tape. Two-inch-width reels were on the way out, and it was now the era of one-inch of the stuff, all curled up on giant spools. The editors were mainly men that came with a hierarchy that was difficult to fathom. All I knew was the biggest and meanest of them manned the most complicated machines. They were like the cockpits of a large jet, with panels of lights, dials and levers all over the place—no mere mortal could possibly understand how you controlled them. These guys, therefore, ran the shop. They got paid pretty well too. I think the introduction of Foxtel in 1995 meant they went to actual pilot wages,[5] just so they would stay on staff. I wondered if I would ever be allowed to sit in their cockpits.

The newsroom staff had their very own editing enclosure, and it was here that I began to make some friends. There were slightly more female editors in news, and not quite the same animal/nerd vibe that big videotape had... but still hard-core. There were even some fully-fledged heroin addicts amongst them. It took me a while to work it out (as usual). These editors looked pretty groggy and red eyed, didn't touch the dials, and seemed to disappear somewhere on a fairly regular basis. I never found out where they went, but it must have been an even darker and danker enclosure underground. If any of the journos caused any problems, the News Edit shift leader soon sorted them out. That was his job. There were some impressive real estate portfolios being built within this group as well, all while being completely fucked up! One of the editors told me they called the journos 'blowies', as in blow flies which hung around sheep faeces on farms. I understood it to mean that the journalists' way of gathering and disseminating information was not well respected by the editors who put it all together in those grubby booths. It was an old-school Australian workplace, with all this slang and devotion to hard-core bludging. What sort of world had I entered? I just wanted to be creative.

Sometimes a journalist was able to break the editor/journo divide (which was huge). The only way was to get down and dirty by taking drugs with them. One journalist, who shall remain nameless, went even further. He would disappear with the hard-core editors at the regularly allocated disappearing times and emerge looking just like them—red-eyed and groggy. But then, it would be time to read his section of the news—live! He would squirt some anti-red-eye stuff into his eyes and get out there in front of the cameras. I personally couldn't think of anything less relaxing than reading from an autocue to a nation of uptight ABC viewers while stoned, and who knows

---

5 I'm thinking pilots from this same period rather than post-global restructuring of the airline industry.

Chapter 10 : March of the Green Men

what else. But he got away with it, many times.

I also wanted to work my way into their hearts for my own nefarious purposes—editing personal stuff! One of the editors I got to know went by the likely but unlikely name of Steve Brown. I talked to him over the phone recently as he settled back on the lounge in his Darwin home.

> It didn't feel like you went to work. The hardest part was just turning up. But the journalists took it all very seriously.
>
> Steve Brown, 2016

I'd remembered how he called the ABC a 'sheltered workshop' and let me get past the shift leader into the edit zone. But Steve had a few of his own interesting memories of the newsroom's hierarchy. One morning early in his career he was left alone in the edit room, when…

> In walks [Steve named a couple of well known journos from this era], who said they wanted to look at some rushes. So, they're sitting there watching the footage and one turns to the other and says, 'I've got this big secret, don't tell anyone…I'm pregnant!' I'm sitting right next to them. That's how it was…you weren't really part of the club.
>
> Steve Brown, 2016

I pondered the legality of what Steve had told me. Then I remembered all the law students that used to come and see the Lighthouse Keepers. Could they be of use here? I messaged Fran Gibson, a constant presence back in our small touring party. Over the years, she turned into a high profile legal eagle (if this term can be used to indicate a status that I am unsure of). Could I use the names Steve gave me? I should have expected the qualified response…

> I cannot give legal advice but I guess you are worried about defamation. Arts Law Centre will give you advice I expect. From 2017 NSW Law Handbook:
>
> > A publication is defamatory if it tends to lower a person's or company's reputation in the eyes of the "ordinary reasonable person".
>
> As for the other bit (forgetting about the law), it might be seen as an intrusion into privacy to reveal people's conversations about pregnancy. I don't know if it would be defamatory. If you are worried get advice.
>
> Fran Gibson,[6] 2018

I messaged back. "These people are journalists! Is not their whole trade built on lowering people's reputation in the eyes of ordinary people? As far as an intrusion—Steve Brown does not exist to them—he is *persona nullius*—so how can his comments have any legal status? Can we get another opinion?"

I hoped this was pro bono work and she wasn't charging by the minute! A few more of the old crowd replied.

> Well, I know nothing about defamation, except for having been sued by a pig dog, but for what it is worth, it doesn't look to me like there is anything offensive in the attachment.
>
> Ben Slade, Principal Lawyer, Maurice Blackburn Lawyers, 2018

> Having worked as a lawyer in the US, where defamation does not seem to exist, I would suggest that if anyone queries it, just claim it's fake news.
>
> Jane Goddard, Practice Leader, Fragomen, 2018

---

6   Fran Gibson BA/LLB, Dip. Crim, LLM who also formed the Cannanes with Hairy from Lighthouse Keepers, who exist to this day. In addition, she attended every Melbourne performance of my musical *Van Park*. In addition to that—Lighthouse Keepers reformed for her sixtieth birthday in 2017.

Wayne McAllister, from ABC days. In the studio with 'One Head Jet'.

The legal answers from the Lighthouse Keepers early fans, came back as clear as mud. I decided to leave the offending journalists names out of it. Who am I to name and shame. I'll leave it to the citizen journalists of social media.

Back in the newsroom in the eighties, we were invisible drones who did the bidding of our superiors. A much more noisy editor was a guy called Wayne McAllister, who was a strapping lad from the country. He wrote poetry and made continual wisecracks for the benefit of the whole newsroom. His poems could be found all over the yellow-tiled toilet walls. They were sort of funny. Somehow, the journos put up with his jibes. I guess they couldn't hear him if they couldn't see him. He had a run as a copy boy, just like myself and Steve Brown.

As a side note—I ran into Wayne the other day. He'd only just returned from a long stint as a cameraman/editor in the ABC's foreign offices in Asia. He'd been shot at repeatedly, filmed thousands of dead bodies in tsunamis and floods and wars, and had an aura of post-traumatic stress. I don't think his training in the newsroom could have been less of a preparation. Spooling through graphic news footage is quite a lot different to being on the ground in a war zone.

But at night during the late 1980s, the ABC TV newsroom was relatively peaceful, almost commune-like. There was a core group of people of similar age and disposition to me. We used to help each other on all sorts of whacky projects once the newsroom had finished for the evening. There were editors, and camera people that would help out if you had a vision they could relate to. We made a lot of video clips and things like that. It was here that I met Paul Clarke, who was a researcher for the *7.30 Report* at the time. He wasn't proud of his work. Amongst us, the ultimate insult was to say it was 'a bit *7.30 Report*'… that meant slow motion, stupid voice-over, horrible production music and an unnecessarily long close-up of an over-serious journalist's face. The comedy *Frontline* was meant to be a satire about a commercial channel, but the current affairs programs at the ABC had a very similar vibe.

I remember one of the gnarled news editors on the night shift looking at us with knowing eyes as we worked on one of our projects.

'You're doing a foreign order, boys.'

I'm imagining a cackle from him that probably didn't occur at the time. But, no, that wasn't what we were doing. 'Foreign orders' were the editors' code for corporate videos they were making on ABC time to get some extra cash. It was even whispered that sometimes they made pornos. He couldn't possibly have understood that we wanted to make our own stuff.

Chapter 10: March of the Green Men

Me and Paul Clarke 'writing'.

I also got to make my first documentary right there in the newsroom. When I say 'I', it was conceived and motivated by Steve Brown, after we'd worked on a few video clips. Steve was a pugnacious, no-nonsense guy. He was extremely dismissive of anything or anyone artsy or pretentious. Most of the editors were a bit like this—they were a cross between dockside workers and hippies. Added to his interesting mix, Steve also had manic depressive issues. I can't remember if this was apparent before or after we made *King Street, Newtown*. He sometimes had manic episodes that would take over his life, and have him either calling or appearing at the News library with some wild projects. On one occasion, I remember him going round the newsroom asking every woman to go out with him, including the journalists. He may not have used polite expressions. This was a complete transgression of the newsroom class and social barriers. A journalist might be friendly on the surface with editors and camera people, but in no way were they an equal. Steve surprised everyone when he approached the female host of the *7.30 Report* at the time. Jane Singleton had an aura of North Shore royalty about her. For once, the shift leader had something to do, and kept Steve employed.

Anyway, in 1994, I was a little surprised when Steve came into our News library and suggested we make a documentary about King Street in Newtown—the old starting point for our Lighthouse Keepers adventures. I tried to think myself out of it, as documentaries weren't my main interest. I was really a frustrated fictional filmmaker, not to mention muso. But try as I might to think otherwise, it sounded like a good idea, and we set about organising a cameraman—our one expense. It might have been $200. We then got our whacky mate Wayne to be a mock journalist. His job was to run down the middle of King Street doing a piece to camera. We interviewed anyone we could find who looked a bit interesting.

In the depths of the night, we beavered away on this documentary about Sydney's biggest traffic bottleneck. Steve and I got a bit tense with each other, as is often the way with these kind of projects. Perhaps you know you're going well when things start getting tetchy. But we got it made without a

Doco makers Greg Appel, left, and Stephen Brown. *Photograph by JAMES ALCOCK*

Voices of Newtown

IN Newtown, where you might find a pierced tongue talking business on a mobile phone, diversity is not only tolerated, it is embraced.

So when filmmakers Greg Appel and Stephen Brown set out to make a documentary about this bastion of bohemia, they concentrated on colourful characters and avoided a straightforward narrative.

Take the opening sequence of vox pops. A man sings a song in Latin. A Hare Krishna muses about his religion: "We are like spiritual policemen." And three lesbians lying in one bed speak their minds.

There are no voice-overs. We simply deduce that these are people of Newtown, in a tale of King Street.

Appel said the film was an independent project made on the cheap over six months in 1994. He composed its original soundtrack, incorporating international instruments — including accordion and sitar — with sirens and traffic.

"The find of the film was probably the guy in the cemetery," says Appel. The character whose narrative is the film's backbone "could speak on any subject for 10 minutes, and ... we thought he was so good we didn't need a voice-over — he held our interest".

So did Wayne — "I'm the king of King Street" — with a running monologue as he jogged the street, dripping beads of street wisdom.

Difference, broadmindedness, community and unpredictability are the talk — not always in glowing terms — of a baker, a bookseller, a barber, the owner of a store that sells leathers and dildos, a municipal councillor and a real estate agent. There is history, from "pre-invasion" days to now. And there's drag artist Simone Troy doing her darnedest to turn King Street into Queen Street, in a suburb that is continually reinventing itself.

King Street, Newtown screens on ABC on Thursday at 10.30 pm.

Sacha Molitorisz

I had learned by then that it was unwise to take the general public Christmas period off. If you kept working, you got paid triple time and the workplace became so lax that you were virtually on holiday anyway. You could choose another time to have a real holiday—when it got busy. I had heard a legend that a few floors above us was the Head Programmer. It was a six-floor building, ugly like the rest of them, but as you ascended, the people got more important, and the offices got bigger.

During this Christmas break I was in extra luck, because usually important people were surrounded by staff who would keep anyone like me, well away. We called them 'program prevention officers' and, indeed, these are one of the few jobs that have expanded in the ABC, along with HR. But they were all holidaying on the North Coast, and I got to knock on a big wooden door. The Head Programmer himself answered it and let me in. Bob Donoghue was an old-school (even then) ABC type with a slightly British accent.

I had a VHS tape of *King Street, Newtown* at the ready, and explained that we had made a documentary and would like to get his opinion. An hour later, I got a phone call from him. He'd pay $2,000 and it would go to air in the Christmas slow season, in a pretty good slot, as I remember. What an excellent fellow. I'm sure he retired with a healthy package not long after that.

The show was a hit. For the ABC, and a documentary, it rated extremely well. So real fight. As anyone who knows me will tell you, I'm extremely easy to work with.[7]

Once we were finished and happy, it fell to me to try and sell the damn thing, but where? I had no idea of how you might sell a program, and we knew of no other channel that might want it except for the one we worked for (or perhaps SBS, the perennial backup). Luckily, however, it was Christmas holidays.

---

7 All true.

much so that it made its way to Parliament House in Canberra. A Senate committee earnestly debated whether viewers had seen real male-to-male fellatio in one of the scenes at the Newtown Hotel. Steve had cut this scene so tightly that you could barely tell what was going on. I looked at that edit again recently when we had a rescreening. Having done a fair bit of editing myself by then, I could see how well Steve had cut it together. And no voice-over! We stuck to our beliefs with that, and it's a fantastic result. In my view, it's one of the best things I've been involved with. It seems so real and entertaining.

After the success of the show, Steve even had the odd journo asking how to get a documentary 'up'. This was very satisfying, but we were brought back to earth when we had a visit from a man from the ABC TV documentaries department. We had unwittingly bypassed this entire bureaucracy by going straight to the Head Programmer. The man gave us a lecture about how this wasn't the way you did things. I know now that it would never have happened if we didn't do it our own way.

But as the program prevention officers gradually returned to work tanned and well read, they begrudgingly let us make a second program, *Maple Street—Maleny*. We felt like we had a budget of enormous proportions. We got $40,000 altogether, and Steve was determined to keep as much of that as he could. And he did—it's probably the most I'll ever make from a documentary, because Steve, being an honest bloke, gave me half of everything we never spent.

But Steve was burnt by this next documentary. Things appeared from above that neither he nor I could believe, even though I've spent so long working in the documentary industry now that I think it's normal. Suddenly we were told we had to write a script! We couldn't believe it as we'd just made one without anything looking remotely like a script. It was a

Still from *King Street, Newtown* documentary.

documentary, for fuck's sake—not a drama. But apparently you had to write out what each character might say, link it all together thematically and make a story arc!

Then there were endless screenings and notes. The 'EP' (Executive Producer) was a semi-insane lady who'd obviously partied hard in the sixties. I've seen a lot of these people now and, in retrospect, she was fairly harmless, but it sent Steve into heavy sedation by the end of the process.

To finish it all off, not long after, there was a series about Australian streets which appeared somewhat suspiciously on SBS. Exactly what we were proposing to the ABC. I won't go into details of who took whose idea. It seems like part of the industry to me now, but back then it seemed Machiavellian. A frustrated Steve Brown went off to work in the Mindil Beach markets in Darwin, as far away as he could get from EPs and documentary scripts, but it was the first 'Spontaneous Production', and this company lives on with my various projects... would it ever produce anything as good as *King Street, Newtown*?[8]

8   Perhaps I'm as big an idea stealer as the rest of them, as I got a nasty email from someone who'd apparently taught me at UTS. He had the name Spontaneous Productions and how dare I use it? Well, I'm sorry. I apologised for the use of a name that I think is more naff by the year, and changed it to Spontaneous Films.

CHAPTER 11

Cruising

Me, Anne Kyle and Andrew Glover at ABC TV.

There is another point in people's memoirs when they skip quite a few years. Things get boring. But as life goes on, sometimes boring can be the better option. And if nothing else, working in the media has taught me how boring people really can be. My mind rewinds through many viewings and clients and producers, back to the days when you actually did rewind tape—then forward again—to the present era, when anybody can change anything with a track change here or a 'tweak' there.

There's a process that has come to be called a 'screening' where a bunch of 'stakeholders' watch a video and give 'feedback'. I'll stop with the inverted commas. But the most common decision in these creative get-togethers is to get rid of weird bits. Although if you get more than three creative types together, these weird bits can be pretty inoffensive.

A media dude who worked in advertising once told me that they give their clients a few options on starting a campaign, ranging from far out crazy to very boring. The

Chapter 11 : Cruising

clients inevitably start with far out crazy and just as inevitably end up with the very boring option, but it's in an advertising company's own interests to have a project get changed as many times as possible. They get paid by the hour. In summary, there is an inherent conservatism in most of the population, but perhaps it's better that way. You'd get pretty sick of an ultra-whacky universe. Unfortunately, I personally enjoy the weird bits. My role in TV often seemed to be as a weird guy. This possibly had a constraining effect on my career.

For me, the weird bits are the 'middle eights' of a program. In music, the middle eight is the part of the song, around about the middle where you deviate from the verse and the chorus. This section might be linked to the composition but it can go almost anywhere. All the hard work of the repeated verse/chorus thing pays off, if done right. My favourite works across all the art-forms, contain these little doorways into other worlds where the unexpected can happen.[1]

Now back to boredom. I have recently run this thought by my partner and mother of our children. Partly because I want to continue to live with her and I am not so insane as to write things to the detriment of our loving union. But I thought back to those days I've been writing about. It was like there was a game of musical chairs going on with sexual partners, and suddenly it stopped. People all paired off. They got serious with houses, got po-faced about careers, and some even had children together. They could be the most unlikely couplings and, of course, the future often did reveal the underlying

problems. But it all seemed to come to an impasse quite suddenly.

For myself, I feel privileged to have ended up with the person I did. Some people grow apart. We have grown together. I think back to what seemed like random events and meetings. I still remember that first fleeting vision of her. I was deeply self-involved at that time (even more so than now[2]). The way people behaved with each other in that insular scene could be quite brutal, and have repercussions that were felt for years. But then, something good might come out of it all. Did some part of me know what lay in the future?

It must have been around the year 2000 that I decided that I would need some more material for my inevitable memoirs. I was

---

1   You want an example? Hmm. Ok, this might throw you, but listen to George Michael's 'Fastlove'—refer to middle eight there. Now there's got to be one in *The Sound of Music*. Maybe where the captain starts crying in 'Edelweiss' during the performance for the Nazi's, or is this whole movie a middle eight? Have I lost the last of the little cred I had left here...

2   I think...

Anders and Zelie at birthday party.

Amanda and Anders at birthday party.

more or less a family man now, and I'm sure my real family didn't want to be dragged into this more than need be. Suffice to say it was going well. Having children can be quite a time-consuming and unexpectedly difficult task for people of my generation. Let's face it— we haven't really had to do much hard work. Australia's relaxed lifestyle, good economy and the self-indulgence handed on to us by our forbears make for some pretty wet citizens. But no excuses—I always wanted to have children and now we have had them. Thank you all concerned.

I had worked on an ABC youth show called *Recovery* for a few years with a good group of people, including Paul Clarke, Bruce Kane and even Sarah MacDonald, who you met earlier when she wrote about our family holidays way back. There's probably a whole other book that could be written about youth TV, but I'm not going to do it. Our show was pretty well received and, on the whole, well remembered. But some of us wanted to go a little harder than the Saturday morning slot seemed to allow. We had side projects, as creative types often do, and after we'd stopped trying to get hip with the kids in our day jobs, we workshopped and beavered away on these projects.

Josh Reed was an editor on *Recovery*, and we both had kids of a similar age. As people of childbearing age, we still had a deep fascination with sex. I think we were trying to pretend we were still free and childless. Sex had no doubt led us to the child predicament in the first place, and sex still gnawed away at my male brain when I wasn't too tired feeding bananas to demanding infants and such activities.

For some reason, Josh and I decided that we'd seriously try and make a porn film. Perhaps to make ourselves feel less seedy, we asked another *Recovery* producer, Anita Jorgensen, to join us. She thought it would be good for a laugh.

So the research and networking began. I remembered my cousin (Pete the Basher) had gone out for a while with a woman who was now head of the Eros Foundation. Fiona Patten dutifully took my call and we had a meeting and everything. She was sort of earnest but husky at the same time, and explained that my old home town of Canberra was where you might film a porno these days. Somehow it was legal, and the appropriately named suburb Fyshwick was now the hub of Australia's adult industry. There were huge warehouses where you could buy dildos of many different

Chapter 11 : Cruising

varieties and a whole lot of unlikely looking sex aids. Anyway, perfect location. I set about organising everything. I never told my parents our plans.

We wanted to make pornography that a couple could watch. I actually didn't watch much myself—although another man made me watch some once. I thought maybe there could be a real plot and less emphasis on gynecological detail. Perhaps this isn't really possible. Men and women view sexuality in such different ways, don't you think? Or do they meet somewhere in the middle, like a love song? I recently asked Josh Reed to refresh my memory on the plot.

My brother Steve, Josh Reed and me in wig, doing some hard core ham acting.

> This was 2000, leading into the Sydney Olympic Games. It was set in the athletes village, where a shipment of anabolic steroids got mixed up with a shipment of ecstasy that was meant to go to a rave. So all the athletes ended up on ecstasy and proceeded to fuck each others' brains out. I believe this is what happens anyway in athletes' villages.
>
> Josh Reed, 2017

But back in that heady year of the Sydney Olympics, the whole project was suddenly undermined when at our pre-production meeting Anita suddenly said: 'are you guys serious?' We looked at each other and didn't really know. It was obvious Anita wasn't fully into it. Just like real pornography, it wasn't that palatable to our female co-producer. In ten years' time, they would make *Game of Thrones* and it would all become family entertainment—but for now, it wasn't to be. Our pathetic dream began to unravel without Anita on the team and we slowly ceased to mention it.

But every cloud has a silver lining. I don't think there could have been a worse time to enter the porn industry. The internet was only just beginning to show its true colours, and today, I imagine it's very difficult for anyone to make a viable pornographic film. It's all out there for free and, again, a man made me watch some.

Post-internet, old-fashioned pornography with any sort of plot seems quaint and old fashioned, but I guess it's crept into dramas like it always should have. We used to have to worry about saying 'fuck' on TV—now it seems like you'd have trouble getting a program going without at least a dozen 'fucks' and a carefully placed 'cunt'. You lucky uncensored viewer.

But I do remember a situation back then, when pornography seemed to be perfectly acceptable in mixed company. A man, this one called Stephen Bunchgrove,[3] brought a hot VHS into the *Recovery* office at ABC TV one day. It was the famous Paris Hilton sex tape that had found its way into the public arena. So we all sat down and watched the whole thing! Paris Hilton looking a bit out of it, having sex with some dodgy guy—just another day at the office.

The ABC is a strange institution—the arts and public service don't mix very well. But there I was on staff, for over a decade, generally trying to do something other than what I was told to do, gradually working towards more interesting material. It's amazing what comes out of that place really, considering the impediments.

---

3   Possibly not his real name.

LONG WAY TO THE TOP

Inspired by the BBC's brilliant history of music documentary series Dancing In The Streets, the ABC commissioned its own six part series documenting the history of Australian rock. Finally finished, it premieres on the **ABC** tonight. **SHANE O'DONOHUE** spoke to producer **GREG APPEL**.

Divinyls

AC/DC

How did the idea for Long Way To The Top come about?
"A group of us were working at the ABC, we'd done Recovery and happened to get this documentary on Australian jazz. The BBC thing [Dancing In The Streets] came out five years ago – the ABC doesn't like to do anything off its own back – and they said they wanted to do one here. It's come out a lot different, but that's how it happened. It's a slow process, not of all that time was spent doing things. I mean they sit around debating for years."

It can't be an easy task, tackling such a huge subject...
"I mean it was harder than what we thought. At first we thought we'd just interview everyone we liked, but in a way it came out better for the fact we didn't because there's some more obscure characters in it. It was hard to compress the main interviews we did. We didn't really start with a clear a plan. I must say it was a lot harder than we

Was that particular people or footage you found impossible to track down?
"It was surprising what we did get. We did get some good stuff. Obviously there's times when things just weren't filmed, so you'll see some re-enactments in there. But I think we really did get some pretty rare stuff in there."

What are your favourite moments in there?
"I sort of tend to like the anecdotes. I tend to like some of the silly stuff. Angus Young was a great interview, Lobby Lloyd was good. People like Michael Chugg were surprisingly entertaining. By the third episode you're getting into that hippy era. There was some horrible music, but there were some great stories."

How did it develop from the original idea?
"A lot of people were working on it to start with, and there

in the end was that good interviews and characters just came to the front and we tried to make the story fit around that, rather than try to chronologically tell the story of when bands started and things like that, which was the original angle. Dancing In The Streets was a good program, but there's something fresh and funny in the way we do it. It's just a bit different, obviously we're a small country and we don't have all the best stuff in the world."

When did you last see it?
"Now that I've had a break – we just had the launch the other day – I hadn't seen it for a while but I saw it the other day and it looked pretty good."

Long Way To The Top screens on the ABC at 8.30pm for the next six Wednesdays, starting tonight (Wednesday 8th).

Having made the Newtown documentary with Steve Brown and then getting it broadcast on the ABC itself meant that the institution begrudgingly allowed me to become a producer, which is how I got to work in Youth TV. I even got to skip the whole internal system that went something like this: dress appropriately, act cool and grovel to become a producers' assistant, then suck really hard with various superiors until, eventually, they let you loose as a producer. It's possible some literal sucking went on here and there. There was a legendary 'Purple Mafia' that reigned supreme (especially in the Arts) around this time. But their day was nearly over and the corporate types were circling.

But the small part I had played in the Australian music industry just wouldn't seem to go away. My career, if you could ever call it that, went from making music to making programs about people making music. I had come to terms with the fact that I was never going to really make it by now—whatever 'it' was—but I would be forced to listen to others who had made it. Some of their music I didn't like, some of it I did, but I would be forced to listen to it regardless—over and over again.

Long Way to the Top is a series I feel proud to have produced, but it is also the one project out of all of them where I really suffered for my art. It was here I both gained (and gave to) the craft of documentaries, and lost a little of my soul. I spent four years on that project, and maybe one and a half were good fun. The editor Andrew Glover was a South African with an aura of a rugby player. You didn't make

Chapter 11 : Cruising

creative suggestions lightly... but sitting inside a small room with him year after year, we became brothers. I'd gladly have him by my side if I ever went over the top in a real battle, and to some degree that's what it felt like in the edit room. Indeed, my favourite episode, the fourth, has a war theme that really suited the material. I think Les Gock from Hush sent us down this track in his interview, by saying being in a band 'was like going to war'.

In the end, the series came out a treat and you could almost say it was groundbreaking. Clinton Walker reappeared in my life here, as well as Tony Barrell, a fantastic old Liverpudlian who'd become embedded in the ABC, and Andy Nehl, another battle weary TV soldier. Is the old saying 'a success has many architects'? Something like that, but there were only a handful of people left in our dank editing room by the end of the process. I've worked with the EP Paul Clarke on and off to this very day. Not to say there weren't other people involved; there were many. Perhaps a few too many at points. But we got there in the end. It was indeed a long way.

Once finally out of the edit booth, the show took on a life of its own. The fifth episode was actually put together relatively quickly in comparison to the earlier episodes, and featured a few of bands I'd met in my former life. I knew by then I could never insert my own band, although if you look closely you'll see a Lighthouse Keepers poster pass in a montage. Such is life! I know there were a few complaints along the lines of, 'Where the hell is Icehouse!?', 'a Stalinist revision of history', etc. I learned that Australians take their music history very seriously. A few of the old 'indie' guard we used to play with were given a chance to be heard. They say there is one sure way to get on to TV. Lindy Morrison from the Go-Betweens got emotional when asked about her days in her own indie war zone. Many years later, I had the chance to ask her about her starring role in that episode.

Me and my close friend Angus.

One of the first things that happened to me when *Long Way to the Top* went to air is that Geoffrey Rush, who I worked with for many years, rang me and said, 'you never cry on camera, Lindy!'

The second thing was that a very good friend of mine said, 'you only cried because you knew you were going to be on television!' But I didn't have to sign the release form. I was truly talking about something that affected me deeply.

Lindy Morrison, the Go-Betweens

As for myself, I felt like crying when I came out the other end of making that series. Indeed, I took a VR—a voluntary redundancy—as I just didn't want to make TV anymore. But of course, I did.

One good thing to come out of the process was meeting a few of Australia's rock and pop stars. I'd say most of them were pretty good people, face to face. I guess when you're asking people to hold forth about themselves during the golden years of their lives, they are generally pleasant.

But, dear reader, I did get to ask a few questions that had been gnawing away at me for many years. And some that I'm sure you would want to know the answers to as well. I hark back to the title of this book. It was a rare chance to get some confessions from these legendary creatures. So, informally, at the end of the interviews, I would throw in a sex question, as in, how much did they get? They were usually in such a good mood after pontificating about themselves that they gave an honest answer.

So. With so many males in *Long Way to the Top*, you'll have to forgive me for the male perspective on this subject. And it appears that the period of most of their sexual success was in the early seventies. This was around the time of the Masters Apprentices, and Jim Keays, the band's front man, was happy to tell us how he'd wake up to twenty girls watching him sleep. His wife of the time wasn't so happy about him doing a re-enactment. But we still managed to do it. In fact, I think we used the hair of my partner and our very young daughter to indicate Jim's waking vision.

But then, as each year went on, things begin to taper off. For instance, Les Gock might complain that only ugly Sharpie girls used to hang around his band Hush as the seventies progressed. He wasn't that interested. But there were still quite a few willing young ladies around. There were some truly scary stories I heard that never made it to air too. A character called the 'Lithgow Leaper' featured in the Ted Mulry Gang's backstage world (and a few more). I often wonder when the eyes that brought down Rolf Harris will turn towards his homeland and the whole *Countdown* era.[4] But then, going right up to my own era and past it to the nineties, we come to a band called Custard. I got the chance to ask my immature sex question of their lead singer. He said that he'd never been approached ever, and he didn't know anyone else that had been either. And this was a good looking guy. A lot better looking than anyone in the Ted Mulry Gang.

Make of that what you will and we'll move on again…

One of Ted Mulry's peers from back in the day, John Paul Young, was a singer I'd always liked. Even though we were watching him through our punky eyes in his heyday, he had seemed to carry himself with dignity in the *Countdown* world every Sunday on the ABC. He was someone I'd get to know in the real world, as time went on. He has a lot of stories too, and some of them I heard a few times in different settings. But he always comes out slightly innocent amongst all the Lithgow Leaper stuff. John's always in a car with someone, then something hideous happens next to him. Or across the room, Ted Mulry is doing something horrible with a dildo.

But most importantly, John's music resonated with me. I like good pop music, as opposed to bad. Perhaps that's what I was trying to create all along. It just came out sounding indie—due to a combination of laziness, budget and random factors beyond my control. Indeed, I think luck plays a huge part in the career of a pop artist.

> I only realise now how lucky I was—when I've seen what my own son has to go through trying to be a singer. I was a sheet metal worker with hair down to my backside. I'd mucked around with a few mates and I knew I could sing, but when Simon Napier-Bell asked me to come and sing over a Vanda and Young track, he hadn't even heard me sing a note. He just met me in a pub and the other singer he had organised dropped out.
>
> John Paul Young, 2015

The English record producer Simon Napier-Bell got John to sing over the top of former Easybeat George Young's vocal track on a demo song. John then had a big hit with 'Pasadena' in 1972, which propelled him to fame. Over the course of many interviews and strange adventures in the documentary busi-

---

4 Since I wrote this, it's getting ever closer…

Chapter 11 : Cruising

ness, I also got to interview Simon Napier-Bell himself. Around 2008, I was trying to make an international program about gay band managers that never quite happened. Simon was one of them. He lived in Bangkok at that point, and after the interview, we went out to lunch. It was a great experience. Some gay men seem to keep the child alive and, though he was a bit older than me, I felt he was a kindred spirit, and we had a very pleasant time. Then there was Bangkok itself! A city of the future, an amazing juggernaut that seems to go on for ever. We got on to the subject which *Long Way to the Top* had spent a long time dissecting—the Australian sound.

> **I don't know if there is such a thing. AC/DC are a sort of second-rate boogie band, but I don't think you could really call that a sound. Status Quo were doing similar things in the UK.**
>
> **Simon Napier-Bell, 2008**

Sacrilegious words to some, I would imagine. But whatever he thought of our nation's music, Simon played a critical part in John Paul Young's contribution to the mythical Australian sound. To illustrate the power of John's music, I have to go back to about 2002 at the ABC. Like many who leave and try and make their way in the scary modern world, I found myself back there from time to time. This time, it was at the end of the documentary series *Love is in the Air*, a sort of sequel to *Long Way to the Top*.

Because John was an integral part of this TV series, they decided he should play at the ABC Christmas party. By this stage, all of the Sydney offices of the ABC were at Ultimo in a big, brutalist modern building in Harris Street, just over the road from the biggest brutalist building of all—my old tertiary institution, the UTS Tower building.

They put John on a stage in the foyer of the ABC building—in the middle of the day. There were austere amounts of white wine, Jatz crackers and cubes of cheese for the staff. The atmosphere was highly corporate-slash-bureaucratic. Anyone who worked there was allowed to attend, or just hang out of their balconies above the vast foyer area.

Slowly, creatures appeared from deep inside the building, lured by the warm free wine. The ABC has some fairly scary types on staff and it looked a bit like the mines of Moria. They glowered down from the balconies above, as John Paul Young started up with his long-term band, the All Stars.

'We're Wiggles for old people!' he yelled to the vast cavern. But then…a magical transformation took place. Somehow, the band cut through the space. Defying all the laws of acoustics, it actually sounded good. The assembled crowd began to begrudgingly tap their feet. And there was more. As John played hit after hit, they started to become increasingly animated. The pinnacle of the performance was the sight of mature women—with a long history of serious public broadcasting—throwing their bras at him! A truly amazing show.

The power of music—displayed on this occasion to perfection—was one of the themes of *Van Park*, a musical I had been beavering away on for quite some time—since I worked at the ABC News library, in fact. Myself and Paul Clarke had an initial meeting with John Paul Young and his manager Phil Manning around this time—to see if John might be interested in playing a cantankerous old rocker called Akbar. It would take years for all the elements to fall into place and actually put the show on.

CHAPTER 12
Shadowlands

Me and Paul Clarke researching *Van Park*.

We've come a long way together, dear reader, and I want to mix things up a little bit as we get closer to the curtain closing. In some ways, *Van Park* ties all the disparate strands of this story together. I will quickly summarise this musical's long history for you, as even I start to fall asleep when I think back… It all started when myself, Paul Clarke and the journalist and very early Lighthouse Keeper, Tim Palmer, were driving past a run-down van park in Leetsvale, NSW. We may have been stoned. Anyway, we snickered as we speculated on how it might be interesting to set a film here—not unlike the way we were fond of trucking music for a few weeks. But this idea just never went away. Perhaps it should have.

Over the years, it transformed into a live stage musical about a group of old musicians who end up living in a van park. When I look at the themes in these 'confessions', they are quite similar to those in the musical's plot—

music, humour, sex and the difficult life of an artist in this sunburnt land. It also appears at a suitable point in the book where I need to get a bit creative. I realise the modern attention span is very short. I know mine is.

One thing I still find particularly hard to concentrate on is scripts. It's really hard to read them and get any feeling for the story. I always find myself wandering away mentally...

SCENE 1. OPENING FLASHBACK MONTAGE

Video montage plays (it's the old editors' trick—when in doubt make a montage). Quirky music starts.

Cut quickly from old-fashioned typewriter clattering away at Windang Caravan Park near Wollongong (circa 1995). Me, Paul Clarke and Wayne McAllister occasionally type things between beers.

Typing shots on all sorts of devices as computers begin to really change and take over the workspace. This goes on for years and years... So much so that...

A quick fight scene in the ABC TV carpark, where my brother Steve physically defends my right to type away at this neverending script in the ABC News Library in 'down' time. (I'd got Steve in on the ABC action at that point.)

Then live readings all over the place, Port Kembla, Darlinghurst Theatre, Newtown...

Different people playing the roles, such as me, Josh Reed, Mikel Simic, Gina Ford, a real-life thespian, John Paul Young.

The years go by, people have children, the children start to grow up...

The script sits in a filing cabinet. Music stops.

Script editor Pete Bradbury sees something there and writes a draft. Music starts again.

Finish on Greg Appel (ME) talking on the phone to Steve Kilbey, a well known Australian musician from such serious outfits as the Church. (A conversation I never thought I'd have)

(continued)

> STEVE KILBEY
>
> Greg, I love it.
>
> I (ME) walking nervously around the house holding a cordless phone. (I did hold this rock star in some awe, despite being a little aussie rock star weary at that point in life.)
>
> ME
> Thanks, Steve.
>
> STEVE KILBEY
> It's really funny, and it's got a lot of musical in-jokes. An old hippy who can't keep the ladies away.
>
> ME
> Yes. Well. When I heard you were looking around for things. I thought perfect! Steve Kilbey.
>
> STEVE KILBEY
> What are you saying?

This is a conversation from memory, although it bears a close relation to the truth— It would be at this point that Steve would test me, by getting prickly. I do remember the next bit clearly.

> STEVE KILBEY
> But this bit about the permanent erection?
>
> ME
> Yes...
>
> STEVE KILBEY
> I'm not walking around with my cock hanging out!
>
> ME
> Well, the script is a work in progress. I only want to suggest the idea. We could do it with special effects...like flashing lights?

Chapter 12: Shadowlands

And that's just what we did for the first run with Steve Kilbey, at the Seymour Centre in Sydney during the Fringe Festival in 2010. It was quite a contraption, worked on by a dedicated team, including my friend's daughter, Bernie McCabe. She was the seamstress. It was always a difficult element to pin down... Yes, this flashing phallic device was responsible for many bad innuendos from those who worked tirelessly behind the scenes, shaping and carving, battery gathering, maintaining and many more penis-related activities.

Steve played the part of Nebauchadnezzar to perfection. He took it further than I had imagined possible, and it gave me great joy to watch this allegedly po-faced rock star letting loose on stage. He channeled his inner Benny Hill, becoming an extremely animated old hippy, with a touch of old-fashioned thespian. He never liked it when I suggested that he could do a great ad for a superannuation fund. But he was that good. Ranting, singing, dancing. He gave it his all—every night. And he did it stoned and more!

While the *Van Park* script had a very long history, the wistful songs written by my brother Steve[1] and myself were a nice contrast to the juvenile humour. And if you look back at the history of theatre, you'll see that the Greeks were running around on stage with phallic enhancements many years ago—and ancient theatre is classy, right? Looking back through very early drafts of the script, there is one illuminating scene that stayed in the musical 'til the end. It's in the van park takeaway shop, run by a character called Gypsy Fire, who was inspired by a real-life woman whose claim to fame was having sex with Bob Dylan in Australia. Cora James took on the part with gusto. She was almost a real-life version of the character. Almost.

Steve Kilbey performing in *Van Park*.

Cora James performing in *Van Park*.

---

1   There were a lot of Steves and Johns involved in this project.

SCENE 2. FROM THE ORIGINAL SCRIPT INT. VAN PARK
SHOP. AFTERNOON

GYPSY FIRE sits behind the counter inside the van park shop. The shop contains a bare minimum of cans and food items, a lot of cheap-looking souvenirs, a small lingerie and bondage section, videos, and a big black dog. GYPSY is overweight and made up with a dyed blonde bouffant. She sings a country ballad to herself. A b&w photo of her past country star success is seen in background. A surfer is hanging around the shop pretending to be looking for newspapers while sneakily glimpsing at pornographic magazines.

                    GYPSY
   Don't think I can't see you!

                    SURFER
   Ay?

                    GYPSY
   Why don't you get out there, and get yourself a
   real woman, instead of glueing paper together?

                    SURFER
   I'm looking for something, alright lady.

                    GYPSY
   Don't look too hard, or I'll charge you, and don't
   make everything sticky. I've got a business to
   run.

SU, the 'love interest' a backpacker from the UK walks in at this point.

                    SURFER
   I'm looking for surfing world. Alright! (looking
   agro)

                    GYPSY
   Don't think I don't mean it.

SU walks around the shop. We catch glimpses of fruit, vibrators and sausages.

                                                   (continued)

> 3.
>
>   GYPSY
>   Now here's a fellow who looks like he needs a
>   good, hard, shag.
>
> SURFER (who has been listening intently) comes over to the
> counter with the offending pornographic magazine curled up
> in a Surfing World and quickly tries to pay. Gypsy forces it
> open, holds it up for everyone to see and slowly reads the
> price.
>
>   GYPSY
>   Stick book!
>
>   SURFER
>   Give it here, moll.
>
> SURFER grabs it leaving the money and scuttles off.
>
>   GYPSY
>   There's nothing more pathetic than a young fella
>   at that time of life. No one wants a bar of them.
>
>   SU
>   Nope.
>
>   GYPSY
>   So they have to buy the old stick books. I'd milk
>   him, if he asked me politely. Put him out of his
>   misery.
>
> SU looks a little distastefully at GYPSY.
> We cut back to the present day.

Genius, hey? We updated it a little as time went on—so instead of stick books there was now a line about surfing the net for porn. The surfer character also became known as 'Panting Dog', and became quite a feature of the show—occasionally one of the young actors was inspired enough to howl in the background. But this script was recited line for line every night. I couldn't say it brought roars of laughter every time, but I feel it captures the soul of Australia somehow; naïve but harsh—like a caravan park.[2] Ugliness in a beautiful landscape. Once in a rehearsal, Cora (who played Gypsy) questioned the line about 'milking' the surfer. John Paul Young told her to stick to the script.

[2] I don't know if it's as good as Gavin Butler's lizard poem referred to in chapter 2.

Washed-up idols hit the right note

The Age
March 20, 2012
Michael Dwyer

Stage comedy *Van Park* finds yesterday's heroes rocking as if there's no tomorrow.

Greg and Steve Appel played out their first rock'n'roll fantasies in caravan parks. Back in the Super 8 1970s, the brothers' ad hoc variety shows brought colour to family holidays in tin-and-canvas resorts along Australia's east coast.

But Greg Appel wasn't thinking about his past when he drove by one such run-down retreat 25 years later. By then he'd retired his rock career with the Lighthouse Keepers and the Widdershins. He was on the road producing the ABC pop history series *Long Way to the Top*.

"We'd been interviewing a whole bunch of old guys who you kind of think of as famous," he says.

"When you meet them you realise they're anything but rich. It's a tough industry if you're older than about 30.

"A lot of them were such great Australian characters, too. It wasn't hard to [imagine] them in a caravan park."

John Paul Young and Steve Kilbey relive the glory days in a scene from the stage comedy *Van Park*.

Ten years later, *Van Park* premiered at the 2010 Sydney Fringe Festival with live music by younger brother Steve and his band King Curly, and starring John Paul Young and the Church's Steve Kilbey as faded rockers in forced retirement.

But Greg Appel says that any social or industrial commentary is purely incidental to the main thrust of *Van Park*. "It's basically a bit silly," he says. "It's meant to be a fun night out that sends you off feeling good.

"When my mother saw it in Sydney I said, 'This is a bit like those shows me and Steve used to put on when we used to go camping, isn't it?' Mum said, 'Yes, it is exactly that.' '

Van Park is at Chapel off Chapel from tomorrow until April 1.

```
SCENE 3. EXT STREETSCAPE MELBOURNE, AUSTRALIA

It's late March 2012 and the author Greg Appel has just
turned 50! His way of dealing with this unpleasant milestone
is to do something complicated and demanding. Attempting to
smother the feelings of impending doom… But for the moment
he walks down Chapel Street in Prahran, a fairly upmarket
Melbourne suburb which has some street cred and a mixed
community of LGBTQIAs, urban professionals and lower socio-
economic denizens. He walks into a newsagent and picks up a
trusty old hard-copy version of The Age.
```

Chapter 12 : Shadowlands

```
                    GREG APPEL
         (Talking to the camera self consciously)

    It seemed that we were off to a good start in
    Melbourne. But Michael Dwyer, the journalist who
    wrote this article, was a big fan of my brother
    Steve's band King Curly, who featured in the show,
    and it didn't really cross my mind that other
    scribes might feel differently. How could they? It
    was a work of genius.
```

Back to the non-script-formatted version of me—coming directly from my head to yours! I strolled down the street in Prahran holding the newspaper as the trams clattered pleasantly around me. We were all staying in nice serviced apartments. Liane Pfister, our production manager, had done a great job of getting an accommodation deal, but it was still expensive. It's not cheap putting up twelve people for two weeks, and we couldn't really ask John Paul Young and Steve Kilbey to have other people in their rooms. They were proper rock stars. I was just a freelance whatever person, with family responsibilities.

John Paul Young was technically the co-director alongside me, by then. I'd had a traditional theatre director for the Sydney run, who really was a traditional theatre director. He shouted at the cast at the end of their last rehearsal and told them they were awful and they were going to disgrace themselves. Afterwards, he turned to me and said in a camp theatrical voice, 'I was always going to say that!'. And what do you know? It worked.

I will at this point make a short detour to note the difference between musicians and actors that I have discovered in my forays into theatre. I have stated before that musicians tend to whinge a lot, but actors will tell

John Paul Young performing in *Van Park*.

the most outrageous lies. I don't know if it's because acting turns pretending into an art form, but an actor can never be late or absent without having an extreme event occur. It's always, 'I'm sorry I'm not going to make it. My mother's dog was run over in front of a police station…'

Stage bow, *Van Park*: Catriona Hamilton, Cora James, Steve Kilbey and John Paul Young.

John Paul Young was from an old school of musical theatre, having played the character Annas, in the Australian version of *Jesus Christ Superstar*, way back. He believed in a disciplined cast, which sounded good to me, so we co-directed the Melbourne run at Chapel off Chapel in Prahran. I also got to know John a lot better during this trip to Melbourne. And, indeed, he was very helpful with crowd wrangling. He'd say things like, 'Melbourne's a hard city, but if you get them on side…it will be your town forever.' John had made Melbourne his own back in the seventies, and some of the creatures from this era started to appear in our early audiences. They were an odd group, mature party animals, who referred to themselves as 'rent-a-crowd'. They had an air of jaded living. The good times were largely behind them, but they were still trying to get a few more parties in. The plot about mature rockers trying to keep the fantasy going in a van park must have felt quite real. I think they liked the show, but it was much harder with a half-empty room than it had been in Sydney. The two-week run, with two shows on some days, stretched before us.

John Paul Young was exactly like his legend. That is—a hard working professional who has a show-must-go-on credo. He was very down on some of the younger members of the cast who would at times come late to rehearsal, forget lines and start 'grandstanding' on stage, but he did tolerate Steve Kilbey's imaginative way of being on time. Perhaps it was because he admired Steve's improvisational skills.

We also had some minor parts that I felt were good for local people—as in local to wherever we were putting on the show. Both because it saved money on accommodation and because it meant you were part of the community straight away. Hopefully, this also meant some of their friends would come to the show. It was one part of the *Van Park* formula that worked exceedingly well. To these ends, I enlisted Fran Bussey, who I knew from the Lighthouse Keepers days, to play Van Park Lady 1 during the excursion to Melbourne. She had moved there and had also become more friendly towards me over time.

> I just wanted to try and remember all the material for dinner parties in years to come. Some of the best things were listening to Steve Kilbey and John Paul Young talk about old times in their changing rooms, about ladies and activities I won't go into to. But my fifteen-year-old daughter Ada came along to one of the shows with her friend and her friend's parents. In his impro section, Steve Kilbey started talking about the Karma Sutra and focused on the girls, and asked them to come back to his caravan. Ada's friend yelled out, 'Yes!'. I was horrified. The parents just disappeared with her straight after the show.
>
> Fran Bussey, 2016

We got to feel like a real family after a while. John's son in the play, Curly (played by Luke Webb), therefore became his real son, annoying him at times. You could feel John's Scottish blood starting to boil at these points. I wouldn't like to get on his bad side.

But my memories of John during this run of *Van Park* were really centered around Pie Face. You know—the takeaway franchise that seems to be under financial stress as I write. We both liked the simple fare served by this establishment after the rigors of the show. And like me, John preferred Carlton Draught to designer beer.

'I stopped going out after shows in the seventies!', John would say. Once the show was over, he'd politely deal with any mature ladies that might want an autograph, chat with any local business types that might be the 'White Knight' that we all dreamed of taking the show to the 'next level'.[3] Then he'd start indicating it was time to go to Pie Face.

Even though his legend has faded a bit since we used to watch him give a steely-faced performance on *Countdown*, he's still John Paul Young. I have a collection of weird old Aussie stars on my phone now, from my various nefarious activities, but when it flashes John Paul Young, it's still kind of unusual—because it's actually him calling. Warwick Capper never calls.

So if I wasn't at Pie Face quick enough after the show for John's liking, the phone would flash accordingly. In this twilight zone of working man's food and beverages, I got to know him. We'd drink a lot after a show, but John was down on anyone having more than three beers during or before a performance. Professional, I think they call it. The band were made up of members of King Curly, as well as Hairy, my old mate from the Lighthouse Keepers. Some of them regularly went way over the three-beer limit, and actually built an island of beer cans as the show's run went on.

They were meant to be a hardened old cover band playing in a derelict pub, and that is indeed the world they created. But I've got to say the music was always excellent. The band stayed just this side of totally plastered. Steve—as trustworthy as only family can be[4] was the Gilligan of Beer Island. The band drunkenly reworked John Paul Young's classic 'Yesterday's Hero', and if nothing worked for the rest of the show, this never failed to get at least a couple of straggly old dancers out of their seats. It's a great song and totally fitted the plot.

---

3   Wow, so many chances for inverted commas in the theatre. 'Theatre speak' is almost a language on its own!
4   Perhaps not all families.

SCENE 4. AGAIN FROM THE ACTUAL SHOW

EXT. RUNDOWN CARAVAN PARK.

> Dear reader—yes, that's you. You should think about listening to some of the music from the soundtrack to get you in the mood. 'Wish I was a Girl', 'Family Man', 'Shadowlands'. All good songs.

The Steve Kilbey character NEBAUCHADNEZZAR has taken it upon himself to mentor CURLY after he is rejected by the love interest. CURLY is a 15-year-old boy and the son of AKBAR played by John Paul Young.

Lights up on NEBAUCHADNEZZAR'S futuristic VAN.

>> NEBAUCHADNEZZAR
> Pretty edgy for her age.

>> CURLY
> You think?

>> NEBAUCHADNEZZAR
> Good looking too. Isn't that always the way? Could be psycho.
> (looks into Curly's eyes)
> Is that the love light I see in your eyes?... It is!

>> CURLY
> Rubbish! Why do you lot always have to make assumptions?

>> NEBAUCHADNEZZAR
> I could help, you know.

>> CURLY
> Forget it. I don't really think I'm her type.

>> NEBAUCHADNEZZAR
> Don't let appearances deceive you! It's what's underneath that counts ...wait till you gaze upon her mound of venus! Then get back to me.

CURLY is not impressed.

>> NEBAUCHADNEZZAR
> Why don't you reveal a little of yourself, my man. Draw her towards the light...All you need is...A LITTLE SONG!

Music builds, suggesting NEBAUCHADNEZZAR is about to burst into song when...

                        CURLY
  A song??

Music drops abruptly.

                        CURLY (cont'd)
I can't write HER a song. She's... She's... too (CREEPY MUSIC) scary!!

NEBAUCHADNEZZAR smiles a 'knowing' smile.

                        CURLY
I can't!! I've just been mucking around. In my head...

NEBAUCHADNEZZAR holds up a hand to silence him. Then puts an arm around his shoulder.

                        NEBAUCHADNEZZAR
If your old man can attract women, you can. You know why he's always been able to pull, Curly?

                        CURLY
He's a pushy sex dwarf?

                        NEBAUCHADNEZZAR
No. And it's not because he's short or persistent, or that he thinks so highly of himself. It's the power of his music.

                        CURLY
Dad is into making noise—and if it happens to coincide with music that's an accident.

                        NEBAUCHADNEZZAR
He makes an ugly noise Curly, yes. But it's a powerful ugly noise, and who says love isn't ugly sometimes? Who says there isn't some wild thing amongst all the flowery stuff? Music is the most powerful implement in the toolbox of love.

                        CURLY
I don't think I'm ready for that box of tools.

You can see there are some familiar themes at work here. The love, the sex and the power of music. I was definitely keeping my own inner child alive. The shows at the Sydney Fringe Festival had been excellent. It was one of the few productions I've been involved with that started to sell out. There was a clear point during that Sydney run, when the phone flow turned in my favour. A rare moment in showbiz. I was able to stop hassling people to come, and they began to call me—almost begging for a scarce seat. It felt great, but it was a moment that I should have enjoyed more at the time. Down in Melbourne, during our two-week run at Chapel off Chapel, the phone flow was back to the usual direction. The performer seeking an audience. It can get to you. But unfortunately for the performer, it's much more comfortable at home watching downloads. Especially for the mature crowd.

Bringing me to a part in this happy tale when I came face to face with an old journo who didn't guffaw at my excellent script. I was feeling reasonably confident when I picked up the first review in the Melbourne *Age*. I wasn't so confident afterwards. Two-and-a-half stars! That didn't seem very good. Worse still, one of the staff at the theatre told me that the reviewer was a kindly soul who tended to write good things. She indeed found a bit of value in the show, along the lines of, 'there's something here, but I don't quite know what.' John Paul Young was a 'trouper'. But as John read the review, even he began to look concerned. She commented on the amateurism and the fact that you could see people crawling around behind the sets. All true. 'She's seen right through our little game!', John muttered to me.

I couldn't help thinking that it was a crushing blow for an original Australian work just trying to find its sea legs. All that fucking work! I began to hate the 'theatre' pronounced with a strong upper-class British accent. If they wanted to keep the nation's stages alive with reruns of *Annie* or Shakespeare with tanks, they could, as far as I was concerned. All the creatures of the thespian world seemed to have conspired against us.

We'd already had the sound and lighting technician call in sick on the first night! I began to see the theatre as a big money trap for the unwitting. If you had a show to produce, they'd take your money. But you wouldn't get out of it lightly. Unlike putting a band on in a pub where, at worst, they'd withhold the free beers, you had to pay to hire the room! Then you had to pay for all these people like ushers, marketing people and technicians. These technicians could take sick days at any moment—as if it was the public service. It's amazing that theatre still exists, as there is barely an audience for it. It's subsidised by

John Paul Young performing in *Van Park*.

those who have a burning desire to put on a show and some scary government arts bodies. It felt like a very in-club, that I would never be part of. I really couldn't sleep now.

> They ripped you off! They knew exactly what they were doing. It was a really long run. It shouldn't have been on for that long, at that time of the year, on that side of town.
>
> Fran Bussey, 2015,
> Van Park Lady 1

But I kept going along every night and watching the show from the audience. It wasn't like it was howled down every time, indeed, some shows seemed quite successful, but it felt like hard work getting these audiences on side. Then I spotted a critic in the audience! I couldn't mistake him—he had a grizzled look that I'd seen on many journalists during my newsroom days. I checked with the theatre people. Yes, he was from the Melbourne *Herald Sun*. I understood this to be a sort of tabloid-type paper, like the *Daily Telegraph* in Sydney.

I waited for my moment at intermission—then pounced.

'How are you going?', I said and launched into some friendly small talk. I can't remember what it was about, but I mentioned the *Telegraph* in Sydney and that didn't go down well, as this guy thought the *Herald Sun* was a whole different thing. But I talked him back onside. I thought our earthy humour might resound better with his audience. Then I got onto the subject of our *Age* review and I talked through that with him. 'I did agree with some of her points about the amateurism, but also felt it was part of the general feel of the show. It even sounded like she sort of liked it. But two-and-a-half stars? That was cruel!'

He seemed to be warming to me, and we talked about English pantomime, music hall

Luke Webb and Catriona Hamilton performing in *Van Park*.

'What? You spoke to him! Never talk to a critic! They're like the policemen of the theatre!'

And perhaps John was right. We got through the run anyway. The reviews certainly didn't help draw crowds. In fact, I'm sure they made it even more difficult. But by the last night, I felt the tide was beginning to turn. I'd stopped looking at the website that monitored every single ticket sale at any given moment. It was driving me insane. I decided to just let it be. I couldn't do much else. I was definitely going to lose some money—but what the hell.

It did seem to be beginning to attract some musicians of a certain vintage. As the Chapel on Chapel run drew to its end—I have a clear but foggy memory of a Wiggle, Steve Kilbey and John Paul Young sitting around a table as we partook of some herbal remedies prescribed by the ancients of Ur after a show. It was like the council of Elrond, with a weird collection of Aussie rock elders. However, the subject matter quickly degenerated. John and Steve have an amazing collection of jokes between them that hark back to *The Two Ronnies* and further to English vaudeville. Some of them are even funny. It is a happy memory amidst a difficult run of shows. Indeed, the experience was pretty unpleasant all round. So I did need that ancient prescription.

and cabaret—that's where this show was coming from. I left him to watch the second half and felt I'd done a nice little bit of work for *Van Park*'s publicity department.

The next day, I got my copy of the *Herald Sun* and opened it eagerly. My journalist friend had indeed found comparisons with pantomime. The rating... two stars. The hack cunt.

I whimpered my sad tale to John Paul Young as he emerged for breakfast.

> I knew John Paul Young but I didn't know Steve Kilbey—it was pretty interesting. I've had a few nights like that with really disparate people and in the back of your mind you're going, 'this is really weird.' Because the Wiggles met a lot of famous people. But you couldn't go to wild parties and do crazy stuff in the Wiggles.
>
> Murray Cook,
> the red Wiggle, 2017

Since Murray is now retired from children's entertainment, I don't think any parents are going to come down on him for enjoying a night out. My sources tell me he had no more than legally available alcohol, anyway. Steve Kilbey is a well-known advocate of ancient remedies and John Paul Young came of age in the seventies. It was also one of the rare occasions Steve Kilbey came out of his serviced apartment to join us. He was usually in the habit of getting wired for the show, putting on an amazing performance and bolting back to his room to avoid the weird sycophants that appeared around him every evening.

The very last show saw more local celebrities poke their heads in. Someone from *Neighbours* was apparently there. My old look alike, Paul Kelly, was even there. But more importantly, there seemed to be a reasonable sized group of people who actually liked the show. I sat at the front and watched Steve Kilbey put in an extremely energetic performance. The band sounded magnificently decrepit. The whole cast were pretty much flawless. When I glanced over at Paul Kelly, he appeared to be smiling. Perhaps it was a karmic response to the Lighthouse Keepers giving him a spot on stage, way back in Perth. And there were many more than the usual straggling bunch of dancers getting out of their seats for the finale.

After it was all over, I tied the *Van Park* set on to the roof racks of our faithful stage manager's station wagon and started the long journey back home. I left feeling fairly hollowed out by the whole theatrical experience.

But then, as I drove back along the freeway, I got a clear message from above! It was a phone call, saying that I'd won an iPad.[5] I couldn't actually remember going in a competition for anything. But I was happy to take it anyway. And I took it as a rather period-specific technological message to keep on writing. And I have. Some of the text you read comes to you from that fairly useful object, dear reader.

But…the hand of God reached down again as I drove. A policeman stopped me! I was indeed carrying drugs at the time. Steve Kilbey had given me his stash (as a fiftieth birthday gift) before he took off on Tiger Airways for Sydney. The policeman informed me that they'd got a call from someone on the road saying that there was unsecure material on my car roof. Indeed, the caller was correct. But instead of searching the car, the kind policeman showed me how to do a truckers' knot like a real man…and I was back on the road, *Van Park* sets no longer flapping in the wind.

Another happier end to the *Van Park* story was our return show. For some reason, a Melbourne promoter, Mark Burchett, who'd been pretty good to us back in the Lighthouse Keepers and Widdershins days, wanted to take a risk on the show and bring it to the Carnival of Suburbia in the appropriately named Caravan Club out in the Melbourne suburb of Oakleigh.

He and the Caravan Club owner, Peter Foley, actually put up some money—as opposed to charging us—and off we went again. To cut a long story short, I still lost a bit of money, but not nearly as much. One of the reasons for this was that I saved on keyboard players by joining the band. It was so much better to be up on stage rather than stressing in the audience or backstage. The show went down a treat both nights, and we had good crowds with laughing and dancing in all the right places. Go *Van Park*! And that's where we leave this show—any White Knights out there who want to take this show to the next level—send me an email. That goes for Lady Guineveres of the arts as well.

---

5   This was early days for iPads, so a bit more exciting than it sounds now.

CHAPTER 13

Return of the King

When I mention White Knights, I must pause to mention they do really exist. I have one. He even helped out with *Van Park* here and there. Peter Hall ran some very successful managed funds and is a bit of an Australian Medici character. His great taste in music and people has helped both me and my brother Steve to make music and put on shows. Pete is still co-director of Spontaneous Films with myself. We made a film about *Bossa Nova*, and another about French music that has bred another whacky musical called *Excuse the French*.

I met Pete through his brother Andy, who was a good mate back in the old punk days in Canberra. They happened to live up the road from us, and both of them ended up pretty well off—due to their skills in stock picking. Pete, in particular, has the ability to 'turn one dollar into two' as he has told me. I wish I had that skill. It seems pretty useful. Pete has funded many arts projects over the years. I asked him once if he'd ever made any money from them. The answer was 'nothing…ever.' I guess he sees it differently to stock picking. He just likes good things and wants to spread his money about. A rare creature in Australia.

Although Peter has helped out with a few things, I've largely survived on my own as a freelancer for the last fifteen years or so. It would take too long to go into all the dif-

Me après *Excuse the French*.

Chapter 13 : Return of the King

ferent projects I've worked on—have a look at my website if you're really interested. To make money in the arts, I've had to go pretty low, at points. But there have also been some highs.

Being freelance is not for the fainthearted. I've worked in both government and non-government organisations, as a permanent employee and a freelancer. I would have to say that I would much prefer to employ myself as a freelancer. When I worked for the ABC on staff, the attitude was often slightly contemptuous towards those who might require my services. It was always going to be done a bit later and I never had much respect for the requester. They were a pretty sad old bunch after all—with some really average ideas. But as a freelancer, nothing is too hard, my service is always provided on time and budget and I'm very pleasant company. Grovelling and obsequious even, but the clients seem to like it that way.

Having said that, I do wonder if there is some middle ground. I don't think a grovelling obsequious employee is necessarily creating the best 'product'. Having to agree with every whimsical idea and follow through with it can be a grind, and some pretty bland outcomes the result. I sometimes wish my career was backwards as well (don't we all wish life could be reversed at points?). Freelance first, then ABC staff 'til retirement. As I get older, it gets pretty stressful having to continually scrabble for work. Media is a very cut-throat industry and there are always younger people who are happy to do it for less, while the technology changes rapidly. I'm pretty amazed I've stayed on top of it. I think wistfully back to ABC Archives, where we could balance a ruler on our noses all day long if we wanted—and still get paid time and a half on a weekend! Unions have done some great work, and made working conditions a lot better for a lot more people. However, today we're left with a split community. People with no rights and no conditions in the freelance world,[1] and those who cling to those old-world positions—waiting for that package. As for young people trying to get going amongst all this, I won't even begin. They're a very ripped-off generation, man. According to some shifting demographic markers, I am classified as a baby boomer, but I don't really feel a part of that generation. I hate Jethro Tull! My parents didn't come home from the war, have sex and beget me.

Just to finish up on that employment thought, while I've had the odd White Knight, it's actually been a lot of Lady Guineveres that have got me through the freelance world with my soul intact. Arts ladies can be scary—they love wearing black after all—but they can also be very loyal. I might even have one living in the house!

A short story for those interested in a career in the arts. I was at my White Knight's office quite a few years ago. It was the height of the financial boom, so, before 2008. The office was very modern and there were well-groomed people doing managed fund stuff all over the place. I got talking to one of his main guys and it turned out he used to work in the Australian film industry, not so very far away from my own little media world. He reflected on his time there, and we agreed you didn't do it for the money. 'But the people!' he said, looking at me with a knowing stare. It was a glazed look that only needed a nod from me to confirm. There are indeed some shocking people who find their way into the creative industries. And the ruthless world of finance just didn't seem to compare. I don't know what it is about 'creativity'—a dubious and highly personal term

---

1 I think they call it 'the gig economy' now—perhaps I should have called this chapter 'we've got a gig'...yuk.

Me inside the Sydney Opera House where I have plied my trade as a 'videographer'.

anyway—but get some people together who think they're creative, and throw in some erratic funding, then boil with as many weirdly titled cooks as you can get together, and what do you get? Something yucky...

A large portion of my career has revolved around the ABC in some way. Inside this complex organisation, there are worlds within worlds.

> **I've never seen anyone get ahead who wasn't ruthless...and not very nice.**
>
> Claudia Taranto,
> ABC Radio National, 2018

But then again, I've met some excellent people in these little worlds—I'd even call them friends. Perhaps it's just how it is in the trenches of a small nation's arts enclave. I remember in my staff ABC TV days, sitting there bored and frustrated, wondering if I ever would reach a position in TV where I could come up with an idea and be able to nurture and feel in control of it. That day never came. In fact, I don't know if I've ever seen anyone achieve it in my working life. I've perhaps personally come closer to that goal with radio and, of course, before that with my life in music.

But in the course of battle, there are moments when it seems to all come together—if only for a moment. It can often be quite unexpected. As I've said, I've never quite been able to stop thinking about music. I had pretty much put the guitar away in the early part of this millennium, only picking it up occasionally to do a bit of background music or some such thing. But it's always in the corner, looking at me yearningly.

As the century turned, it so happened that I was living south of Sydney in the pleasant Illawarra region with school-age children. We'd ended up there by way of Sydney's real estate problems and a half-assed *Good Life* attempt (as in the old British TV show). Our kids went to the local government primary school, Thirroul Public. You would think you were back in the 1960s there, with the sun shining on yellow and grey clad chil-

Chapter 13 : Return of the King

dren, who were almost all white (if a little tanned). It was not unlike the Sutherland Shire, where, in fact, a large portion of the population had migrated from.

But as we looked around the quadrangle while waiting awkwardly for our children, it became apparent that there were a lot of muso exiles from the very time I've been writing about. Scattered amongst this nervous group were Rob Younger from Radio Birdman, Jodi Phillis from the Clouds, Tim Oxley, one of the Oxley clan, and even Johnny Batchelor from the Dropbears! Gradually, we began to introduce ourselves and the kids would play with each other. Eventually, we were invited into the homes of these musical exiles.

One of the other parents, Liane Pfister, was a bit of a music fan and saw potential for a musical night that would raise money for the school. Naturally, we were all horrified, but agreed to do it, as Liane was very persuasive—and why not?

So we all appeared at the local pub one night. Liane dealt with the delicate task of who went on and in what order. It all went pretty well, and there was polite applause. Some of the parents appeared to be enjoying it. There was no question of who would go on last. Rob Younger got up with a band of local musicians. With twin electric guitars at full volume they launched into the first of series of covers from punk and Detroit's heydays. It was stuff like MC5, the Damned, and Iggy Pop.

I have rarely seen such a crowd reaction in my life. These people didn't really know the material. I think they were under the impression that this was Radio Birdman, but a few songs into the set, those same people that had waited uncomfortably around the school for their kids with us were taking off their shirts and getting sweaty. Rob put on quite a show, and took those parents on a trip to Suffragette City and back. It was a perfect rendition of all of these songs—one of those unexpected shows where you realise why you got into music.

Rob Younger proved to be a hard-core music fan. He's got an amazingly broad knowledge and is a religious vinyl person. My mind sometimes travels back to Canberra and that Radio Birdman album lying on the floor, caked in blood at Trogg's house. Rob is probably an example of how difficult it is to be a musician in Australia—but he's the real thing and will go for as long as he can. He's also a nice man, and I should not fail to mention his lovely family.

On to another project that came down to me from above. It might be due to age, but I find myself overwhelmed at times with religious-type questions. I'd had vague thoughts about using the structure of a traditional Christian church service in a more lateral way. One day, I was overcome by the urge to actually do something about these thoughts. I didn't think the Illawarra was quite ready for this concept, so I met up with Andrew Errington, one of the reverends at St Stephen's in Newtown, Sydney—just near King Street. He seemed to think it was a good idea.

What I did discover in the course of trying to publicise the project was depth of anti-religious feeling out there in our secular world. It was like Facebook poison, at least to my particular 'friends'. If I posted anything about the event, I was greeted by an overwhelming absence of likes. I think people thought I was trying to convert them, or had some hidden agenda. I was only interested in the meaning of life! I lost some respect for my Facebook pals after this. I let them get back to something simpler, like whining about Tony Abbott. It was that era. And as I write, Donald Trump has spectacularly filled that void.

Steve Kilbey at St Stephen's Church, Newtown.

the love Jesus had for us all, etc. But even then, I knew he was wrong. Maybe the first three Beatles albums were all he'd heard. After that, the love they sang about took a very religious turn. I won't go into my thing about the Beatles becoming a real religion in a hundred years, actual video evidence … John Lennon's shooting … a set of beliefs enshrined in lyrics … the Indian phase … a good set of hymns…I could go on… But I do think love songs, a tradition that I myself dabbled in, filled the gap left by an absence of religion. I just don't know if they really did the job that well.

> **But if at church they would give some ale**
> **And a pleasant fire our souls to regale.**
> **We'd sing and we'd pray all the live-long day,**
> **Nor ever once from the church to stray**
>
> William Blake[2]

Although I was confirmed into the Church of England at a somewhat innocent age, I would now call myself an agnostic on a good day and an atheist on a bad day. The C-of-E is only a small step away from atheism anyway. One thing the sixties took away from us in first world countries was any sort of solid religion. As a young boy, I clearly remember a priest talking to us about the Beatles in the Garran Primary School hall after Sunday school. It was a seventies, triangle-y concrete building that served as a temporary place to practise our alleged religion, as this new suburb had no church yet. The priest told us that when the Beatles were singing about love, it wasn't real love, like

So the idea was to use the structure of a church service to do something meaningful. The event was called 'The Meaning of Life', it referenced Monty Python in a roundabout way. It turned into something like one of those old jokes where an Irishman, a Scotsman and an Englishman walk into a bar….So we had a Buddhist, an atheist and an Anglican each talking for ten minutes about the meaning of life, broken up with some songs from the band that played in *Van Park* (appropriately named the Living Dead).

We had only recently worked with Steve Kilbey when he played the Nebuchadnezzar character in *Van Park*, and I thought the church service would be an ideal place for him to make a cameo, as Steve's impro section was always fun. So I contacted him and he agreed to make an appearance.

But when he turned up on the day, I could see that he was wondering what the hell this

---

2 Yes, I interviewed William Blake.

was all about. I explained as best as I could that it was a show, I didn't know what was going to happen and that was a good thing. I just wanted him to improvise on religious themes in the style of Nebuchadnezzar, the old hippy character he had recently played. He still wasn't too keen. Steve also needed his medicine. Liane, my ever-faithful stage manager, frantically tried to procure some marijuana from the nearby festival to calm his nerves. It didn't happen. He was in a difficult mood and I offered him some of a bottle of whisky I had hidden in the priest's side room, which I was going to use to sooth my own nerves. As the show started up, Steve and his girlfriend took over this room, grabbing the whisky bottle and shutting the door. I had no idea whether he was going to come out.

Steve hardly ever drinks, but as the show started up it seemed like he was making an exception. The band played a couple of songs and a couple of the speakers did their thing. All good. Occasionally, I'd hear a disturbing noise coming from the priest's room.

Nebuchadnezzar's moment came. The door opened and out came Steve. He looked angry—maybe channelling an Old Testament Jehovah. Off he went on his rant. He went up every single pew in the church picking out people to riff off—or at. I was starting to think I might have to go and stop him when one of the congregation got up.

This was a real church-goer who happened to come along out of interest. He accosted the ranting Steve in the middle of an aisle and told him it was 'self indulgent verbal masturbation' and something unchristian sounding. Afterwards we found out this guy thought Steve was for real! I had to intervene urgently. Steve quickly finished up and left the church (yes, synergetic wording).

Our improvised church service finished up with a heartwarming rendition of the

And so we enter the new world: a fake selfie after 'The Meaning of Life' at St Stephen's in Newtown, 2014.

Beatles' 'All You Need is Love', and everyone went away fully entertained. The head priest was a little disturbed, but that's show business. When I went to get my scotch bottle, I saw that the demon drink had played a large part in Nebuchadnezzar's rant. It was nearly empty. Steve Kilbey's girlfriend wrote on Facebook that he'd been a 'very naughty boy'. A reference to *Monty Python's Life of Brian*, younglings. To me, it was all part of the show. I really didn't know that was going to happen. It was certainly interesting. They also let us pass the collection plate around and keep the money for the entertainers. And what do you know? People were quite generous and the show was income positive. A rare day in the arts.

I will finish this chapter with an unexpected glimpse into an arts bureaucracy that actually works! As the years went by, my (*de facto*) partner Amanda and I found ourselves working together in the broader arts world. We have had the good fortune to work with a great group of people in the Aboriginal art sector. It's one of the most rewarding areas of the arts I've been involved with. Around 2014, Amanda and I, and a small group from a large NSW institution, found ourselves in

Recording at Buku–Larrŋgay Mulka Arts Centre, Yirrkala.

Yirrkala, at the tip of Arnhem land in the Northern Territory, looking out over the Arafura Sea. We were documenting and researching an exhibition that was to travel to Sydney.

After an extremely turbulent flight to nearby Nulunbuy, we found ourselves in a different world. It felt a long way from the Australia I had grown up in. At school in Canberra, we learned very little: Arnhem land was a mysterious different coloured section of the map. I had formed an idea back then, that this was the last place where Aboriginal people led a 'traditional life.' Being there and seeing the culture alive in the contemporary world was an adult educational experience for both of us. You could learn a lot by just listening and observing. The landscape was full of meaning, and indeed, made itself known. In the wet season, the climate is literally electric, permanently drenching you in sweat if you walk outside. While if you attempt to cool down, the warm blue ocean is filled with things that want to kill you. It was indeed this magnificent sea that saw me end up in Nhulunbuy Hospital after I slipped on a rock while filming its beautiful lapping!

But the real surprise was waiting at the Buku–Larrŋgay Mulka Centre at Yirrkala. The local Yolgnu community run this arts centre and have kept the same manager for over twenty years. Will Stubbs just happens to be one of the original Lighthouse Keepers fans from way back in Canberra, where he studied law at Australian National University. Yes, a white guy. It's a long story how Will ended up at Yirrkala, but it sounds

Chapter 13 : Return of the King

like a TV series to me. A drunken, pigtailed, defence lawyer, travelling around the Northern Territory having a head spin every episode, 'til he marries a Yolgnu woman and ends up in Yirrkala.

Will appeared to us to be fluent in Yolgnu, though he described his linguistic level as 'taxi-driver'. He was very much part of the community and is fascinated by Yolgnu culture and the post-colonial history of Yirrkala. We asked him one question on camera, and an hour later, he finished. Quite a journey of an answer, but both entertaining and enlightening. Still, he remains sentimental about his earlier life. I was personally introduced to anyone who would listen, as a rock star. Little did the Yolgnu know.[3] But this brings me to the arts bureaucracy in place at Yirrkala. Long recognised as a thriving arts community, works from Yirrkala are exhibited in galleries around the world. The Buku Art Centre has been a big part of that success.

As we stayed there, we began to learn about the arts centre's system of paying artists. This is how I understand it. The Yolgnu people employ the arts centre staff. Everyone in the community who wants to make a piece of art can sell it at a negotiated price. Therefore, much art is created and the art centre is a place of continual activity. People coming in with barks, painting *larrakitj* (hollow logs), working in the various studios and doing all sorts of artsy things. Cheques were continually being handed out at the front desk. In Yirrkala, everyone who wants to be an artist and makes art, is paid for their art. Somehow, the forces of supply and demand work to make sure there was enough high quality work coming in from

Will Stubbs, Co-ordinator, Buku-Larrŋggay Mulka Centre.

the better artists. I can't quite explain how this works, but it does. Then there are all sorts of corporate types in tropical gear circling, paying a lot of money for big collections of *larrakitj* to go in their skyscraper foyers.

Have the Yolgnu come up with the perfect arts bureaucracy? Where the system might break down in the big city arts world, is with money sharing. Yolgnu artists often divide their earnings with extended families. So a good *larrakitj* artist might be supporting ten people, a hundred kilometres away. In this community, art can actually provide an income without a form in sight. The obvious next step would be to disband the Australia Council, and split all the money saved, between anyone who made an artwork in Australia. They might have to sign it in blood to show they were legit. But I guess you've got to have someone to supervise this process and the whole thing begins again. They need support staff…

---

3   Will Stubbs is related by marriage to Mandawuy Yunupingu. A real rock star. Sadly we went to his funeral ceremony while at Yirrkala. An honour to attend this community event that went for many days.

CHAPTER 14

Love Beacon

James Cruickshank.

I remember a recent article entitled, 'Australia—too boring?' from some British (of course) online source. However, it did ring true, and brings me to the conundrum facing all those who live in this lovely place, especially the artists who try to eke out a living here. I grew up in Canberra, which must be the ultimate concrete tribute to the nation's lust for dullness. It's easy to criticise Canberra, and the current inhabitants don't like it if you do but, then again—why are they so touchy?

Chapter 14: Love Beacon

I am fond of Australia, and you may find it hard to believe, but Canberra was a small child's dream world. Only one problem: it could get a little boring. Perhaps that's where my need to put on shows, create stuff and generally do things all came from. I have met many fellow Australian creative adventurers along the way now trying to do the same thing. They might not come from Canberra, but Australia itself is incredibly suburban. While the ethnic mix of Australia has changed, the culture is still all about lifestyle and houses.

But do artists have to suffer? I certainly didn't. I might suffer a little psychological hardship now and then but, as you've read, I've had a pretty good run. I've spent much of my life seeking pleasure, which must be some sort of Australian credo. I've listened to a lot of speculation on why it's so hard in the arts here. There's not enough people, the weather is too good, a high rate of smartphone addiction, the people are too lazy and so on. It's always better somewhere else. Like the surf. My studies tell me that musicians automatically get the dole in France, and it's not even called the dole—it's *le* something pretty respectable. Or is America where it's at? Maybe not just at the moment. Perhaps China? Even New Zealand seems to produce a lot more good stuff than we do.

But as on that slightly tragic night many years ago in Hamburg, when my two Australian band mates were fighting in front of me, I have always wanted to come home. But the arts in Australia? You've got through a fair bit of bellyaching, dear reader. Is there anything we can take away with us?

Do the general population want art or music? They don't really seem to care that much. On the one side, government-funded arts is a nightmarish world. Then, on the other, the average person who might pay for a bit of something is almost impossible to get out of their chairs and away from their many screens. American product is omnipotent. Sport is the one obvious exception. You only have to go to any reasonable-sized sporting event, then down to a bar to see one of those things still called bands, to realise where people's heads are at. I don't know if I can blame these sports lovers either. It's a lot more of a clear-cut outing to see a couple of good teams going for it than some self-absorbed band bleating about nothing much. And, of course, there are bands that are actually popular…

But the rest of us struggle on. I guess that's a positive. Occasionally, you do see someone doing something good. There might be twenty people who like it, there might be more. Again, it helps to be young. There are new generations continually entering that period when they really want to get out of the house and meet someone… even if it means going to a live show.

Not so long ago, I was doing a phone interview with Warren 'Pig' Morgan as research for a rock documentary. He was the keyboard player for John Paul Young's All Stars from way back in the 1970s and has played with all sorts of people over time. The All Stars are still a touring band and quite an inspiring act. All getting on in years, they produce an incredibly powerful pop/rock sound—based around an amazing collection of Vanda and Young songs.

Pig had come along to see John Paul Young, who was in *Van Park*, when we performed at the Sydney Fringe Festival some years ago. He knew I'd been involved and made some nice comments about it. During the interview, I told him I'd written the show. His tone changed to a mixture of admiration and sympathy. 'You're on the ship and you can't walk away.'

I'd often felt John's real band were like living versions of what we'd tried to recreate in *Van Park*, with its storyline about a gaggle of musicians who are forced into budget accommodation, yet refused to give up the dream. And perhaps my own story has elements of this, although in reality I can't complain about my housing situation. While talking with Pig in that disembodied way that modern communications brings with it, the feeling of a shared path was mutual. I often find mature musicians have lost the plot somewhere in their thirties, and they can get bitter, but John Paul Young's band just get better with age.

In the UK, if you've done something, you're on a pillar forever. In Australia, it's like—isn't that the cheesy person I liked when I was teenager? You can't like them anymore...unless you're Paul Kelly.[1]

Tim Pittman, promoter

I have quite a few comrades who've persisted with the artistic struggle in Australia's suburban wastes—with mixed results.

Not long ago, James Cruickshank, my luckiest friend, took me by surprise. The following conversation was recorded after he'd had some pretty heavy medical news. I had gone to see him in person and was surprised by his relatively good mood. I asked if he still had the young girlfriend that I'd last seen him with. No, he'd got rid of her as he didn't want to go through his adolescence again. So it must be hard to deal with this alone, I wondered. But he told me he did still have company. Apparently, three different women would rotate on call, to hop into bed with him and help him through it all. Even in these circumstances, he had a bit of his old luck left.

Men aren't that good with this sort of thing. They're a bit awkward and just want to know if you're still drinking.

James Cruickshank, 2015

So we sat there drinking some tea, as he ingested his cannabis oil. We had the best conversation we'd had for years. I thought he was taking it all really well, amazingly well. Strangely, some of the more astral philosophies that he'd spouted now sounded meaningful. Anyway, I'm trying to put this conversation in perspective. I had told him I was putting this book together, but I wasn't intending to record anything. Just catch up with him and see how he was going. But at one point, we both thought what the heck, and switched on the digital device everyone carries with them now.

The question I wanted to ask him went something like this: he'd been in the Widdershins with me, and was part of a whole group of people around us who were trying to do something—struggling away. Making music, selling records, doing creative stuff. Then James suddenly made it. He became a real rock star with the Cruel Sea and made the Australian Top 10. He even got a heroin habit at thirty. So how did it feel?

"Really?" he said, (denying we wanted to be famous). "I guess we did have those crumbs, like the Go-Betweens or the Triffids—our peers had been to Europe and made it... there was evidence that you could actually do it."

"But," I said, "you went further than them, in that you had actual chart hits in Australia... but I guess you never really had the overseas cred."

Maybe I was just a typical jealous muso, trying to undercut his international image.

"Well, that's not quite true, Greg. We had a profile in Europe. We just worked pretty much flat out for all that time. There was a time when we first had a hit in Australia, a guy upstairs was playing our record all the time, driving me crazy, but I didn't want to say, 'stop it!'."

---

1 Yes, another Paul Kelly reference! Let's just leave that one hanging there.

Chapter 14 : Love Beacon

I pressed him on why he became a heroin addict. No clear reason. It seemed like that was just what you did and he had some examples in the band to follow.

And so it went on 'til I came back to the rock star thing. What about the naked women, the great drugs? Didn't he enjoy that?

"A lot of it's just work... I think one per cent of actors and musicians are living that life... but I still think that music is the greatest thing you can do...even scientists have proven it, Greg. Nothing lights up that part of your brain like music."

"Not even a good shot of heroin?"

"No, nothing like music."

"What if you've had a good shot, you've got a naked woman on top of you and great music is playing in the background?..."

But he backed away from my adolescent inquiries.

"No, the life I've had is just extraordinary because of it... though in Australia, it was never enough to be an artist, people always wanted to know what else I did."

I changed tack...

"As a musician, I often felt slightly resentful of people that made it, but I never felt that about you and the Cruel Sea."

I was starting to get a bit emotional (I was only drinking tea, remember). James continued to talk positively...

"I'm very grateful for all that, I couldn't do anything else—I'm totally useless as a human being in terms of the workforce. I think it's a really wonderful thing making music. Like making interesting air. I think music's just a wonderful window to other dimensions."

Other dimensions do sound interesting. On a good day, I might agree with James... on a bad day, maybe it sounds like drivel. I do know that I've had a lot of fun at these artistic portholes to another dimension, real or imagined. To be immersed in the moment seems to be about the closest I've come to feeling anything meaningful. James's funeral was a few weeks later. It was an eclectic gathering of people from his life.

> I spoke at James's funeral. He knew I would. So did I. In a cottage on a hill, I viewed his body. I'd only spoken to him days before. He wore a lovely pinstripe suit that he had bought for the occasion. I patted his cold forehead, beaded with a slight thaw on such a spectacular Spring day.
>
> With encouragement from family and friends and James himself, I lifted the lid on his life and we explored the maddening contradictions of the luckiest man in the room.
>
> At the wake, I discovered that every single person had spoken to James in the last days! He had worked the room like he was backstage with a vodka and orange. I felt slightly betrayed but had to laugh to think that he could manage to annoy me even in death. He had left, surrounded by women—sister, mother, friend and lover, at home and the last thing he did was eat a bowl of Coco Pops. And while it's a cliche, I know now that there is no better way to go out and I pray I should be so lucky.
>
> Ken Gormly, Cruel Sea, 2017

Like Ken, I was also asked to speak at James's funeral. It was one of the hardest things I've ever done. I don't know if our generation has come to terms with death. I certainly haven't, have you? A valium helped me through. It was a surreal setting, amongst fountains, with the bright Australian sun beating down. The congregation were an odd collection of inner-city musos of a certain vintage. But I think James would have been impressed. Who knows? There's a very small chance he was hovering over the coffin.

CHAPTER 15
Hoogle Waltz

The Lighthouse Keepers reunion in 2011: `pling (Kevin William Prideaux), another lost comrade, taking a photograph. This photo taken by Jake Lloyd Jones.

And so we come to nowadays, although it's almost pointless trying to capture that moment, as it changes quickly. Or does it? Back in my youth, we looked forward with overly optimistic glasses. People landed on the moon when I was in primary school, so of course you would expect to be holidaying there in the reasonably near future.[1] I look around now. Things look more or less the same. A few more cars, a few more people, a lot more racial variety, but the same mix of ugly

1 No one really knew what we were going to do up there.

Chapter 15 : Hoogle Waltz

what does the Top 40 sound like now, compared to the ones I pulled out for you earlier? Is there such a thing? I don't think people could concentrate for forty songs anymore.

So to finish off, I'm going where few older people dare to tread. The Australian Record Industry Top 10 for 2017. I'm going to listen to all the songs, at least a few times and see what's happening out there…

ARIA TOP 10 2017	
1. SHAPE OF YOU	Ed Sheeran
2. DESPACITO	Luis Fonsi & Daddy Yankee feat. Justin Bieber
3. CASTLE ON THE HILL	Ed Sheeran
4. PERFECT	Ed Sheeran
5. SOMETHING JUST LIKE THIS	The Chainsmokers & Coldplay
6. THUNDER	Imagine Dragons
7. GALWAY GIRL	Ed Sheeran
8. HUMBLE	Kendrick Lamar & Skrillex
9. GLORIOUS	Macklemore feat. Skylar Grey
10. THERE'S NOTHING HOLDIN' ME BACK	Shawn Mendes

buildings and suburban waste set amongst Australia's harsh natural beauty. People even seem to listen to the same music—it's hard to avoid in supermarkets. A loop from my teenage years follows me everywhere.

Of course, computing and gizmos have really intruded where we might have previously had Space Invaders, two channels on TV and limited access to our parents' home phone. But somehow, these new devices inhabit another dimension, connected to a void we are all being drawn into. Let's hope it's a nice place we're going.[2]

But I still wonder at the continuing re-branding of older styles in faster loops. And

I had been dreading this experiment, but thought I should give it a go to be balanced. So first, the good news. It was far better than I expected. From the first dong of Ed Sheeran's 'Shape of You', I realised that I'd actually heard this diabolically catchy riff. I guess these things play in the background of the world I am still part of. In fact, Ed Sheeran[3] has four out of the ten songs—so I heard a fair amount of this artist. He's got red hair too! *Revenge of the Nerds* was a truly prophetic film. While

---

2 Even since I wrote the first draft in 2015, the mood has changed. The internet has become darker. That feeling of surveillance is becoming more oppressive. *1984*'s 'big brother' turned out to be us all along. Everyone is watching, everyone's a journalist, everyone's got an opinion on everything… please give my book five stars. (and even since I wrote this footnote! – it's 2020; say no more – I think I'll be updating this for a while to come).

3 Time has moved on but it didn't really matter what year I listened to the Top 10. Since writing this, Ed has toured Australia and played to some ridiculous proportion of the population. I learned via my son's girlfriend that he played the whole concert himself! Now there's a musician making money still. But see previous footnote re 2020…

I don't think I'll be going out of my way to download his music, he has a good voice and the songs are almost moving…almost. I guess he is the one who has taken up that sensitive but rocking baton that I referred to way back at the start—U2 being the prime exponent. He doesn't seem to be political, not in the four songs I got to know, but still… In this vein, I noticed Coldplay were hanging in there with a co-song. This pairing up seems to be a common thing nowadays. That's nice that musos are putting aside their personal animosity.

The more negative news. Remember, I'm getting on in years. I'm left with a feeling of blandness. I think those earlier charts had a bit more variety. One song that did jump out was 'Humble', rapped by Kendrick Lamar, remixed by someone called Skrillex. This one sounds like something the Linda Blair character from *The Exorcist* might sing at the height of her possession. It seems like you can say 'fuck' as much as you want in the pop charts now: it's just like TV! The lyrics remind me of what some country town audiences used to yell at Juliet during our inland tours with the Lighthouse Keepers. You can't quite make it out, but it doesn't sound very polite. While I have mixed feelings about rap and hip-hop, you have to admire its resilience as a genre.

To continue with the negatives. Has music production improved since the eighties in this pop end of the market? Not much. Quincy Jones got it right with *Thriller*. There is also a tendency for young male vocalists to use what I'll call a baby voice, too often. Try saying 'baby', like 'beebee', and then sing every word in this accent and you'll be getting close. But overall, better than expected. People keep making music and the pop machine keeps rolling.

If a tree falls in the forest, will anybody hear it?

Ken Gormley, Cruel Sea, 2017

This is a quote from a conversation I had with Ken at his café in Marrickville. He was referring to the fact that as we age, we don't really listen to anything that's current, if anything at all. Perhaps that's why talk-back radio is so big with the oldies. They find music too loud and annoying.

Many of the people from the period when the Lighthouse Keepers had their crack at the scene are thoroughly neutered. For instance, I've been to a few parties for people reaching significant ages, full of record industry luminaries from back in those days. At the time, I would have been all a-quiver with how to approach them as they held forth to their sycophants and revelled in their powers. But now, nothing. You can go up and talk to them like normal people. In some ways, this is relaxing, in other ways a bit of downer. Maybe we have all kind of given up?

I find ex-music industry people often have similar stories to my own, if taken on different paths, with different levels of notoriety. And even my own small successes can seem like quite a career to an outsider. Yet I know from the inside that it doesn't always feel like that.

But now, dear reader, I bring you in a full circle. Like a waltz. Returning to my own family as we finish this tale. Because within it lies the full music biz journey, and conveniently, it's where I began the story. My daughter, Zelie, speaks at a family gathering:

Sometimes, I worry that music isn't really progressing like it used to.

Jane Wexler, my (de facto) father-in-law's third wife replies:
'Thank goodness you said that!'

Jane has been involved in the music business as a singer/pianist. She voices an opinion that many older people share about the state of music today.

But as we talk, I realise that in the room, we had someone who had lived the whole

Chapter 15 : Hoogle Waltz

thing. Jane's husband, my partner's father, Brian Peacock, has followed a similar trajectory to me in some ways, yet in an earlier era. He's a real baby boomer,[4] and became a lot more famous than I ever did. Especially in New Zealand, that country just across the Tasman Sea. It's kind of like Australia with better geography. With arts and music, you'd have to say New Zealand has done pretty well too. But Brian humbly admits he began his career as a pure Beatles imitator. I couldn't resist pulling out a handy gizmo and interviewing Brian. So I'll let him tell his story.

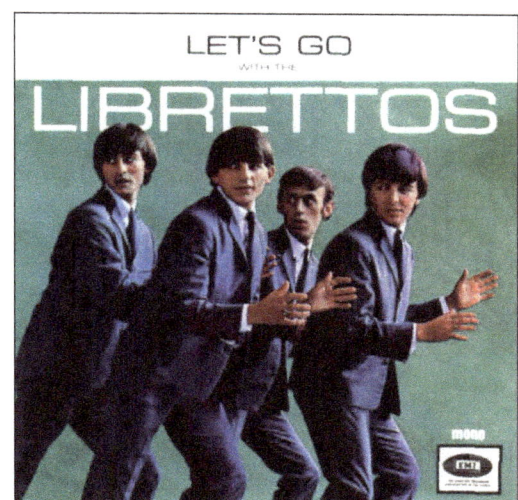

Brian Peacock (far right).

> I grew up in the fifties with the tail end of the old straight pop music of the forties and then the blast of rock'n' roll. From the age of ten, I knew that was what I really wanted to do. New Zealand at the time was one of the most isolated places on earth, it had less than two million people. Growing up in a small town in the South Island, the only entertainment you had was the radio. You had no exposure to any public performance of rock.
>
> I built my first bass guitar. I guess there were people who played piano but I didn't know anyone who played the guitar. I taught myself from scratch, just listening to the radio. I identified that there was some instrument playing the bottom line in the recordings. I didn't know how to play guitar, but I worked out the bass line.
>
> Brian Peacock, 2016

It was a cunning move to learn the bass. To me, the archetypical bass player does have a slightly Machiavellian touch, pragmatic might be a better word. So Brian was scouted by the Librettos, New Zealand's top band, who happened to be blatant Beatles imitators. You could call them groundbreaking in the cover band genre that was to sweep nearby Australia in a few decades, a genre that has grown to be one of the mainstays of the local music industry. Back to Brian's tale.

> We were just kids, really. We had the grey suits and imitation Beatle haircuts. We had our own TV show *Let's Go With The Librettos*. It was a great demonstration of the power of television. Suddenly, we were a household name and I went from playing in a bar band to being recognised in the street from television. When we toured, the whole town would come out to see us.
>
> We played some amazing shows, like supporting Roy Orbison and the Rolling Stones on their first New Zealand tour. Then the (real) Beatles came through and we played with them. I remember sneaking into their dressing room in the bowels of the Wellington Town Hall. There was no security, and we picked up their guitars and played them while they weren't around.

---

4   Unlike me, who's been reclassified after the fact—which is annoying as it's a horrible pair of words—my argument for not being a baby boomer is Billy Idol's first band was called Generation X. Now, Billy is older than me, and he wouldn't name his band anything other than the most current generation, would he?

Brian Peacock (right).

Pam and Brian, with a very young Amanda.

The Librettos took Brian to Australia. At some point, he fathered my partner with Pam Peacock (then Pam Irving), just when Melbourne was becoming a rock'n'roll hot spot (at least in the southern hemisphere). Brian and Pam really lived the sixties like you see in re-enactments. When I look at their photos from this period, they almost look fake.

They were amongst a small contingent that did the sixties thing in Australia—in the actual sixties. There was a lot of money coming into the music industry then. Pam told me that some of it was criminal money. She had direct experience of this when she was a Playboy bunny. She worked in the Melbourne Playboy club and, the way she tells it, the criminals looked after her real good and made sure the customers didn't get too frisky with the rabbits.

The Mafia that ran that club were the best people I've ever worked for.

Pam Peacock, 2017

Pam and Amanda.

Pam Peacock.

Chapter 15 : Hoogle Waltz

There's always been a criminal fringe to the music business. Legend goes that a lot of London's seed finance in the swinging sixties was based on money laundering. It was there that Brian had a period playing with Normie Rowe from 1966, an Aussie teen sensation who had got a bit old. He was now into his twenties and trying to crack the UK. Normie wanted a backing band that would make him look groovier! Normie Rowe and the Playboys toured with some unlikely combinations like Gene Pitney on the same bill as the Troggs! It didn't quite happen, but out of the remnants of Normie's band, Brian formed Procession. This was a more original group, but they still had a strong Beatles influence—*The White Album*—now.

The UK mansion.

> I did meet some of the Beatles. Most of the night-life in London happened in the very early hours of the morning. After all the regular gigs were over, all the British rock royalty would congregate in these small clubs like the Bag O'Nails and the Speakeasy, where Procession often played. At about one in the morning, they'd all start rolling in. We'd be playing and you'd have Paul McCartney on one side and George Harrison on the other. Or Eric Clapton—anyone you could imagine—all just hanging out. My daughter Amanda—your partner—was with us when we moved into a big country mansion.

After living the sixties rock star life in the mansion, Brian and Pam then moved to Australia and did the real hippy commune thing. They lived with 'the Universal brotherhood' in rural Western Australia. Again, they were part of a small authentic group of Australian hippies. These people were trying to get back to nature and mixed it up with a bit of reinterpreted Christianity. But unlike the American variety of communes, this one finished without a massacre, just a whole lot of craziness. By the end of it all, the marriage was over.

Amanda and friend.

Brian Peacock rehearsing.

But Brian kept going with all sorts of jobs in the music industry—from roadie to manager. He managed a few Australian eighties bands like the Eurogliders and Wa Wa Nee. The Lighthouse Keepers were very anti these kind of bands. They were successful and lived in a different world to us. I can still safely say I don't feel much for Aussie new romantics—or British ones for that matter. Anyway, Brian was part of that whole coke-snorting,[5] back-slapping world that I was not part of. They were having the last party before it all fell in a heap.

> What happened to the music industry was a really early example of the disruption that's happened in nearly every industry. It happened before anyone recognised it. The digital era changed the ownership of the rights to music—artist rights, songwriters' rights have been trashed—making it much harder to make a living.
>
> While I think people are still doing it, they're having to go back and rewrite the book of how you do it. They're experimenting at the moment. At one point, you could claim to be a bit of an expert on how to be successful in the music business—not anymore.

And as a side note, another family member, my brother Rob, was involved in the music business at the same time as Brian. He was a dot.com millionaire for a while with Chaos Music, a pioneering Australian online music site. For a while, you could see Chaos.com signs all over buses in Melbourne and Sydney, and he ran a big office full of groovers in a refurbished warehouse in Surry Hills. No doubt he mixed in the same circles as Brian. Rob was a direct part of all the 'disruption', and possibly working against the interests of both me and our brother, Steve, in King Curly. I remember him talking to me about what was over the horizon for musos—and it wasn't much money. It turned out to be all the iTunes and Spotifys and the ever-shrinking physicality of recorded music. Never mind—we did have some family shares in Chaos. Rob found the whole industry pretty ugly, and is now much happier as a Telco[6] millionaire. Hopefully, he can keep his money this time.

After all his music experience Brian Peacock ran Export Music Australia out of a government department. Maybe the straights had taken over. But Brian enjoyed his life in an industry that was disrupted and crushed, and still remains resolutely positive.

> It was a fantastic experience to have a working life in the music industry and seeing it from so many different vantage points. Experiences like Jimi Hendrix's first show when he came over to London—in a tiny club, supported by Fats Domino! People can't imagine what it was like. The main negative is seeing success followed by failure further down the line. I've seen

---

5 I don't think Brian was a coke-snorting type, BTW.

6 It's impossible to keep this up to date, as time moves on. No longer the case as of 2019, but house in Sydney purchased with proceeds from this Telco period.

Chapter 15 : Hoogle Waltz

so many become successful but not be able to sustain it—for so many reasons. I've seen it myself as a songwriter... I have come very close to having an international hit.

In some ways, Brian is now living his original counter-culture dream, but in more comfort, in a Victorian cliff-top house overlooking Bass Strait. As whales romp in the distance, he tends the organic garlic patch. he doesn't like to relive the past. So I was lucky to interview him.

> You can be so good you break through by sheer force of talent, but a lot of people get there by hard work and a modicum of talent. You can do that, and a lot of luck comes into play...maybe it's lucky for my bands that we didn't succeed, because once you have success, you have to sustain it. There are many different levels of success, and even to be great and not successful—there's no dishonour in that. There are a lot of ways to be successful without fame and fortune.

But Brian isn't the only positivist amongst music industry veterans. Tim Pittman, the slightly dour,[7] Alice Cooper-looking promoter, still makes a living through live shows. He also ran a CD label for a while. The Lighthouse Keepers were one of the bands he put out as reissues. I knew the recording industry had been disrupted when I got an email from Tim saying he was shutting down the label. Not long ago, I went and retrieved a few boxes of Lighthouse Keepers CDs that he couldn't sell anymore. No one buys them, they barely pay for a download. We talked about how they still hadn't come far enough with holograms to disrupt live music just yet—according to him it's still a healthy scene:

> There's so much good music out there now, same as there ever was.

Repressed Records: Nick with a Lighthouse Keepers CD.

I responded that it didn't seem like there were many places left to play, especially in Sydney, and the whole music industry had more or less collapsed...

> It's hard in any era. You have to be good enough to cut it.

Perhaps a lot of it is about knowing when you don't cut it, and bowing out gracefully. Australia is still a warm place to curl up in. Many musicians find themselves back in their country of birth. So I will leave you with some thoughts on music, and life in the Antipodes.

> When I came back in 1988, I was shocked by this world where the Indigenous people were up in arms, but no one else seemed to care. I didn't really want to come back. The only reason I decided to come back to Australia was to have a baby. It's so much easier in Australia. In London, you're poor and you're in a freezing house. Here you don't freeze. It's a huge thing. If you're making a decision about bringing up a child, you're going to choose Australia, because you know it's going to be easier.
>
> Lindy Morrison, 2016

---

[7] Tim is also an honest promoter and remains a music fan. Both not that common in the trade.

Zelie Appel and Murray Wiggle.

Then there were the people that used to come to our shows. Academic and rock writer David Nichols was one of them. He didn't seem to think Australia's warm climate affected the creativity of the nation when I asked him.

> The climate? There's plenty of creative people in Australia. I don't know why you'd ask that question. All artists have to compromise—how can they not? What counts against Australia perhaps is its small population. But isolation works for us overall. I think we're in a very privileged position as we can view other places and make our own version that references things and other parts of the world. Because we're relatively well educated.
>
> David Nichols, 2016

So perhaps Australia is an arts paradise! The Australian indie scene from the eighties, which formed the core of this book, did have some unexpected reverberations on the wider world. While you wouldn't call the Wiggles 'indie', they had their roots in that same Sydney scene.

> In America, it sometimes seemed like 'pinch me' stuff for the Wiggles. Round about 2002–2008, we were on the Disney Channel in America and it just went through the roof, we played Madison Square Garden and things like that—6,000-seat arenas. The kids were the same everywhere but in America, the parents could be quite loud… and it was because of that one record the Wiggles made at uni.
>
> Murray Wiggle, 2017

The Wiggles have also sidestepped any highbrow rock criticism, or mental daggers from jealous musos.

> A lot of musicians were quite proud of us—I feel fortunate. I think we found a niche that no one else did. Taking it to America was really the key to ongoing financial success.
>
> Murray Wiggle, 2017

John Paul Young might refer to his music as 'Wiggles for adults', but the real Wiggles have regenerated like Doctor Who and have replicas out there earning money. For myself, the Wiggles' music can cause flashbacks to the previously mentioned difficult-child-rearing-period. And by the end of the process of writing this book, I'd enlisted my own Wiggle-sat child, Zelie, as part of the information-gathering process. She interviewed Murray herself, along with a few of the other interviewees who have appeared, like Lindy Morrison, who was ready with some career advice.

> Would I go into music as a young person? I certainly didn't want my daughter to do it. It was a terribly hard life. I just fell into it. I was acting and playing the drums and I was very political. I was just caught up in the punk movement in Brisbane. I think it's so very hard to make money in the music industry—there are so many factors—so I probably wouldn't be encouraging young people. Lots of people still work in the industry but, to be a musician, there are so many sacrifices. It's such

Chapter 15 : Hoogle Waltz

Lighthouse Keepers reunion gig.

a gamble, whether or not you're going to keep making a living, particularly as you get older. Okay, interview done.

Lindy Morrison,
the Go-Betweens, 2017

And I return for one last time to the musings of my fellow band members from the Lighthouse Keepers.

> I enjoyed being a musician immensely, though I suppose I didn't know what I really wanted. I suspended my disbelief and went for the ride. I would say it was good sort of thing. In terms of money and property, I'd say no—though I never saw myself as a 'professional' musician but a 'full-time' one. I kept playing, recording and touring in bands after the Lighthouse Keepers, and even when I moved overseas, I still occasionally played publicly. A feature of the intervening years has been a radical change in the music scene; not only the expected changes in tastes, but more importantly the slow death of the live scene.

Blue, Lighthouse Keepers

If you want to know what happened to the rest of the Lighthouse Keepers; Hairy went on with his partner Fran Gibson to play in the Cannanes for the last thirty years or so, while Steven Williams became a sauna mogul in Queensland. Juliet wanted me to make her into a mysterious figure that disappeared into the ether. But I was talking to her on the phone just the other day…

> I was just sorry that I couldn't enjoy it more. But that's what youth is about. I was an unhappy girl a lot of the time. But I was happy while I was singing. I

found performing incredibly cathartic and I've made some fantastic friends. I think music is a language and when you find people that can speak that as well, it's incredibly rewarding experience. And it probably nearly killed me a few times as well.

Unhappy talk again? I wanted to understand what Juliet was talking about before I finished this book. We'd spent six years living together. She was making me unhappy in a historically revisionist kind of way…

There is a thing you do when you're younger and you practise playing with emotions and practise being depressed, you create a little drama so you can play the jilted whatever. What hit me like a truck was a real thing that was going to happen and I couldn't believe it was real. I'm talking about my brother and trying to cram so much love down his throat in a short time, which scared him too.

Juliet's brother Barnaby was both haemophiliac and HIV positive and lived longer than many people expected. I remember after Juliet and I split up, I sometimes saw her with him. They were very physical together and got around in matching animal tails for a while. It was quite a look and they obviously had an intense relationship that had grown over time. Unfortunate yet again, Barnaby just missed the new antiretroviral HIV drugs. But his own music[8] has proved resilient and Juliet keeps the flame alive.

I don't see Juliet very often, but we stay in touch. We are all a bit wary of playing with the Lighthouse Keepers again. I don't think we wanted to tamper with something that was special for us. But we have occasionally, and it's been a largely positive experience. You feel a little of the power of those acts like John Paul Young who can trigger overwhelming nostalgia with their music. In our case, it's to

8 As Baterz and with the Bedridden.

Chapter 15 : Hoogle Waltz

a smaller audience, but nonetheless enthusiastic. They seem to want the same shambolic sounds, delivered in the same unprofessional way. And for us, it's also powerful. We are taken back thirty years. Songs come back to life, hands form guitar chord shapes automatically, and we look awkwardly at each other across the stage once again. I remember how I lived in the moment, so much more than I do now. Damn that brain wiring once again.

My mother said to me recently, 'What happened to you? You were such a happy child?' Still something of a child, I didn't answer her. I just thought to myself, 'It's pretty obvious, you idiot. I was crushed!'[9] On reflection, it's not quite so simple. I did have a fantastic childhood. So good, it's probably sickened a few readers. On top of this, I had creative dreams I wanted to pursue, once I'd passed through the black hole of adolescence. But to be honest, these dreams were a bit vague. A lot of people will tell you to be true to your dreams. I don't really subscribe to that philosophy, as it can send you on some disappointing roads. I think for me it was a succession of crushings, then re-inflatings. My dreams have good and bad days. This can wear you down. But although I am a little road weary, I also know I have had a pretty good journey so far. I'm just not very good at acknowledging that.

And so, we suddenly come to the conclusion. It's been so good having you, dear reader. It's difficult to say goodbye. I guess my own advice would be to always have a back up-plan, I just can't quite remember what mine was. Something to do with accountancy. There have been a couple of times I've gratefully pulled out of accountancy courses over the years when some more interesting work comes along. I do know I am lucky to have a beautiful family. And my daughter had this advice for me on a particular day that comes round every year. Which I will share with you, without permission...

---

9 Sorry, mum.

Dear Dad,

Once again, it is your birthday. Also once again, you seem to be quite stressed—how many calming birthday cards will I need to write before you agree to de-stress? Maybe you could have some vitamin B—I hear it is very helpful!

But the point is, you really don't need to worry. Think instead about everything you have achieved, which is so much. (Why else would you be writing an autobiography?!)

You've chosen the noble, creative path in life, and hasn't it turned you into a far greater and happier person?—the object of admiration and interest for all my friends.

PS Jack was just the other night marvelling at the wonders of your cassette collection. ('Greg and I just have the same music taste!')

Hey, maybe you could make a documentary about those who chose 'the noble route'.

Anyway, before I run out of space, HAPPY BIRTHDAY!

Thank you for being such a loving and supportive father, who is also great company!

I really appreciate it. Lots of love from your daughter,

Zelie xoxoxo

APPENDICES

Discography

The Lighthouse Keepers

Gargoyle / Demolition Team / Quick Sticks
Guthugga Pipeline Records GPR 001
7-inch single
Released March 1983
(500 more pressed late 1983)
Picture sleeves stamped and painted by the band.

The Exploding Lighthouse Keepers
Guthugga Pipeline Records GPR 004
12-inch EP
Released 1983
Recorded at Dream Studios, Haymarket, Sydney.
Engineered and produced by Keith Hale.
Whisky & Gin recorded in bathroom at Hugo Street, Chippendale.
Hand coloured wrap-around sleeve with lyric insert.

SIDE ONE
- Springtime
- Again
- The Beat (I Want My Loving Back)

SIDE TWO
- Bad Mood
- Narvel Felts Goes to Town
- Whisky & Gin

Gargoyle / Demolition Team / Quick Sticks
Hot Records HOT 713
7-inch single (reissue)
Released May 1984

Ocean Liner / A Sad Tale
7-inch single
Hot Records HOT 720
Released November 1984

Confessions of a Lighthouse Keeper: Greg Appel

Tales of the Unexpected
12-inch LP
Hot Records HOT 1011
Released November 1984

SIDE ONE
- Wheels Over the Desert
- Lip Snipe Groin
- No Reason
- A Time of Evil
- Jazz Song
- Power Ring
- We've Got a Gig

SIDE TWO
- Ocean Liner
- Love Beacon
- Big Noise
- Lighthouse Keepers
- Wilder Beast
- Evil Touch
- Torture Road

Ode to Nothing / Seven Years
Hot Records HOT 724
7-inch single
Released August 1985

Imploding
Waterfront DAMP 33
12-inch LP compilation
Released November 1986

SIDE ONE
- Gargoyle
- Demolition Team
- Quick Sticks
- Springtime
- Again
- The Beat (I Want My Loving Back)

SIDE TWO
- Seven Years
- Bad Mood
- Narvel Felts Goes to Town
- Whiskey & Gin
- Mr Wicked
- Lair
- Ode to Nothing

Lipsnipegroin
Phantom Retrospective Series
PHDCD-19
CD compilation
Released 1992

DISC ONE
- Gargoyle
- Cigarettes & Whisky & Wild, Wild Women
- Bad Mood
- Ode to Nothing
- A Time of Evil
- On the Jetty
- Lipsnipegroin
- Mr Wicked
- Narvel Felts
- Jazz Song
- The Beat (I Want My Loving Back)
- Again
- Demolition Team
- We've Got a Gig
- A Sad Tale

DISC TWO
- Ocean Liner
- Seven Years
- No Reason
- Springtime
- Lair
- Wilderbeast
- Power Ring
- A Fool Such As I
- Whisky & Gin
- Lighthouse Keepers
- I've Been Getting Down
- Evil Touch
- Love Beacon
- Big Noise
- Wheels Over the Desert
- Legless
- Torture Road

Appendices : Discography

Ode to Nothing
Feel Presents FEEL 009
CD compilation
Released September 2011
- Lip Snipe Groin
- Springtime
- Gargoyle
- Love Beacon
- Wheels Over the Desert
- A Time of Evil
- Ocean Liner
- Lighthouse Keepers
- No Reason
- Wilderbeast
- Evil Touch
- Torture Road
- Ode to Nothing
- Seven Years
- Whisky & Gin

Appearances on compilations

No Worries
Hot Records WORRIED1
Released 1984
- Gargoyle

Distant Violins Tape 2 (recorded live)
Released 1984
- A Time of Evil
- Big Noise
- To Sir With Love

A cover version of the Georgie Fame song 'Yeah Yeah' was included on the cassette release, *Distant Violins* 17, released some time in the 1980s.
An original composition entitled 'Lip Snipe Groin' was included on the cassette release *Let's Sea*, issued by K in Olympia, WA, USA, released in 1986.
The original composition 'Gargoyle' was included on the LP release *No Worries*, released by Hot Records in 1984.

This Is Hot
Hot Records HOT1
Released 1985
- Gargoyle

This Is Hot Too
Hot Records HOT2
Released 1986
- Seven Years

High Temperature: A Collection of Hot Records 1982-1985
White Hot L 44001, L 44002
Released 1986
- Ocean Liner
- Seven Years

BLUNT Who Cares Wins: A Biased History of Australian Rock
CD included with the book
Published 2001
- Springtime

Tales From the Australian Underground – Singles 1976-1989
Feel Presents FEEL 001, 336142
Released February 2004
- Ocean Liner
- Inner City Sound

Laughing Outlaw
LORICS-001
Released October 2005
- Springtime

Souvenirs from Egg Records
Egg Records UK eggrest015
Released October 2006
- Springtime

A live version of 'Gargoyle' from the benefit concert was included on the CD release: *Life's What You Make It*, a tribute to Linda Gebar. Released by Audrey Studios in the Melbourne in 2009.

The Widdershins

Now You Know / Dishwashing Liquid
Waterfront Records DAMP 53
Released 1987
7-inch single

Bottle Man's Wife
Waterfront Records DAMP 76
Released 1988
12-inch EP

Return Of The King / Bugle Call
Waterfront Records DAMP 98
Released 1989
7-inch single

Ascension
Waterfront Records DAMP 97
Released 1989
Album

Now You Know
Egg Records (4) eggrest019
Released 2006
CD single

Good Songs 1987–1989
Egg Records (4) eggrest017
Released 2005
Compilation album

One Head Jet

Chains Of Water
Phantom Records (3) PHCD 51
Released 1995
CD

Snickedy Palace
Phantom Records (3) PHMCD-23
(CD)

Juliet Ward

Jessamine
Released 2014
CD

THE LIGHTHOUSE

Once upon a time I was nineteen years old and a heartily immature rock writer; I used to run around imposing my opinions on everyone, "that band is the best band in Sydney" and "they're the worst band in Melbourne" and so on and on.

Now I'm a little older and a little wiser (still nineteen but). I sit back and listen to others chat about music, which, let's face it is pretty horrendous these days. However whenever the words, The Lighthouse Keepers are heard some of that old enthusiastic sparkle glimmers in my eye, and I cannot help but say, "They're a good rockin' band." Forgive me if I get too controversial, but I reckon The Lighthouse Keepers are a better band than Wham. Better than ELO. Better than Pink Floyd. Better than Aztec Camera. Superior to disco. And Swamp music. And the Hoodoo Gurus. Anyway, better stop that before I get hurt in the name of hard-hitting music criticism. Just take it from me; they are incredible. Greg Appel's songs are so great I used to think they were cover versions. A compliment.

Actually it was David McComb who suggested that to me and it was he also who told me they were a good rocking band and not what I thought they must have been when I first heard of them, "Oh a part-time Particles spin-off", which just goes to show what sort of suspicious mind I have. Up until early this year, Stephen, Steven and Blue of the Lighthouse Keepers were also involved in that much older but far less wiser pop band. Few would deny that the 'Keepers had come out the better after what Greg calls "the divorce".

These days the band has a single (Ocean Liner sounds great on the radio), an album (Tales of the Unexpected-fifteen rocky tracks) on the now slightly tepid Hot Records. They have faithful followers who like to call out for To Sir With Love at the end of the set... they have people who think they are the best band in Australia. Perhaps They Are. I think the proof of the pudding is in Greg's soaring licks in a song like say, A Time Of Evil which is propelled by a jangly twelve-string idea. Greg's songs can be classic. The reality of how he writes them is a bit depressing. He sends Juliet away and for a couple of days sticks songs together. Then he adds what he calls "horrible lyrics"... well maybe all the best tunes are made that way. Such is his lack of confidence in his lyrics that he

Appendices : Discography

KEEPERS

predicts, "There will be a lot more instrumentals from now on". Maybe he's embarrassed about being so obsessed in his songs.

True, constant references to evil notwithstanding, the Lighthouse Keepers' songs do stick in a relatively traditional format. But that is their trick, they're not afraid to experiment with old ideas. Their music is made from what might be love, but though it might imitate older styles it can also escalate far above them. With this band daring to be so oddly good it might not surprise one (it may even bore one) to find that they arose out of a punk band (Guthugga Pipeline) and a dead little city (Canberra). Stephen and Greg played in Guthugga Pipeline in the late seventies - the astute may notice this is the name of their label, the one that their first two records came out on. The band wrote a book about itself, a copy of whic which apparently lies in our National Library. It recently reformed to do one show, and may do so again. Greg gave up music for awhile and he and Juliet moved to Sydney - when Stephen came to Sydney to play with the Particles, they were playing as Tex Truck and the Semis. Blue was already in a band at the time and Stephen joined first as a drummer, later changing to (primarily) bass when Steven joined. It's a wild tale. Like The Moodists and probably quite a few other bands they had an early long since departed bassist whose whose name is never mentioned and who sometimes gets joked about - this particular bassist was friends with The Church apparently.

Live, the Lighthouse Keepers make a few mistakes, just like all really good bands. They make small jokes in between songs and swap their instruments around. I saw Woodstock on the weekend and the faces of the wild guitarists there made me think of the expressions Greg assumes when he plays his guitar, he looks like he's having a tough time. They do a lot of covers though they no longer need to (I mean, they have enough originals)... they seem to enjoy it... they do Fever, Fire (not the U2 one), To Sir which is quite a hit these days but I think it started as joke, Big Noise which is great - the pounding drums (well they are pounding even if it is a cliche) at the beginning make me go all hot and cold. Or something. Nowadays people call out for Springtime which is a bit retrograde, I hate it when the audience wants hits, although people always have been rather moronic in my experience of them.

We can tell the Lighthouse Keepers are going to hit the big time soon because they're attracting groupies. Once Stephen was at the Strawberry Hills and keeping to himself and some girls came and talked to him. And in Newcastle recently (I was told) a girl said to Greg, "I think your really spunky, do you want to come to a party?". This is the very essence of rock'n'roll. Fandom... all over Australia young people in suburban bedr bedrooms are listening to Lighthouse Keepers records and thinking, "they're really spunky" or more suitably, "these people are poets". In fact there are some poems on the lyriceless lyric sheet inside the album just to prove this. Maybe they feel something, have more feeling than most musicians do these days. They are not the Lighthouse Keepers for the sake of an attitude, or because they hate or love the world. In fact they won't tell you why they're here. I guess they must like music. Sounds a bit simple.

They rehearse on Sundays in a Chippendale house, and seeing people walk past and wonder at the music is a bit like the Beatles' Get Back rooftop performance... actually most people look annoyed. Maybe they think they think they're missing out on something. I think the Lighthouse Keepers are better than the Beatles. Blue can talk on any subject for any length of time. Recently in Canberra he was interviewed on radio and the foolish DJ ran out of questions, he had to say, "Well I have nothing left to say"... Blue talked for the next half an hour. Fortunately he is not boring. The Lighthouse Keepers generally do rotten interviews. They seem to scared of overstating or even thinking about the future, they will only venture to say that they would like to record a single early next year. Currently they only have three "new" songs (actually only a few months old anyway) but seem intent on getting down to the matter at hand in 1985 now that Greg has ended his tertiary education.

Their album was certainly achievement enough for '84. It was recorded at midnight-to-dawn sessions, and has settled the band nicely in debt. Of the fifteen tracks, one (Big Noise) is a cover, and two (Lighthouse Keepers, Jazz Song) are instrumentals. A Jazz Song is by Stephen O'Neill who up until now has not written any LHK material. The other songs are mainly sung by Juliet. They seem quite content with the album, as are their record company Hot. The band's relationship with Hot is quite different to most band/record company relationships. They spend quite a bit of time talking about Hot and whether that label is boosting or destroying the "independent" scene. The band was at first very independent, their first record Gargoyle was packaged in a way no major label could ever cope with, each copy with an individual sleeve, hand drawn. For the second Guthugga Pipeline release, The Exploding Lighthouse Keepers 12" Ep, the covers were printed and then hand-painted. The band coped well when they were independent, selling roughly a thousand copies of each release, but they needed Hot to finance a new record. The "sellout" was minute and, I suppose, necessary - remember Hot is affiliated with CBS.

Then again Hot is doing things like releasing singles off albums these days. The purchaser of Ocean Liner gets exactly the same song that is on the album. Not a new concept obviously but Juliet still feels that this is cheating the loyal fans, and her vote was cast against this idea (the others in the band disagreed). She is probably right. The b side is Greg's radio play A Sad Tale, it runs for more than ten minutes. Incidentally this tale is also a short story and a video. Yes, they should have a TV show made about them. And now, with your permission I will end this rousing drama with;

Lighthouse Keepers Discography

Gargoyle/Demolition Team+Quick Sticks (released twice on Guthugga Pipeline, then a third time on Hot)
The Exploding Lighthouse Keepers 12" Ep (Guthugga Pipeline)
Tales of the Unexpected (Hot) Lp
Ocean Liner/A Sad Tale (Hot)
Gargoyle (No Worries comp-Hot)
A Time Of Evil, Big Noise, To Sir With Love (Distant Violins tape 2-recorded live STUC early 1984)

Halton Elbit.

The Musical Web

Guthugga Pipeline
1978–present

Other members of Guthugga Pipeline include Gavin Butler (Gus), Jack Woodrow, Wayne Millar, Nick Ketley, Dave Phillip, Mark Fraser, Lindsay Dunbar, Graham Steadman.

The Grant Brothers
1978

GREG APPEL

STEPHEN 'HAIRY' O'NEIL

TONY SHANNON

STEPHEN 'HAIRY' O'NEIL
bass
1982–84

The Lighthouse Keepers
1983–86

JULIET WARD
vocals, guitar

GREG APPEL
vocals, guitar

STEPHEN 'HAIRY' O'NEIL
vocals, bass, guitar

Rainlovers 1986–87
Widdershins 1987–90

JULIET WARD
vocals, guitar

GREG APPEL
vocals, guitar

BARRY TURNBULL
bass

Skullduggery 1992

Juliet Ward, Peter Timmerman, Simon Kain, Jason Kain.

One Head Jet
1992–97

STEVE APPEL
vocals, guitar

GREG APPEL
vocals, guitar, keyboard

DAVE APPEL
vocals, guitar

King Curly
2000–present

The Living Dead 2012 (Van Park band)

Greg Appel, Stephen 'Hairy' O'Neil, Steve Appel, Evan Mannell (drums), Elmo Reed (guitar), John Hibbard (trombone, keyboards), John Paul Young (vocals). Performers: Steve Kilbey, Cora James, Hannah Raven, Catriona Hamilton, Luke Webb, Jodi Phillis, Remi Slade-Caffarel.

The Particles 1977–85

 **PETER WILLIAMS** guitar, vocals

 **ASTRID SPIELMAN** vocals, keyboards, percussion 1979–85

 **ALEX HAMILTON** trumpet 1982–83

 **NICOLE MENZIES** trumpet 1984

 **STEVEN WILLIAMS** drums 1978–81

 **MICHAEL 'BLUE' DALTON** harmonica 1984

The Cannanes 1984–present

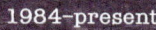
see next page

 **STEVEN WILLIAMS** drums

 **MICHAEL 'BLUE' DALTON** harmonica, slide guitar, bass

The Honeys 1987–88

 **PETE TIMMERMAN** drums

 **JAMES CRUICKSHANK** guitar

John Kennedy's Love Gone Wrong 1984–86

 **PETE TIMMERMAN** drums

Other members of One Head Jet include Duncan Kimball (bass), Sarah Peet (bass), Wayne McAllister (percussion).

The Cruel Sea 1987–2015

Thanks to Roger Griffin for creating The Musical Web.

Confessions of a Lighthouse Keeper: Greg Appel

The Cannanes
1984–present

FOUNDING MEMBERS
Frances 'Sputnik' Gibson (vocals, bass, Casio, flute, synthesizer: Getting Us Places)
Stephen 'Hairy' O'Neil (guitar, vocals, Casio, sad trumpet: Persistence)
Hairy's other bands include: Alternative TV, Flywheel, Jamalia, Ashtray Boy, Sleater Kinney, El Duende, and ors

REGULARS
Andrew Coffey (bass, drums, guitar, vocals: Technical Genius!)
Bon King (drums, vocals: Inspiration)
David Nichols (art, drums, vocals, programming: Ideas and Inspiration!)
Guy Blackman (bass, keys)
James Dutton (guitar, bass, vocals: Rockin')
Nick Ketley (bass and maybe the sax?)
Penny McBride (trumpet, flugelhorn, maracas: Goodness)
Stephen Hermann [aka 'Explosion Robinson'] (bass, guitar, keyboards: Studio Production)
Stewart Anderson [aka 'Steward'] (drums, guitar, keys, percussion, vocals: The UK Connection)

GOLD STAR CONTRIBUTORS
Annabel Bleach (lead vocals: Early Years)
Ben Donaldson (muse/member)
Francesca Bussey (bass, keys, vocals: Inspiration)
G Roy Gavin 'Gus' Butler (bass, guitar: Grunt)
Greg Wadley (synthesizer, drums, live sound: Vision)
Ian McNeil (bass)
Jen Turrell (bass, drums: Red Square Records honcho)
Jim Woff (bass)
Mia Schoen (bass)
Michael Nichols (co-writer/dancer/interviewer)
Michelle Cannane (tambourine and vocals – perhaps guitar?)
Miranda Picton-Warlow (bass? guitar? percussion + BVs)
Nick Kidd (bass and French horn)
Randall Lee (bass, guitar, vocals: Enthusiasm)
Sally Cameron (vocals, keys)
Simon Williams [aka 'Crayola', aka 'Crayola Sarandon'] (bass)

CASUAL LIGHTHOUSE KEEPERS
Glad S. Bag: trombone
Beat Boy: baritone sax
Hugh Veldon: drums
John Papanis: mandolin and banjo
Mick Smith: bass
Penny McBride: trumpet
Peter Timmerman: drums 2012
Rod Bradbury: drums
The Boy Soprano: soprano
The Palmer Street Trio: Annabel, Fran, Lee, Wadey
Tim Oxley: drums/harmonica
Tim Palmer: bassist (early days)
Dave Appel: drums

INDEX

A
ABBA (band) 31, 33, 48
Abbott, Tony 195
AC/DC (band) 105, 112, 175
The Age (Melbourne newspaper) 19, 188
Alpha House (venue) 56, 61–64, 79, 84–86, 91
Altar Ego (band) 107
Alt-J (band) 20
The Andrews Sister 96
Appel, Anders 82–83, 170
Appel, David 24, 25
Appel, Denis (my father) 23
Appel, Jan (my mother) 22–25, 27, 33, 145, 182, 215
Appel, Margie 3, 27
Appel, Rob 27, 210
Appel, Steve 27, 29, 31, 104, 171, 179, 182, 185, 192, 210, 222
Appel, Zelie 3, 11, 14, 154, 170, 206, 212, 216
Aria Hall of Fame 19
Arms & Legs (band) 88, 90
Askin, Robert 103
Association of Modern Education School 37
Australian Broadcasting Corporation (ABC)
    ABC as an 'institution' 171, 175
    ABC commissioning documentaries 167
    ABC production office 168
    ABC television 158, 172
    ABC van borrowed by James Cruickshank 160
    Archives 158, 161–162, 193
    Bellbird (television series) 79
    Christmas breaks at the ABC 166
    Commmissioning of *King Street, Newtown* 166
    Countdown (television series) 48, 174, 185
    Four Corners (television series) 154–155
    Frontline (television series) 164
    Greg Appel working with ABC 5, 14, 19, 27, 45, 158–162, 164, 173, 175, 193, 194
    GTK ('Get To Know', television series) 47
    News library 161
    Radio National 194
    Recovery (television series) 170–171
    7.30 Report (television program) 164–165
    'sheltered workshop' 163
    Triple J (radio station) 19
    Van Park script 177
    Walkley Award, Tim Palmer 44
Australian Crawl (band) 83, 102
Australian Labor Party 4, 19, 22, 74
Australian National University Bar 32, 64–66, 71, 83, 111, 114–115

B
Baby, Dave 116
'Bad Mood' (song) 7, 86
The Bad Seeds (band) 135
Bag O'Nails (venue) 209
Bapu Mamoos (band) 75
Barnes, Jimmy 54
Barrell, Tony 173
Bartley, Don 50
Bayley, Karen 98
The Beasts of Bourbon (band) 95
Beat Boy (musician) 110, 116
The Beatles (band) 26, 38, 109, 117, 196–197, 207, 209
    'All You Need is Love' (song) 197
    The White Album (*The Beatles*) 209
The Bedridden (band) 92, 214

Behind Enemy Lines (venue) 56, 82, 83, 104
The Benders (band) 129
'Big Noise from Winnetka' (song) 96
Bill Haley and the Comets 26
Bill the Busman 34, 35
The Birthday Party (band) 134–135
Blake, William 196
Bleach, Annabel 57, 142
'Blood on the Saddle' (song) 37
'Blue' (Michael Dalton)
    asked to join the Triffids 81
    Cobar recollections 114
    cooking and diet 94
    diary entry by Steven Williams 119
    diary entry in 'Eating Guide To Roadhouses Of The World' 120–122
    discussing homosexuality in the 1980s 75
    discussing John Cooper Clarke 80
    discussing the 1980s 46–48, 65–68, 70, 73–75, 86, 90, 213
    Europe tour 16, 124–125, 136–137
    first meeting with Juliet Ward 42–44
    harmonica 44, 63
    Lighthouse Keepers disbanding 141
    living with James Cruickshank 153
    Marxist politics and anti-capitalism 46, 51–52, 75, 105, 125
    meeting with Lemmy 139
    Melbourne tour 106–108
    origins of the band name for SPK 90
    recording of *Tales of the Unexpected* 110–111
    Redfern share house 87
    reunion with Greg Appel in 2008 45
    stopover in Sri Lanka 122
    Western Australia tour 95, 97–101
Bossa Nova: the sound that seduced the world (documentary) 5
The Bottle Man (short film) 147–148, 152–153, 154
Bowie, David 118
    'Let's Dance' (song) 118
Box of Fish (band) 64–65
The Brady Bunch (television series) 23
Bristow, Tim 103
Britannia Hotel 46, 48, 58, 60–61, 69, 71, 75, 77
Brown, Steve 163–165, 167, 172
Bubbalouie (dog) 43, 87

Buku–Larrŋgay Mulka Arts Centre 198
Bunchgrove, Stephen 171
Burchett, Mark 191
Bussey, Fran 142, 146, 185, 189
Butler, Gavin (Gus) 21–22, 32, 38–39, 43, 88, 181

C

The Canberra Times (newspaper) 23, 32
The Cannanes (band) 141, 163, 213
Captain Coco (band) 114
Caravan Club (venue) 191
Casey, Martyn 15, 131
Cassidy, Shaun 29
Castanet Club (venue) 75
Castanets (band) 75
Cave, Nick 20, 54, 81, 102, 131, 134–135, 140
The Celibate Rifles (band) 54
Chamberlain, Lindy 38
Champions (band) 104
The Change (band) 111
Chaos (dog) 36–37, 43–44, 61, 74, 116
Chaos Music 210
Chapel off Chapel (theatre) 182, 184, 188
Chapman, Geraldine 124
The Church (band) 4, 45, 177, 182, 196
Clapton, Eric 209
Claringbold, Dave 153
Clarke, John Cooper 79–80
Clarke, Paul 154, 164–165, 170, 173, 175–177
The Clash (band) 50
Clear As Day (band) 114
Cline, Patsy 50
The Clouds (band) 195
Cocker, Joe 83, 136
The Cockroaches (band) 105–106, 111–112
Cody, Chris 78
Coe, Sue 73
Coldplay (band) 20, 205–206
Coloured Stone (band) 115
Confessions Of (television series) 9
Cook, Murray 4, 62, 72, 190, 212
Cooper, Alice 211
Coupe, Stuart 90
Cranfield, Mr. (music teacher) 25
Cream (band) 31
'Crolucks' 146–147
The Cruel Sea (band) 4, 159, 160, 202–203, 206

Cruickshank, James
    discussing drugs 203
    'enigma head' 154–155
    first meeting with Bjarne 157–158
    first meeting with Greg Appel 79
    funeral 203
    in studio location 200
    luck 160, 202–203
    medical diagnosis 202
    selection of surname 79
    with the Cruel Sea 160, 202
    with the Widdershins 153, 159
    working at the ABC 160–161
Cruise, Tom 26
Crystal Set (band) 69, 113, 115, 156
Custard (band) 174

D
Dadednyne (band) 77, 79, 106
The Daily Telegraph (newspaper) 189
Dalton, Michael *See* 'Blue' (Michael Dalton)
The Damned (band) 195
Deebles (family friends) 29
The Deer Hunter (film) 67
Dexys Midnight Runners (band) 56
Diamond, Neil 26
Diddy Wah Hoodaddys (band) 96
Dire Straits (band) 83
    'Twisting by the Pool' (song) 83
Distant Violins (fanzine) 49
Doctor Who (character) 212
dole, unemployment benefits 47–48, 79, 151, 201
Domino, 'Fats' 210
Donaldson, Ben 111
Donoghue, Bob 166
Doors Ajar (band) 97
Do-Ré-Mi (band) 48, 60
Dream Studios 50, 82
Duran Duran (band) 49
Dylan, Bob 30, 179
Dynamic Hepnotics (band) 32, 112

E
The Eagles (band) 136
EastEnders (television series) 135
The Easybeats (band) 174
Eating Guide to Roadhouses of the World (diary) 16
Elton, Ben 96

Eros Foundation 170
Errington, Andrew 195
The Eurogliders (band) 112–113, 210
Excuse the French (musical) 192
The Exorcist (film) 206
Export Music Australia 210

F
Field, Billy 109
    'Bad Habits' (song) 109
Fifth Corruption (band) 114, 115
Flying Doctor (band) 104
Foxtel 162
Francis, Connie 63
Frankie Goes to Hollywood (band) 112–113
Franklin, Aretha 137
Funny Stories (performance comedians) 75, 79

G
The Gadflys (band) 115
Game of Thrones (television series) 171
Garema Place, Canberra 34
Gare, Sophie (Sophie Elton) 96
The Gargoyles (band) 79
Garran Primary School 38, 196
Garrett, Leif 29
Gas Babies (band) 105
Gibson, Fran 163, 213
Gibson, Mel 56
Glad S. Bag (musician) 110, 116
Glasgow Arms Hotel 42
Glengarry Castle Hotel 58, 63–64, 66, 69
Glover, Andrew 168, 172
The Go-Betweens (band) 8, 12, 14, 16, 19, 20, 54, 81, 111–114, 135, 144, 173, 202, 213
Gock, Les 173–174
Goddard, Jane 163
Goldsboro, Bobby 70
Gormly, Ken 4, 160, 203
Goulburn Jail 40
Graham Parker and the Rumour (band) 32
Grant Brothers (band) 38–39, 50
Graphic Arts Club 8, 140
Greville (store) 51
Grierson, Roger 86
Griffin Centre (Canberra) 38–39, 106
Guthugga Pipeline (band) 33–36, 38, 43, 50, 82
Guthugga Pipeline Records 82
Guy Delandro Band 111

H

'Hairy' (S. O'Neil)
  borrowing money from parents 50, 52
  Canberra 19, 40
  Ceduna Hotel performance 101
  cover design of *Tales of the Unexpected* 111
  diary entry from 1985 116, 119, 121
  discussing Dream Studios 50
  Europe tour 124–125, 136
  Grant Brothers 38–39, 50
  Guthugga Pipeline 33, 43, 50
  Norseman Hotel performance 99
  on-stage brawl in Hamburg 12–13, 16
  origins of nickname 50
  performing in *Van Park* 185
  performing with the Cannanes 141, 163, 213
  performing with the Lighthouse Keepers 49, 60, 76
  performing with the Particles 56
  punk music 37
  receiving 'Gargoyle' vinyl copies 51
  recording of *Tales of the Unexpected* 110–111
  short-changed by Hopetoun Hotel 78
  singing 'To Sir, With Love' 61
  stopover in Sri Lanka 122
  taking Alice on Perth tour 93
Hale, Keith 50, 110
Hall, Andy 43, 129, 192
Hall, Peter 192
Halstead, Marko 68
Hamburg (Germany) 6, 11–13, 16–17, 137, 139, 201
Hamilton, Alex 110
Hamilton, Catriona 184, 190
Hammerhead (band) 45
Hammersmith Clarendon (venue) 127, 129
Hammond, Sonny (television character) 29
Happy Days (television series) 9
Harold Park Hotel 104, 107, 115, 152, 154
Harrison, George 209
Harris, Rolf 174
Hatzel, Aurora 22, 33
Hawke, Bob 74, 103
Hendrix, Jimi 210
The Herald Sun (newspaper) 189–190
Hilton, Paris 171
Hip Hop Club (venue) 114–115
Hoffman, Dustin 34
Hoi Poli (band) 115
'The Honeymoon is Over' (song) 160
Le Hoodoo Gurus (band) 95, 113
Hopetoun Hotel 8, 77–78, 115, 156
Horn, Trevor 112
Hot Records 51, 109, 116, 127–129
Hudson, Bob 47
Hunters and Collectors (band) 48, 112
Hush (band) 173, 174

I

I Am Vertical (band) 140
Icehouse (band) 19, 173
Idiom Flesh (band) 79
Iggy Pop and the Stooges (band) 50
  Pop, Iggy 195
Inner City Sounds (book) 52
INXS (band) 109, 112–113, 134

J

Jackson, Michael 38, 83–84, 113
  'Billie Jean' (song) 83–84
  'Thriller' (song) 113, 206
James, Cora 179, 184
The Jam Tarts (band) 96, 140
Jelly Babies (band) 61, 64–65
Jennings, Martin 109, 116, 127, 129, 137
Jesus and Mary Chain (band) 130
Jesus Christ Superstar (stage play) 184
JFK and the Cuban Crisis (band) 66
Jimmy and the Boys (band) 32
John, Elton 32, 48, 83
John Kennedy's Love Gone Wrong (band) 221
John Paul Young and the All Stars (band) 175
Jones, Howard 85
Jones, Ignatius 32, 90
Jones, Quincy 206
Joplin, Janis 88
Jordan, Gregor 154
Jorgensen, Anita 170–171
Just A Drummer (band) 107, 115–116

K

Kane, Bruce 170
KC and the Sunshine Band 38, 83
Keays, Jim 174
Kelly, Paul 8, 78, 139, 140, 191, 202
Kennedy, John 66, 153

Kilbey, Steve 45, 183, 184, 185, 190, 191
    'Nebauchadnezzar' (stage character) 179, 196–197
    Sydney Fringe Festival 179
    'The Meaning of Life' (event) 196
    Van Park review 182
    Van Park script 177–178, 186–187
Killer Sheep (band) 16
The Killjoys (band) 155
King Curly (band) 31, 182, 183, 185, 210
King Henry VIII 22
'King of the Road' (song) 37
King Street, Newtown (documentary) 7, 61, 84, 165, 166, 167
Kragh, Bjarne 157, 158
Kristofferson, Kris 81
    'Sunday Morning Coming Down' (song) 81
Kuepper, Ed 8
Kyle, Anne 168

L

La Femme (band) 56
Lamar, Kendrick 205, 206
'Land of the Boons' (song) 102
Lansdowne Hotel 58
The Laughing Clowns (band) 8, 109, 111
Lawall, Gaspar 129
Lawson Square Infirmary (band) 129
Leans (family friends) 29
Lee, Graham 14, 15, 19, 32, 78, 80, 101, 126, 127, 131, 144
'Lemmy' (German fan) 131, 137, 138, 139
Lennon, John 38, 196
Let's Go Naked (band) 117, 140
The Librettos (band) 207–208
    Let's Go With The Librettos (television series) 207
Liebknecht, Karl 90
The Lighthouse Keepers (band)
    anti-technology (music) 56
    'A Sad Tale' (song) 87
    becoming well-known 83, 91
    Ceduna performance 100
    comparisons with the Go-Betweens 20
    cover songs selection 70
    creative work afterwards 18
    description 5
    diary entries 88, 91–92, 97, 107, 119
    disbanding 140, 145, 153, 213
    disruption in music industry 211
    drug usage 63
    'Evil Touch' (song) 88
    The Exploding Lighthouse Keepers (album) 82, 85
    Facebook page 34
    fan base in Adelaide 114
    fan base of lawyers 49, 163–164
    friendship with Will Stubbs 198
    'Gargoyle' (song) 9, 35–36, 50–52, 57, 65, 68, 86, 126, 156
    Hamburg (Germany) 11–13, 16
    Imploding Lighthouse Keepers (album) 5
    inclusion into *Long Way to the Top* (documentary) 173, 182
    lack of support from critics 19
    meeting Paul Kelly 191
    memories of Canberra 34
    memories of the band 60
    music critics 81, 129
    music styles and tastes 210
    nervous on stage 12
    Newtown subculture 165
    'Ocean Liner' (song) 5, 8, 63, 84, 87, 109
    'Ode to Nothing' (song) 11, 116–117
    onset of 1984 86
    on tour 94, 102, 136
    origins of 'Gargoyle' song 9
    origins of the band 36, 45
    performance in The Netherlands 131
    politics 45, 65, 74
    preparing for Perth tour 93
    recollections
        from 1980s 57
        from Annabel Bleach 142, 206
        from 'Blue' 43–44, 47, 51, 65–68, 70, 73–75, 80–81, 87, 90, 125–126, 137, 213
        from Clinton Walker 54
        from Fran Bussey 142
        from 'Hairy' 50–51
        from Juliet Ward 48, 58, 71–72, 76–77, 81, 135, 141, 145, 147
        from Murray Cook 72
        from Nick Mainsbridge 128
        from Rob McComb 70
        from Tanya Plibersek 8
    recording of final single 117

The Lighthouse Keepers (band) cont.
    release of 'Gargoyle' 36
    reunion 141–142, 155, 163, 204, 213–214
    review by Clinton Walker 90, 124
    self-indulgence 147
    style of music 13, 49, 65, 81, 84–85, 116
    Tales of the Unexpected (album) 5, 87, 109–111, 116
    transition to the Widdershins 145, 158
    working with Mark Burchett 191
    working with the Particles 69, 97
Like Unruly Children (band) 61
The Living Dead (band) 196
Loggins, Kenny 112–113
Long Way to the Top (documentary) 5, 7, 14, 19, 172–175, 182
'Love Beacon' (song) 7, 84, 200
Love Gone Wrong (band) 153
Love is in the Air (television series) 175
Lunar Circus (band) 115
Luxemburg, Rosa 90
Lydon, Johnny (aka Johnny Rotten) 37

M
Macdonald, Sarah 4, 27–28, 29
The Machinations (band) 60
Maestros & Dipsos (band) 85, 114
Mainsbridge, Nick 117, 128, 131
Manning, Phil 175
Maple Street—Maleny (documentary) 167
The Masters Apprentices (band) 174
Maynard F# Crabbes (performer) 75
MC5 (band) 195
McAllister, Wayne 164–165, 177
McCabe, Bernie 179
McCartney, Paul 209
McComb, David 70, 81
McComb, Rob 4, 15, 70, 126, 131–132
'The Meaning of Life' (event) 196
Melbourne Comedy Festival 19
Men Love Sex (book) 52
Menzies, Nicole 54
Michael, George 112–113, 169
Middle Harbour Skiff Club 66, 92
Midnight Oil (band) 113
The Modern Lovers (band) 34, 50
Mondo Rock (band)
    'Come Said the Boy' (song) 112–113
Monty Python 32, 196–197
Monty Python's Life of Brian (film) 197

The Moodists (band) 101
Mop and the Dropouts (band) 117
Morgan, Warren 'Pig' 201–202
Morrison, Lindy 4, 14, 16, 20, 135, 144, 173, 211–213
Mozart, Wolfgang 19–20, 158
    Amadeus (film) 20, 158
Mulry, Ted 174
Mutant Death (band) 75, 83
Myxo (band) 34

N
The Nansing Quartet (band) 140
Napier-Bell, Simon 174–175
Native Rose Hotel 57, 87
Nehl, Andy 173
Neighbours (television series) 191
New Musical Express (newspaper) 5, 32, 84, 126
Newtown Hotel 167
Nichols, David 4, 49, 84, 212
1984 (novel) 205
The Nomads (band) 130
Non Fiction (band) 61, 110
No Night Sweats (band) 79
Norseman Hotel (venue) 98–99
NSW Institute of Technology 44, 159
Nullarbor Plain 94, 100

O
O'Callagan, Jackie 33
Old Melbourne Hotel (Perth) 94–95, 98
One Head Jet (band) 31, 45
O'Neil, Stephen *See* 'Hairy' (S. O'Neil)
On The Street (newspaper) 147
Orbison, Roy 207
Orwell, George 86

P
Painters & Dockers (band) 114
Palmer, Tim 44, 60, 176
Papanis, John 110
Paradise Studios 109
Parini, Jay 8
Parsons, Gram 50, 81
The Particles (band) 54, 56, 61, 63–64, 66, 69, 71, 75, 79, 82–83, 87, 93–100, 102–103, 106, 142
The Past is a Foreign Country (book) 73
Patten, Fiona 170
Peacock, Amanda 3, 11, 152, 154, 170, 197, 208–209

Peacock, Brian 197, 207–211
Peacock, Pam 208–209
Perkins, Tex 159
Pfister, Liane 3, 183, 195, 197
Phantom Records (store) 51
Phillis, Jodi 195
Phoenician Club (venue) 114, 116
Pickworths (family friends) 29
Pickworth, Simon 29
Pilot to Bambadier (band) 107
Pink Floyd (band) 38, 129
    'Another Brick in the Wall' (song) 38
Pittman, Tim 49, 70, 136, 202, 211
Plan 9 from Outer Space (film) 87
Plibersek, Tanya 4, 8, 19
`pling (Kevin William Prideaux) 204
poker machines 58, 64
Police (band) 56, 83
Pooley, Justin 159, 205
Pop Up Toasters (band) 106
Presley, Elvis 26, 68
    'Suspicious Minds' (song) 68
Price, David 109–110
Prince (musician) 34
The Prince of Wales (Prince Charles) 65, 126, 130
The Prince of Wales (venue) 102, 114
The Princess of Wales (Princess Diana) 38, 65
Procession (band) 209

R
Rabbits Wedding (band) 155
Radio Birdman (band) 39, 195
The Rainlovers (band) 45
Redeye Records (shop) 8, 51
'Red Fox' (gang leader) 39, 147
Red Parrot (venue) 97
Reed, Josh 170–171, 177
REM (band) 20
Revenge of the Nerds (film) 205
Reyne, James 102
Rhinoceros Studios 109
Richman, Jonathan 77–78
'Rock Against Roxby Downs' (event) 74
Rocky Horror Picture Show (film) 31
The Rolling Stones (band) 159, 207
Rowe, Normie 209
Ruby My Dear (band) 114

Rushdie, Salman 36
Rush, Geoffrey 173

S
Safehouse (band) 66
Salieri, Antonio 19–20
Samurai Trash (band) 115
Sandman (performer) 75
Sandringham Hotel 8
Scant Regarde (band) 79
Scared Weird Little Guys (band) 18
The Scientists (band) 95
Scratches (store) 51, 84
The Seaview Ballroom (venue) 100–102, 105–107
Secret Seven (band) 140
Sekret Sekret (band) 77, 107
The Sex Pistols (band) 50, 65
    'Anarchy in the UK' (song) 37
    'God Save the Queen' (song) 65
Sham 69 (band) 32
Shane Shane 56
'Shape of You' (song) 205
Sheeran, Ed 205
The Shindiggers (band) 107
The Shining (film) 102
Shock Headed Peters (band) 130
Sinatra, Frank 26
Singleton, Jane 165
Sitch, Rob 140
six o'clock swill 58, 61, 66
Slade, Ben 163
Smith, Patti 36, 88, 105
    Horses (album) 105
Soggy Porridge (band) 66
The Sound of Music (film) 31, 169
Space Invaders (computer game) 38, 205
Spartacist Party (Germany) 90
Special Broadcasting Services (SBS) 166–167
    Rock Around the World (television series) 86
Spector, Phil 25
Spectres Revenge (band) 115
Spielman, Astrid 54, 63, 94, 103
Spielman, Ingrid 63, 103
SPK (band) 89, 90, 105
Spontaneous Productions 167, 192
Starkie, 'Bongo' 105
Status Quo (band) 31, 175
Steiner-Schober, Brigitte 124
Steppenwolf (book) 137

Stevens, Cat 26, 30
Stiff Little Fingers (band) 43, 88
'St James Infirmary Blues' (song) 37, 81
Stoned Crow (venue) 97, 98
Strangelings (band) 75
The Stranglers (band) 32
Strawberry Hills Hotel 8, 66, 69–70, 75, 77, 83, 90–92, 104, 107, 111, 113, 115, 142
    name change from Southern Cross Hotel 64, 66, 69
St Stephen's Church 195–197
    'The Meaning of Life' (event) 196–197
Stubbs, Will 198–199
Studdert, David 34
Studio 301 50
Swayze, Patrick 104
Swinging Tees (band) 111
Sydney Fringe Festival 19, 182, 188, 201
Sydney Gay and Lesbian Mardi Gras 76
Sydney Morning Herald (newspaper) 23, 90, 162

T

The Tactics (band) 34
Taranto, Claudia 194
Taylor, Sarah 59
The Team That Never Played (documentary) 5
Ted Mulry Gang (band) 174
Tex Deadly and the Dum Dums (band) 68
Tex Truck and the Semis (band) 44
Thorn, Tracy 135
The Thought Criminals (band) 86
Tillett, Louis 87, 147
Timmerman, Peter 153
Tiny Town (band) 135
'To Sir, With Love' (song) 61
Trade Union Club 8, 77, 79–80, 88–90, 102–104, 106–109, 160
Tribe (band) 113
The Triffids (band) 5, 8, 12, 15, 19–20, 54, 61, 69–71, 78–81, 83, 90, 93–95, 97, 101, 104, 106, 109, 112, 115, 126–132, 135, 144, 202
    Born Sandy Devotional (album) 127, 132
    Treeless Plain (album) 94
'Trogg' (Canberra punk) 39, 40, 195
Tropfest 154
Trump, Donald 195
Turnbull, Barry 153, 160
Tu Tu Z (band) 114
2SER (radio station) 47

Two Hands (film) 154
The Two Ronnies (television series) 190

U

U2 (band) 20, 206
The Undertones (band) 32
University of Technology, Sydney 44–45, 61, 87, 167, 175
Upsidedown House (band) 79

V

Vacant Lot, the (band) 34
Vanda, Harry 174, 201
Van Park (stage play) 7, 18, 161, 163, 175–176, 179, 182–185, 189–192, 196, 201
    'Akbar' (stage character) 175
Vergona, Lee 110
Violent Femmes, the (band) 8, 104
Vulgar Beatmen (band) 75

W

Waiting for Brasso (band) 79
Walker, Clinton 15–16, 16, 52, 54, 56–57, 81, 84–85, 88, 90, 91, 134–135, 155, 173
Wallner, Peter ('Pete the Basher') 26–27, 39–40, 170
Ward, Barnaby 91, 110, 214
Ward, Juliet
    accident in 'Chuffy' the car 90
    attitudes about music and fashion 48, 58, 81, 105
    billing with SPK 89
    Chaos (dog) 36, 44, 61, 116
    Cobar tour 114
    departing Sydney 157
    diary entries 86, 88–89, 91, 94, 96–97, 99–101
    discussing the 'Crolucks' 146
    drawing covers of 'Gargoyle' records 51
    Europe tour 123–125, 129–131, 135
    first meeting with Barjne 157–158
    first meeting with 'Blue' 42–43
    first meeting with Greg Appel 33, 36–37
    friendship with Keith Hale 50
    heckling from audiences 67, 206
    in 'Blue's diary entry 106
    in 'Ocean Liner' video clip 87
    in Steve William's diary entry 119
    in Virgin Megastore 132
    Lighthouse Keepers disbanding 18, 140–141
    living through teenage years 76

Ward, Juliet cont.
    on stage persona 12, 72
    performance on stage 144
    performing in Student Union talent quest 44
    recalls Barnaby Ward at Strawberry Hills Hotel 91
    recollections
        about the Lighthouse Keepers 213–214
        from 'Blue' 74–75, 137
        from Fran Bussey 146
        from Tanya Plibersek 8
    relationship to 'Gargoyle' song 35
    relationship with audiences 98
    relationship with chickens 146
    relationship with Greg Appel 17, 36, 40, 42–43, 47, 52, 61, 76–77, 84, 104, 140–141, 145, 214
    singing on stage 63
    smoking cigarettes 59, 115
    South Australia tour 120–121
    stopover in Sri Lanka 122
    the Widdershins 157, 159
    vocal skills 92, 109, 117
    Western Australia tour 71, 93, 108
    witchcraft 145
    worshipped by lesbians 75, 76
Watusi Now (band) 88
Wa Wa Nee (band) 210
Webb, Luke 185, 190
Weddings Parties Anything (band) 114
Wedd, Neil 139
The Wet Taxis (band) 61, 107, 109, 111
Wexler, Jane 206–207
'Who's Sorry Now' (song) 63
The Widdershins (band) 4, 7, 45, 144–146, 152–160, 182, 191, 202
    Ascension (album) 145
    Bottle Man's Wife (mini-album) 152–153
    'March of the Green Men' (song) 7, 153, 156–157
The Wiggles (band) 4, 112, 190, 212
'Wilderbeast' (song) 84
Wilkes, Jane
    New Musical Express 5, 129
Wilkins, Richard 19

Williams, Steven
    band transportation 90
    bookings and management 72, 93, 99, 103, 107, 108, 119, 140–141
    diary entry 119
    Donna (girlfriend) 87
    drumming with the Particles 56
    first performance with the Lighthouse Keepers 66
    life after the Lighthouse Keepers 213
    managing Alpha House 62
    meeting with Lemmy 139
    on-stage brawl in Hamburg 12–13, 16
    playing cricket with the Triffids 71
    Western Australia tour 93, 108
Wimmen & Boys (band) 75, 82, 85, 102
Winter, Chris 47
Wood, Ed 87
Woodentops (band) 130
Wran, Neville 103
Wrong Kind of Stone Age (band) 75
Wyman, Bill 159

X
X-Ray Spex (band) 32

Y
Yirrkala 198–199
Yolgnu 198–199
Young, Angus 64, 173
The Young Docteurs (band) 34
Younger, Rob 39, 195
Young, George 174
Young, John Paul 7, 174–175, 181–186, 188–191, 201–202, 212, 214
    'Pasadena' (song) 174
    'Yesterday's Hero' (song) 185
Yunupingu, Mandawuy 199

Z
Zero Hour (band) 113

www.ingramcontent.com/pod-product-compliance
Lightning Source LLC
Chambersburg PA
CBHW061810290426
44110CB00026B/2844